ESSAYISTS ON THE ESSAY

ESSAYISTS *on the* ESSAY

Montaigne to Our Time

EDITED BY CARL H. KLAUS AND NED STUCKEY-FRENCH

University of Iowa Press, Iowa City

University of Iowa Press, Iowa City 52242

www.uiowapress.org
Printed in the United States of America

Design by April Leidig-Higgins

The University of Iowa Press is a member of Green Press Initiative and is committed to preserving natural resources.

Printed on acid-free paper

Library of Congress Cataloging-in-Publication Data
Essayists on the essay: Montaigne to our time / edited by Carl H. Klaus and Ned Stuckey-French.
p. cm.
Includes bibliographical references and index.
ISBN-13: 978-1-60938-076-2 (pbk.)
ISBN-10: 1-60938-076-2 (pbk.)
1. Essay. 2. Essay—Authorship. 3. Essays. 4. Essays—Translations into English. 5. Essayists. I. Klaus, Carl H. II. Stuckey-French, Ned. III. Title.
PN4500.E724 2012
808.84'9357—dc23 2011031860

To Kate, Jackie, and Elizabeth

Contents

Preface

A brief glance at our table of contents might suggest that this book is essentially a collection of pieces about the essay by essayists from Montaigne to the present. But beyond the collection, it is also a guide to hundreds of additional pieces on the essay, as one can see by consulting our bibliography and the thematic guide that follows it. With the aid of this bibliographical guide, we hope to stimulate research and commentary that might lead toward a poetics and analytics of the essay, as suggested by our introduction, Toward a Collective Poetics of the Essay."

Our decision to produce this source book is the result of a conviction that despite the extraordinary growth of interest in the essay during the past twenty-five years—thanks to such important projects as Robert Atwan's *Best American Essays* series, Phillip Lopate's *The Art of the Personal Essay*, John D'Agata's *The Next American Essay* and *The Lost Origins of the Essay,* and G. Douglas Atkins's recent books on the essay—the essay has largely been ignored in the world of criticism and theory. By virtue of being the handmaiden of criticism, the medium in which other forms of literature, art, and culture are interpreted, the essay perhaps has seemed to need no explanation. As if it were transparent as a pane of glass. How else to account for the fact that during the past twenty-five years only a handful of academic books have been devoted to defining it or interpreting it?

But essayists themselves have not been reticent about the nature, form, and purpose of the essay, reflecting on it in columns, prefaces, introductions, letters, and reviews, as well as in essays on the essay and occasionally in book-length works about it. All in all, they have produced an extensive body of commentary that constitutes the heart of our concern in this source book. Our collection offers a historically and culturally representative sampling, dominated during the early centuries by English essayists, who were then more self-consciously concerned with the essay than their counterparts elsewhere in the world. But during the twentieth century, as our collection reflects, American, Latin American, and European essayists became increasingly concerned with the nature and significance of the genre. Likewise, women writers became more concerned with the genre during the twentieth century, as our table of contents reflects.

Some of the pieces in our collection are reprinted here in their entirety, others are excerpts that we have made because they embody significant issues, themes, or points of view in the history of thinking about the essay. Each selection is prefaced by a headnote that provides information about the author's life and works and about ideas in the piece itself.

Our bibliography includes not only essays on the essay but also a wide variety of other titles, ranging from brief prefaces and reviews to book-length works that reflect on some aspect of the essay or the essayist, or both. We wish it had been possible to reprint more of the pieces that appear in the bibliography and that we mention in the introduction, but the collection is meant to be representative rather than exhaustive. On the other hand, our guide to the bibliography offers a broad range of thematically related pieces for further study.

Though precursors of the essay can be found in ancient Greece, Rome, China, and Japan, our collection begins with Montaigne, for he is the first essayist to reflect on the nature and form of the essay and is its major progenitor, having named it and produced such an enduringly influential book of essays. We have in turn devoted this source book solely to the commentary of essayists who have published at least one collection or the equivalent, because as practitioners of the form they know it and understand it from the inside. Thus we have not included or listed scholarly or textbook material on the essay, unless it was authored by an essayist.

While we refer to Montaigne and his successors as essayists, it is well to remember that most of them have not earned their living by penning essays. Montaigne was a statesman and diplomat, Bacon a barrister and member of Parliament, Boyle a scientist, Lamb a bookkeeper. Even when they have been professional writers, essayists have usually identified themselves not as essayists but as philosophers, critics, playwrights, and more recently novelists, editors, or professors. Thus we are keenly aware that most essayists have a life and a living beyond the essay that often inform their thinking about it in one way or another. But for the purposes of this book, an essayist is someone who has written essays and written something about the essay itself, which we seek to highlight in our individual headnotes.

Our bibliography grew out of the work of an essay study group at the University of Iowa. For their assistance in discovering and discussing commentary on the essay, we are very grateful to our former colleagues in that group—Maura Brady, Cassie Kircher, Michele Payne, John Price, and Dan Roche.

For their excellent assistance in procuring permissions and compiling the manuscript, we are grateful to Christina Rivera, Misty Bravence, and Ann Robinson of Florida State University. For its generous support of the project, we are grateful to Florida State University. And for its excellent production of the book, we are grateful to the staff of the University of Iowa Press, particularly our editor Joe Parsons and managing editor Charlotte Wright, as well as our free-lance copyeditor David Chu.

Toward a Collective Poetics of the Essay

CARL H. KLAUS

Though the essay has yet to find its Aristotle, essayists have often written about it with the certitude of a poetics—in prefaces, introductions, letters, journals, and essays on the essay. A hint of that self-reflective tendency can be heard in musings of the fourteenth-century Buddhist monk Yoshida Kenko: "What a strange, demented feeling it gives me when I realize I have spent whole days before this inkstone, with nothing better to do, jotting down at random whatever nonsensical thoughts have entered my head" (30). Montaigne, on the other hand, was so enthralled by his pathbreaking literary venture that he repeatedly sought to describe it, explain it, justify it, celebrate it, and sometimes even denigrate it in digressive passages that can be found in 26 of his 107 essays. So many digressions, sometimes rambling on for several hundred words, increasing in length with each successive edition, that in his final essay Montaigne exclaimed, "How often and perhaps how stupidly have I extended my book to make it speak of itself!" (818).

Contrary to that self-deprecating outburst, Montaigne and his descendants have produced a significant body of commentary on a wide range of interrelated topics—the nature of the essay, the purpose of the essay, the form, length, and variety of the essay; the style of the essayist, the voice of the essayist, the personality, mind, and knowledge of the essayist; the essay and the article, the essay and the theme, the essay and the story, the essay and the lyric. Though their interests vary as widely as their backgrounds, essayists so often concur on a few crucial issues that their convergence suggests the key elements of a collective poetics.

The most striking and significant consensus can be seen in the tendency of essayists from every period and culture to define the essay by contrasting it with conventionalized and systematized forms of writing, such as rhetorical, scholarly, or journalistic discourse. In keeping with this contrast, they often invoke images and metaphors suggestive of the essay's naturalness, openness, or looseness as opposed to the methodical quality of conventional nonfiction. Likewise, they typically conceive of the essay as a mode of trying out ideas, of exploration rather than persuasion, of reflection rather than conviction. Montaigne is the first to invoke the contrast, in passages that highlight both his uncertainty and his unmethodical manner: "The scholars distinguish and mark off their ideas more specifically and in detail. I, who cannot see beyond what I have learned from experience, without any system, present my ideas in a general way, and tentatively. As in this: I speak my meaning in disjointed parts" (824). In a similar vein, Bacon, whose formal and pithy essays have often been regarded as the antithesis of Montaigne's, refers to his pieces as "fragments of my conceites" (238), and in *The Proficience and Advancement of Learning* he concludes a defense of the aphoristic mode, typical of his essays, by contrasting it with methodical writing: "And lastly, aphorisms, representing a knowledge broken, do invite men to inquire further; whereas methods, carrying the show of a total, do secure men, as if they were at furthest" (173). Though Montaigne seeks to mirror his mind in action while Bacon aims to provoke the minds of others, both describe their prose in antimethodical terms such as "disjointed" and "broken" that clearly distinguish essayistic form and purpose from the methodical discourse that dominated classical rhetoric and medieval scholasticism.

The early influence of that dichotomy can be seen in Bacon's contemporary William Cornwallis, who defined the essay as "a manner of writing well befitting undigested motions" and compared the essayist to "a scrivener trying his pen before he engrosses his work" (190). The persistence of the contrast—one might even say the codification of it—is exemplified by a surprising statement in one of Joseph Addison's *Spectator* papers: "Among my Daily-Papers, which I bestow on the Publick, there are some which are written with Regularity and Method, and others that run out into the Wildness of those Compositions, which go by the Name of Essays" (IV: 186). Beyond its pointed contrast of "Regularity" and "Wildness," this passage contains a notable revelation—that, contrary to most descriptions of his work, Addison did not consider all of his *Spectator* papers to be essays. Anything "written with Regularity and Method," as he indicates elsewhere, he considered to be "a set Discourse" (II: 465) in contrast with "the Looseness and Freedom of an Essay" (II: 465). Having asserted and reiterated the contrast, Addison subsequently expanded it by distinguishing between the composing processes he followed in each case: "As for the first, I have the whole Scheme of the Discourse in Mind, before I set Pen to Paper. In the other kind of Writing, it is sufficient that I have several Thoughts on a Subject, without troubling myself to range them in such order, that they may seem to grow out of one another, and be disposed under the proper Heads" (IV: 186). And as if to solidify the distinction, Addison identifies the antecedents for each type: "*Seneca* and *Montaigne* are patterns of writing in this last Kind, as *Tully* and *Aristotle* excel in the other" (IV: 186). Given his neoclassical bias, it is not surprising that Addison favored methodical discourse, yet he also knew enough from his firsthand experience of writing to acknowledge that the essay allowed him the "Freedom" to explore ideas and to engage material "that has not been treated of by others" (II: 465).

By the time that Samuel Johnson compiled his *Dictionary of the English Language*, the contrast had become so well established that he echoed it in his pithy definition of the essay: "a loose sally of the mind; an irregular, indigested piece, not a regular, orderly performance." Johnson's antithesis is tinged, of course, with neoclassical scorn, much as his extended discussion in the *Rambler* gives an ironic account of the essay's advantages over lengthy and learned forms of writing:

> The writer of essays escapes many embarrassments to which a large work would have exposed him; he seldom harasses his reason with long trains of consequences, dims his eyes with the perusal of antiquated volumes, or burthens his memory with great accumulations of preparatory knowledge. A careless glance upon a favourite author, or transient survey of the varieties of life, is sufficient to supply the first hint or seminal idea, which enlarged by the gradual accretion of matter stored in the mind, is by the warmth of fancy easily expanded into flowers, and sometimes ripened into fruit. (201)

Hasty and careless though the essayist appears to be in this account of an essay's gestation, Johnson's piece just as quickly expands his seminal idea about the essay into two paragraphs of reflection on the unpredictable and uncontrollable aspects of composing an essay, which segues into a meditative essay on the uncertainties of life. Thus in the very form and content of his piece Johnson tacitly endorsed the ease of the essay, much as his neoclassical sympathies inclined him against its lack of extensive learning.

Nineteenth-century essayists, on the other hand, were quite receptive to the contrast, not only because it spoke to their interests in a more natural or seemingly freer form than methodically structured writing, but also because it embodied such a clear-cut endorsement of impressionistic rather than definitive thought. Charles Lamb was so in tune with the contrast that he turned it into a sustained distinction between two mental archetypes, one of which he acknowledged to be the basis of his Elian persona:

> There is an order of imperfect intellects (under which mine must be content to rank). . . . The owners of the sort of faculties I allude to, have minds rather suggestive than comprehensive. They have no pretences to much clearness or precision in their ideas, or in their manner of expressing them. Their intellectual wardrobe (to confess clearly) has few whole pieces in it. They are content with fragments and scattered pieces of Truth. (135)

In a more exuberant spirit, the midcentury writer Alexander Smith extolled the essayist's wayward and imperfect intellect: "The essay-writer is a chartered libertine, and a law unto himself. A quick ear and eye, an ability to discern the infinite suggestiveness of common things, a brooding meditative spirit, are all that the essayist requires to start business with" (27).

Given such a "libertine" view of the essayist, it is hardly surprising that by century's end Agnes Repplier went even further and expounded a hedonic view of the essay: "It offers no instruction, save through the medium of enjoyment, and one saunters lazily along with a charming unconsciousness of effort. Great results are not to be gained in this fashion, but it should sometimes be play-hour for us all" (233). By this point, it would seem that the dichotomy had become so conventionalized and attenuated as to result in a trivialization of the essay as escapist writing, espoused both by Repplier and other genteel essayists such as Richard Burton, who conceived of the essay as "mood and form" and thus considered "the theme unimportant in itself" (87).

During much of the twentieth century, however, essayists invoked the contrast to define and affirm a quite different kind of freedom—not just from the conventionalized structures that prevail in other forms of discourse, but also from any kind of generic strictures that inhibit the mind itself, as Cynthia Ozick makes clear in her definition of the essay "as the movement of a free mind at play." Such a wide-open conception of the genre tacitly implies a freedom from any kind of form, which suggests that strictly speaking the essay is an antigenre, a heretical form of writing in the universe of discourse. Or as Theodor Adorno puts it, "the law of the innermost form of the essay is heresy" (171).

The heretical impulse can be seen most clearly in a pointed contrast between the essay and the article that dominated the thinking of essayists throughout the twentieth century. Howells invoked the distinction in 1902, as if it were already a commonplace, lamenting the time "when the essay began to confuse itself with the article, and to assume an obligation to premises and conclusions" (802). Though Howells does not venture to say when the change took place, he distinguishes the article's "premises and conclusions" from the essay's "wandering airs of thought" (802), harking back, in effect, to the long-standing dichotomy between methodical discourse and essayistic rambling. By midcentury, however, the dichotomy was cast in more up-to-date terms when Joseph Wood Krutch called the essay "man-made as opposed to the machine-made article" (19). Hoagland, in a similar spirit, asserted that "essays don't usually boil down to a summary, as articles do, and the style of the writer has a 'nap' to it, a combination of personality and originality and energetic loose ends that stand up like the nap on a piece of wool and can't be brushed flat" (25–26). Thus the contrast was reframed in terms of a dichotomy between organic and mechanistic form, and by extension between humanistic and technological values.

Twentieth-century essayists often echoed and expanded upon that dichotomy by distinguishing between the personal orientation of the essay and the factual mode of the article. In one formulation or another, this distinction has roused essayists more than any other issue. Some of their intensity can be traced to the fact that many editors and readers had been lured away from the essay by the utilitarian appeal of the article. With the onset of World War I and the economic, political, and social upheavals that followed, magazine editors found themselves compelled to satisfy a widespread demand for highly informed articles about the most pressing and complex issues of the day. By the early 1930s, magazines had become so dominated by articles that Katharine Fullerton Gerould decried "the spectacle of the old-line magazines forsaking their literary habit, and stuffing us month after month, with facts, figures, propaganda, and counter-propaganda" (393). Gerould's outburst provoked so many letters to the editor that the *Saturday Review of Literature* featured them for two consecutive weeks in a "Plebiscite for Mrs. Gerould."

The essayists' quarrel with the article, though provoked in part by competition for magazine space, was rooted in their conviction that it allowed no room for the personal experience, personal thought, or personal voice of the essayist. Thus they depicted the article as being out of touch with human concerns. Or, as Krutch put it, "The magazines are full of articles dealing statistically with, for example, the alleged failure or success of marriage," but "one man's 'familiar essay' on love and marriage might get closer to some all-important realities than any number of 'studies' could" (19). Krutch's remarks also reveal that essayists were aroused by a distrust of specialized studies, heavily reliant on factual information that they regarded as symptomatic of an ill-placed confidence in the reliability of systematized and impersonal approaches to knowledge. Ultimately, then, they depicted the article as embodying a naively positivistic approach to knowledge, an approach out of touch with the problematic nature of things. William Gass is especially emphatic on this score in his satiric portrait of the scholarly article: "It must appear complete and straightforward and footnoted and useful and certain and is very likely a veritable Michelin of misdirection; for the article pretends that everything is clear, that its argument is unassailable, that there are no soggy patches, no illicit references, no illegitimate connections" (25). In keeping with his attack on the certitudes of the article, Gass portrays the essay as having a disinterested engagement in the play of ideas and thus as making no special claims about the truth of its observations: "It turns round and round upon its topic, exposing this aspect and then that; proposing possibilities, reciting opinions, disposing of prejudice and even of the simple truth itself" (25).

The most fully developed depiction of the essay as inherently skeptical and antimethodical can be found in the work of Theodor Adorno, who offers an extensive set of variations on the theme of the essay's "heresy":

> Luck and play are essential to the essay (152). The essay does not obey the rules of the game of organized science. . . . [T]he essay does not strive for closed, deductive or inductive, construction. As the essay denies any primeval givens, so it refuses any definitions of its concepts (159). In the essay, concepts do not build a continuum of operations, thought does not advance in a single direction, rather the aspects of the argument interweave as in a carpet (160). The essay . . . proceeds so to speak methodically unmethodically (161). Discontinuity is essential to the essay. (164)

Though radical in its opposition to any systematized form of thought, Adorno's conception of the essay is the logical extension of Montaigne's contrast between the "system of the scholars" and his "disjointed parts." Indeed, the continuity of their thought is reflected in Adorno's equation of "the neo-positivists," whom he opposes, "with Scholasticism," which Montaigne rejected (160). Adorno's echo of Montaigne, like Gass's critique of the article, highlights the ultimate yearning of essayists to be free from any systematized form of thinking or writing. Thus Díaz-Plaja claims that "the essayist remains free of the systematic demonstration of a treatise" (237), much as Hoagland asserts that "because essays are directly concerned with the mind and the mind's idiosyncrasy, the very freedom the mind possesses is bestowed on this branch of literature that does honor to it, and the fascination of the mind is the fascination of the essay" (27). So it might be said that above all else essayists conceive of the essay as a place of intellectual refuge, a domain sacred to the freedom of the mind itself.

Given this collectively shared view, one might well be moved to wonder what essayists have to say about the formal essay, that long-honored subgenre that frequently turns up in literary handbooks, histories, and encyclopedias. Surprising as it may be, the formal essay does not seem to figure in the thinking of essayists, not even in the commentary of William Hazlitt, Leslie Stephen, and Virginia Woolf, who survey the work of their predecessors and might well have considered academic distinctions between the formal and informal essay. In fact, this contrast is discussed only by Phillip Lopate, and he brings it up only to call it into question, noting that "it is difficult even now to draw a firm distinction between the two," though he also acknowledges having excluded Bacon and Emerson from his anthology of the personal essay because he "decided in the end that they were not really personal essayists but great formal essayists whose minds moved inexorably toward the expression of impersonal wisdom and authority, regardless of flickering references to an 'I.'" The closest that any other essayist comes to making such a distinction is Smith's assertion that "Bacon is the greatest of the serious and stately essayists—Montaigne the greatest of the garrulous and communicative" (40), or Huxley's discussion of three different kinds: those that focus primarily on "the personal and autobiographical," those that turn their attention outward to the "concrete-particular" aspects of "some literary or scientific or political theme," and those that "work in the world of high abstractions" (v–vi). But in elaborating their distinctions, neither Smith nor Huxley refers to the "formal" essay, or to any of the logical, systematic, and tightly organized qualities that are usually associated with it. Ultimately, most essayists probably do not recognize the formal essay, because it embodies the very antithesis of what they conceive an essay to be. For much the same reason Paul Graham offers an extensive set of distinctions "between real essays and the things one has to write in school."

Most essayists do not attempt to classify essays in any fashion, and the few who do make gestures in that direction offer little more than casual listings, such as Hardwick's observation that "most incline to a condition of unexpressed hyphenation: the critical essay, the autobiographical essay, the travel essay, the political—and so on and so on" (xiii). Classifications more rigorous than these would be inconsistent with a conception of the essay as being allied to the free play of thought and feeling. In keeping with this view, White playfully suggests the hopelessness of trying to classify essays: "There are as many kinds of essays as there are human attitudes and poses, as many essay flavors as there are Howard Johnson ice creams" (vii).

Despite their resistance to methodical systems of thought and discourse, most essayists consider the essay to be a disciplined form of writing. Indeed, their insistence on its freedom from conventionalized form and thought probably makes them all the more intent on dispelling any notion that the essay is a free-for-all kind of writing. White is especially pointed on this issue: "And even the essayist's escape from discipline is only a partial escape: the essay, although a relaxed form, imposes its own discipline, raises its own problems, and these disciplines and problems soon become apparent and (we all hope) act as a deterrent to anyone wielding a pen merely because he entertains random thoughts or is in a happy or wandering mood" (viii). Montaigne, "disjointed" though he professes himself to be, sounds the same note of caution: "I go out of my way, but rather by license than carelessness. My ideas follow one another, but sometimes it is from a distance, and look at each other, but with a sidelong glance" (761). Even Adorno makes a point of asserting that the essay "is not unlogical; rather it obeys logical criteria in so far as the totality of its sentences must fit together coherently" (169).

Adorno's view of coherence, like White's and Montaigne's, is predicated not on mere surface continuity from one statement to the next but on a deep interconnection among ideas, on a cohesion so powerful, as Montaigne implies, that related ideas seem to be animated by an affinity for each other no matter how far apart or seemingly unrelated. Given this view of coherence, the essay evidently requires a delicate set of mental adjustments, attuned both to giving the mind free rein and to reining it in, so that the form of an essay will appear to reflect the process of a mind in action, but a mind that is always in control of itself no matter how wayward it may seem to be. In other words, the essay is predicated on an idea akin to organic form, yet also on an idea of artful artlessness, or as Montaigne exclaims, "Lord, what beauty there is in these lusty sallies and this variation, and more so the more casual and accidental they seem" (761). Addison hints at this complex combination of the organic and the artful when he says that in writing an essay "it is sufficient that I have several Thoughts on a Subject, without troubling my self to range them in such order, that they may seem to grow out of one another, and be disposed under their proper Heads" (IV:186). Gerould reaffirms this complex idea of essayistic form in her assertion that "the basis of the essay is meditation, and it must in a measure admit the reader to the meditative process. . . . An essay, to some extent thinks aloud; though not in the loose and pointless way to which the 'stream of consciousness' addicts have accustomed us" (Essay 412). Gass affirms the same principle when he speaks of Emerson as having "made the essay into the narrative disclosure of thought . . . but not of such thinking as had actually occurred. Real thought is gawky and ungracious" (34). Huxley redefines it as "free association artistically controlled" in trying to account for the "paradoxical secret of Montaigne's best essays" (vii). And Adorno codifies the paradox in his assertion that the essay "proceeds, so to speak, methodically unmethodically."

In keeping with this idea of form, essayists tend to see the significance of an essay as residing primarily in its display of a mind engaging ideas. Gass, for example, declares that "the hero of the essay is its author in the act of thinking things out, feeling and finding a way; it is the mind in the marvels and miseries of its makings, in the *work* of the imagination, the search for form" (19–20). In a similar vein, Hoagland asserts that "through its tone and tumbling progression, it conveys the quality of the author's mind," and thus he concludes that "the fascination of the mind is the fascination of the essay" (27). John D'Agata likewise asserts that "the essay is the equivalent of a mind in rumination" (9), much as Ander Monson claims that "stepping into an essay is stepping into the writer's mind." In each of these statements, as in others, essayists focus so persistently on the image of the author in the process of thinking that they tend to perceive the essay as embodying the drama of thought, or what Elizabeth Hardwick refers to as "thought itself in orbit" (xviii). Lopate, for example, maintains "that, in an essay, the track of a person's thoughts struggling to achieve some understanding of a problem is the plot, is the adventure" (1). Adorno shifts the dramatic focus from the essayist thinking to thought in action by asserting that "the thinker does not think, but rather transforms himself into an arena of intellectual experience, without simplifying it" (160–61). And Lukács views the drama in such abstract terms that he does not even allude to the essayist, but conceives of the essay instead as enacting the experience of thought itself: "There are experiences, then, which cannot be expressed by any gesture and which long for expression. From all that has been said you will know what experiences I mean and of what kind they are, as immediate reality, as spontaneous principle of existence" (7). But not even Lukács goes so far as to remove the essayist from the scene of the essay, explicitly noting that "the hero of the essay was once alive, and so his life must be given form; but this life, too, is as much inside the work as everything is in poetry" (11).

Most essayists give special attention to the role of the essayist in the essay, not only in their concern with the flow of an author's thoughts but also in their preoccupation with an author's implied personality or persona. The importance of personality is reflected in the fact that essayists generally make it a defining feature of the essay. This emphasis on personality is reflected in a tendency, especially among nineteenth-century essayists, to discuss their predecessors primarily in terms of the changing moods or aspects of personality that they find in their essays, occasionally even judging them for what they deem to be an inappropriate manner, as in Hazlitt's derision of Johnson for being "always upon stilts" (101). Hazlitt's view of Johnson is reflective of norms that have prevailed throughout the nineteenth and twentieth centuries, the basic premise of which, as Leslie Stephen puts it, is that "no literary skill will make average readers take kindly to a man who does not attract by some amiable quality" (69). According to these norms, "the charm of the familiar essayist," in Arthur Benson's view, "depends upon his power of giving the sense of a good-humored, gracious and reasonable personality" (59). In keeping with such norms, Woolf asserts that "the voice of the scold should never be heard in this narrow plot" (217), and Hardwick observes that "pompously self-righteous, lamely jocular forays offend because an air of immature certainty surrounds them" (xvii). As these remarks suggest, and as Gass makes clear, "this lack of fanaticism, this geniality in the thinker, this sense of the social proprieties involved (the essay can be polemical but never pushy) are evidence of how fully aware the author is of the proper etiquette for meeting minds. . . . If there is too much earnestness, too great a need to persuade, a want of correct convictions in the reader is implied, and therefore an *absence of community*" (24).

Given their concern for engaging readers, "for meeting minds," it should come as no surprise that essayists tend to offer problematic definitions of the persona or personality of an essayist. Woolf hints at the complexity when she speaks of personality as "the essayist's most proper but most dangerous and delicate tool" (222). A few sentences later she defines the complexity in terms of another paradox: "Never to be yourself and yet always—that is the problem" (222). In a similar spirit, Vivian Gornick tells of discovering the need for a persona "who was me and at the same time was not me." And Nancy Mairs likewise declares that "I am not the woman whose voice animates my essays. She's made up. . . . But I am more the woman of my essays than I am the woman of my fiction." This paradoxical conception of the essayist's persona as being at once an authentic reflection and a fictionalized construction of self can be traced in part to the practices of the periodical essayists, whom Hazlitt describes as having "assumed some fictitious and humorous disguise, which, however, in a great degree corresponded to their own peculiar habit and character" (95). Even in the absence of self-evidently fictitious disguises, essayists tend to discuss personality in terms that suggest they see it as involving a subtle combination of actual and fictional qualities. In an unpublished review of Hazlitt, for example, Lamb notes that "this assumption of a character, if it be not truly (as we are inclined to believe) his own, is that which gives force & life to his writing" (303). Similarly, Benson's previously cited remark about the essayist's "power" to create a pleasing personality suggests that it is not necessarily an authentic reflection of the author but a textual quality that the essayist is capable of projecting. Weeks likewise observes that "style is at once the man himself and the shimmering costume of words which centers your attention" (81). This complex interplay between the essayist's authentic self and the self in costume is vividly delineated by E. B. White: "The essayist . . . can pull on any sort of shirt, be any sort of person, according to his mood or subject matter. . . . [he] cannot indulge himself in deceit or in concealment, for he will be found out in time" (vii–viii). So it would seem that essayists explicitly recognize an intimate connection between role-playing and essay writing, even as they affirm that the roles they play must be deeply in tune with their innermost sense of themselves.

The complexity of role-playing is further complicated by the challenge of doing so at the same time that one is projecting the impression of a particular "meditative process." At first thought, of course, there might appear to be no problem here, since the two impressions presumably must be in harmony with each other—the persona or personality giving direction to the meditative process and the meditative process in turn revealing the most distinctive aspects of personality. But as essayists define personality, it seems to refer to a public or exterior aspect of self, something that one can put on and take off as easily as if it were a "costume" or "garb" or "shirt," whereas a meditative process is centered in one's mind or consciousness and thus involves the most private and interior aspect of one's self. Paradoxically, then, essayists apparently conceive of the essay as embodying a multistable impression of the self, in the process of thought and in the process of sharing thought with others. Interiority and exteriority simultaneously manifest. Or, as Gass says, "The unity of each essay is a unity achieved by the speaker for his audience as well as for himself, a kind of reassociation of his sensibility and theirs" (35). Considered in this light, the essay, rather than being a straightforward and transparent form of exposition, is a highly complex and problematic kind of writing—an enactment of thought and a projection of personality that use language dramatically, as in a monologue or a soliloquy, and that thereby call for literary interpretation. To explain and illustrate what might be entailed in such analysis is clearly beyond the scope of this piece, but it does suggest that a methodology for understanding the essay is long overdue.

Works Cited

Adorno, T. W. "The Essay as Form." Trans. Bob Hullot-Kentor. *New German Critique* 31 (Spring–Summer 1984): 151–71.

Anonymous [Virginia Woolf]. "Modern Essays." *Times Literary Supplement* 30 (November 1922): 1–2.

Bacon, Francis. *The Proficience and Advancement of Learning.* Oxford: Oxford English Texts, 1974.

Benson, Arthur C. "The Art of the Essayist." *Modern English Essays*. Ed. Ernest Rhys. Vol. 4. London: J. M. Dent, 1922. 50–63.

Cornwallis, William. "Of Essays and Books." *Essays*. London: n.p., 191–202.

D'Agata, John. "1500 B.C.E." *The Lost Origins of the Essay*. St. Paul: Graywolf, 2009. 9.

Díaz-Plaja, Guillermo. "Los límites del ensayo." *La Estafeta Literaria* 582 (February 15, 1976): 236–39.

Gass, William. "Emerson and the Essay." *Habitations of the Word*. New York: Simon and Schuster, 1985. 9–49.

Gerould, Katharine Fullerton. "An Essay on Essays." *North American Review* 240.3 (December 1935): 409–18.

Gornick, Vivian. *The Situation and the Story*. New York: Farrar, Straus and Giroux, 2001.

Graham, Paul. "The Age of the Essay." http://www.paulgraham.com/essay.html

Hardwick, Elizabeth. Introduction. *The Best American Essays, 1986*. Ed. Elizabeth

Hardwick. Series ed. Robert Atwan. New York: Ticknor and Fields, 1986. xiii–xxi.
Hazlitt, William. "On the Periodical Essayists." *The Complete Works of William Hazlitt*. Vol. 6. London: Dent, 1931. 91–105.
Hoagland, Edward. "What I Think, What I Am." *The Tugman's Passage*. New York: Random House, 1982. 24–27.
Howells, William Dean. "The Old Fashioned Essay." *Harpers* (October 1902): 802–3.
Huxley, Aldous. Preface. *Collected Essays*. New York: Harper, 1960. v–ix.
Johnson, Samuel. *A Dictionary of the English Language*. London: W. Strahan, 1755.
———. "Rambler No. 184." *The Complete Works of Samuel Johnson*. Ed. W. J. Bate and Albrecht B. Strauss. Vol. 5. New Haven: Yale UP, 1969. 200–204.
Kenko. "Essays in Idleness." *The Art of the Personal Essay*. Ed. Phillip Lopate. New York: Anchor Books, 1994. 30–37.
Krutch, Joseph Wood. "No Essays, Please." *Saturday Review of Literature* (March 10, 1951): 18–19, 35.
Lamb, Charles. "Imperfect Sympathies." *Essays of Elia*. Iowa City: U of Iowa P, 2003. 133, 147.
———. Unpublished Review of Hazlitt's *Table Talk*. *Lamb as Critic*. Ed. Roy Park. Lincoln: U of Nebraska P, 1980. 299–307.
Lopate, Phillip. "The Essay Lives—In Disguise." *New York Times Book Review* (November 18, 1984): 1, 47–49.
Lukács, Georg. "On the Nature and Form of the Essay." *Soul and Form*. Trans. Anna Benstock. Cambridge, MA: MIT P, 1978. 1–18.
Mairs, Nancy. "But First." *Carnal Acts*. New York: HarperCollins, 1990.
Monson, Ander. "Essay as Hack." http://otherelectricities.com/swarm/essayashack.html
Montaigne, Michel de. *The Complete Essays of Montaigne*. Trans. Donald M. Frame. Stanford: Stanford UP, 1957.
Ozick, Cynthia. "She: Portrait of the Essay as a Warm Body." *Quarrel and Quandry*. New York: Vintage, 2001.
Repplier, Agnes. "The Passing of the Essay." *In the Dozy Hours*. Boston: Houghton Mifflin, 1895. 226–35.
Sanders, Scott Russell. "The Singular First Person." *Essayists on the Essay: Redefining the Genre*. Ed. Alexander Butrym. Athens: U of Georgia P, 1989. 31–42.
Smith, Alexander. "On the Writing of Essays." *Dreamthorp: A Book of Essays Written in the Country*. Portland, ME: Thomas Bird Mosher, 1913. 23–46.
The Spectator. Ed. Donald Bond. 5 vols. London: Oxford UP, 1965.
Stephen, Leslie. "The Essayists." *Men, Books, and Manners*. Minneapolis: U of Minnesota P, 1956. 45–73.
Weeks, Edward. "The Peripatetic Reviewer." *Atlantic Monthly* (August 1954): 81–82.
White, E. B. *Essays of E. B. White*. New York: Harper, 1977.
Woolf, Virginia. "The Modern Essay." *The Common Reader*. New York: Harcourt Brace Jovanovich, 1953.

ESSAYISTS ON THE ESSAY

MICHEL EYQUEM DE MONTAIGNE (1533–92), though widely recognized for his philosophic skepticism and his pathbreaking, free-ranging *Essais*, was known in his own time for his statesmanlike moderation of the prevailing religious conflicts between Catholics and Protestants. Even after retiring from public life in 1571 to work on his essays and to travel, he was called back into service as mayor of Bordeaux. But Montaigne incessantly wrote and revised his self-oriented essays—"I am myself the subject of my work"—in defiance of literary conventions that scorned such writing. His self-absorption was ultimately motivated by a distinctively modern preoccupation with the complexity of his inner life, with the flow of his thoughts, as he makes clear in the excerpts that follow: "What I chiefly portray is my cogitations, a shapeless subject that does not lend itself to expression in actions. It is all I can do to couch my thoughts in this airy medium of words."

From "Of Practice," "Of Repentance," and "Of Vanity"

From "Of Practice"

What I write here is not my teaching, but my study; it is not a lesson for others, but for me.

And yet it should not be held against me if I publish what I write. What is useful to me may also by accident be useful to another. Moreover, I am not spoiling anything, I am using only what is mine. And if I play the fool, it is at my expense and without harm to anyone. For it is a folly that will die with me, and will have no consequences. We have heard of only two or three ancients who opened up this road, and even of them we cannot say whether their manner in the least resembled mine, since we know only their names. No one since has followed their lead. It is a thorny undertaking, and more so than it seems, to follow a movement so wandering as that of our mind, to penetrate the opaque depths of its innermost folds, to pick out and immobilize the innumerable flutterings that agitate it. And it is a new and extraordinary amusement, which withdraws us from the ordinary occupations of the world, yes, even from those most recommended.

It is many years now that I have had only myself as object of my thoughts, that I have been examining and studying only myself; and if I study anything else, it is in order promptly to apply it to myself, or rather within myself. And it does not seem to me that I am making a mistake if—as is done in the other sciences, which are incomparably less useful—I impart what I have learned in this one, though I am hardly satisfied with the progress I have made in it. There is no description equal in difficulty, or certainly in usefulness, to the description of oneself. Even so one must spruce up, even so one must present oneself in an orderly arrangement, if one would go out in public. Now, I am constantly adorning myself, for I am constantly describing myself.

Custom has made speaking of oneself a vice, and obstinately forbids it out of hatred for the boasting that seems always to accompany it. Instead of blowing the child's nose, as we should, this amounts to pulling it off.

> Flight from a fault will lead us into crime.
>
> Horace

I find more harm than good in this remedy. But even if it were true that it is presumptuous, no matter what the circumstances, to talk to the public about oneself, I still must not, according to my general plan, refrain from an action that openly displays this morbid quality, since it is in me; nor may I conceal this fault, which I not only practice but profess. However, to say what I think about it, custom is wrong to condemn wine because many get drunk on it. We can misuse only things which are good. And I believe that the rule against speaking of oneself applies only to the vulgar form of this failing. Such rules are bridles for calves, with which neither the saints, whom we hear speaking so boldly about themselves, nor the philosophers, nor the theologians curb themselves. Nor do I, though I am none of these. If they do not write about themselves expressly, at least when the occasion leads them to it they do not hesitate to put themselves prominently on display. What does Socrates treat of more fully than himself? To what does he lead his disciples' conversation more often than to talk about themselves, not about the lesson of their book, but about the essence and movement of their soul?

From "Of Repentance"

Others form man; I tell of him, and portray a particular one, very ill-formed, whom I should really make very different from what he is if I had to fashion him over again. But now it is done.

Now the lines of my painting do not go astray, though they change and vary. The world is but a perennial movement. All things in it are in constant motion—the earth, the rocks of the Caucasus, the pyramids of Egypt—both with the common motion and with their own. Stability itself is nothing but a more languid motion.

I cannot keep my subject still. It goes along befuddled and staggering, with a natural drunkenness. I take it in this condition, just as it is at the moment I give my attention to it. I do not portray being: I portray passing. Not the passing from one age to another, or, as the people say, from seven years to seven years, but from day to day, from minute to minute. My history needs to be adapted to the moment. I may presently change, not only by chance, but also by intention. This is a record of various and changeable occurrences, and of irresolute and, when it so befalls, contradictory ideas: whether I am different myself, or whether I take hold of my subjects in different circumstances and aspects. So, all in all, I may indeed contradict myself now and then; but truth, as Demades said, I do not contradict. If my mind could gain a firm footing, I would not make essays, I would make decisions; but it is always in apprenticeship and on trial.

I set forth a humble and inglorious life; that does not matter. You can tie up all moral philosophy with a common and private life just as well as with a life of richer stuff. Each man bears the entire form of man's estate.

Authors communicate with the people by some special extrinsic mark; I am the first to do so by my entire being, as Michel de Montaigne, not as a grammarian or a poet or a jurist. If the world complains that I speak too much of myself, I complain that it does not even think of itself.

But is it reasonable that I, so fond of privacy in actual life, should aspire to publicity in the knowledge of me? Is it reasonable too that I should set forth to the world, where fashioning and art have so much credit and authority, some crude and simple products of nature, and of a very feeble nature at that? Is it not making a wall without stone, or something like that, to construct books without knowledge and without art? Musical fancies are guided by art, mine by chance.

At least I have one thing according to the rules: that no man ever treated a subject he knew and understood better than I do the subject I have undertaken; and that in this I am the most learned man alive. Secondly, that no man ever penetrated more deeply into his material, or plucked its limbs and consequences cleaner, or reached more accurately and fully the goal he had set for his work. To accomplish it, I need only bring it to fidelity; and that is in it, as sincere and pure as can be found. I speak the truth, not my fill of it, but as much as I dare speak; and I dare to do so a little more as I grow old, for it seems that custom allows old age more freedom to prate and more indiscretion in talking about oneself. It cannot happen here as I see it happening often, that the craftsman and his work contradict each other: "Has a man whose conversation is so good written such a stupid book?" or "Have such learned writings come from a man whose conversation is so feeble?"

If a man is commonplace in conversation and rare in writing, that means that his capacity is in the place from which he borrows it, and not in himself. A learned man is not learned in all matters; but the capable man is capable in all matters, even in ignorance.

In this case we go hand in hand and at the same pace, my book and I. In other cases one may commend or blame the work apart from the workman; not so here; he who touches the one, touches the other.

From "Of Vanity"

I go out of my way, but rather by license than carelessness. My ideas follow one another, but sometimes it is from a distance, and look at each other, but with a sidelong glance. I have run my eyes over a certain dialogue of Plato, a fantastic motley in two parts, the beginning part about love, all the rest about rhetoric. The ancients do not fear these changes, and with wonderful grace they let themselves thus be tossed in the wind, or seem to. The titles of my chapters do not always embrace their matter; often they only denote it by some sign, like those other titles, *The Maid of Andros*, *The Eunuch*, or those other names, Sulla, Cicero, Torquatus. I love the poetic gait, by leaps and gambols. It is an art, as Plato says, light, flighty, daemonic. There are works of Plutarch's in which he forgets his theme, in which the treatment of his subject is found only incidentally, quite smothered in foreign matter. See his movements in "The Daemon of Socrates." Lord, what beauty there is in these lusty sallies and this variation, and more so the more casual and accidental they seem.

It is the inattentive reader who loses my subject, not I. Some word about it will always be found off in a corner, which will not fail to be sufficient, though it takes little room. I seek out change indiscriminately and tumultuously. My style and my mind alike go roaming. "A man must be a little mad if he does not want to be even more stupid," say the precepts of our masters, and even more so their examples.

A thousand poets drag and languish prosaically; but the best ancient prose—and I scatter it here indiscriminately as verse—shines throughout with the vigor and boldness of poetry, and gives the effect of its frenzy. To poetry we must certainly concede mastery and preeminence in speech. The poet, says Plato, seated on the tripod of the Muses, pours out in a frenzy whatever comes into his mouth, like the spout of a fountain, without ruminating and weighing it; and from him escape things of different colors and contradictory substance in an intermittent flow. He himself is utterly poetic, and the old theology is poetry, the scholars say, and the first philosophy. It is the original language of the Gods.

I want the matter to make its own divisions. It shows well enough where it changes, where it concludes, where it begins, where it resumes, without my interlacing it with words, with links and seams introduced for the benefit of weak or heedless ears, and without writing glosses on myself. Who is there that would not rather not be read than be read sleepily or in passing? *Nothing is so useful that it can be of value when taken on the run* [Seneca]. If to take up books were to take them in, and if to see them were to consider them, and to run through them were to grasp them, I should be wrong to make myself out quite as ignorant as I say I am.

Since I cannot arrest the attention of the reader by weight, it is all to the good if I chance to arrest it by my embroilment. "True, but he will afterward repent of having wasted his time over it." That may be, but still he will have wasted his time over it. And then there are natures like that, in whom understanding breeds disdain, who will think the better of me because they will not know what I mean. They will conclude that my meaning is profound from its obscurity, which, to speak in all earnest, I hate very strongly, and I would avoid it if I could avoid myself. Aristotle somewhere boasts of affecting it: blameworthy affectation!

Because such frequent breaks into chapters as I used at the beginning seemed to me to disrupt and dissolve attention before it was aroused, making it disdain to settle and collect for so little, I have begun making them longer, requiring fixed purpose and assigned leisure. In such an occupation, if you will not give a man a single hour, you will not give him anything. And you do nothing for a man for whom you do nothing except while doing something else. Besides, perhaps I have some personal obligation to speak only by halves, to speak confusedly, to speak discordantly.

The Complete Essays of Montaigne, 1580; translated by Donald Frame, 1958

SIR WILLIAM CORNWALLIS THE YOUNGER (c. 1579–1614) served in Parliament, in the king's privy chamber, and as a diplomatic courier for his father, who was ambassador to Spain. But he lived so extravagantly that his wife and eight children were impoverished when he died. His two collections of essays (1600, 1601) appeared shortly after Bacon's first collection of 1597, yet differed markedly in their plainness, directness, and sometimes personal stance, as in the opening of his piece "Of Alehouses": "I write this from an Alehouse, into which I am driven by night." His thoughts on the essay, excerpted below, are similarly frank in declaring himself at the outset to be in effect the first genuine essayist, because, unlike those who preceded him, his pieces were not "strong, and able to endure the sharpest trial"—a clear allusion to the root meaning of essay as a trial or attempt.

From "Of Essays and Books"

I hold neither Plutarch's, nor none of these ancient short manner of writings, nor Montaigne's, nor such of this latter time to be rightly termed essays, for though they be short, yet they are strong, and able to endure the sharpest trial: but mine are essays, who am but newly bound prentice to the inquisition of knowledge, and use these papers as a painter's boy a board, who is trying to bring his hand and his fancy acquainted. It is a manner of writing well befitting undigested motions, or a head not knowing his strength like a circumspect runner trying for a start, or providence that tastes before she buys: for it is easier to think well then, to do well; and no trial to have handsome dapper conceits run invisibly in a brain, but to put them out, and then look upon them: if they prove nothing but words, yet they break not promise with the world; for they say but an essay, like a scrivener trying his pen before he engrosses his work; nor to speak plainly, are they more to blame then many other that promise more: for the most that I have yet touched, have millions of words to the bringing forth one reason, and when a reason is gotten, there is such borrowing it one of another, that in a multitude of books, still that conceit, or some issued out of that, appears so belabored, and worn, as in the end it is good for nothing but for a proverb.

Essayes by Sir William Cornwallis, the Younger, 1600–1601, modernized by Patrick Madden, http://essays.quotidiana.org

FRANCIS BACON (1561–1626), the first English essayist, was a prolific author who wrote a utopian novel entitled *New Atlantis* (1626), as well as substantial works on philosophic and scientific methodology, contributing to the development of what is now known as controlled research. Bacon was also trained in the law and rose to become Lord Chancellor of England in 1618, before being stripped of his office on charges of corruption in 1621, for the then-common practice of accepting gifts from legal petitioners. Bacon's pithy essays, first published in 1597 and expanded in 1612 and 1625, differ markedly from Montaigne's, not only in their brevity and rigorous focus but also in their complete self-effacement and their notably pragmatic outlook. In the following passage from *The Proficience and Advancement of Learning* (1605), Bacon offers a detailed rationale for "writing in aphorisms," as he did in his essays, rather than "in method."

From *The Proficience and Advancement of Learning*

But the writing in aphorisms hath many excellent virtues, whereto the writing in method[1] doth not approach.

For first, it trieth the writer, whether he be superficial or solid: for aphorisms, except they should be ridiculous, cannot be made but of the pith and heart of sciences; for discourse of illustration is cut off; recitals of examples are cut off; discourse of connection and order is cut off; descriptions of practice are cut off. So there remaineth nothing to fill the aphorisms but some good quantity of observation; and therefore no man can suffice, nor in reason will attempt, to write aphorisms, but he that is sound and grounded. But in methods,

> "Tantum series juncturaque pollet,
> Tantum de medio sumptis accedit honoris,"[2]

as a man shall make a great show of an art, which, if it were disjointed, would come to little. Secondly, methods are more fit to win consent or belief, but less fit to point to action; for they carry a kind of demonstration in orb or circle, one part illuminating another, and therefore satisfy. But particulars being dispersed do best agree with dispersed directions. And lastly, aphorisms, representing a knowledge broken, do invite men to inquire further; whereas methods, carrying the show of a total, do secure men, as if they were at furthest.

1. By "writing in method" Bacon means "a systematically organized and methodically interconnected mode of presentation."

2. The numerous connections make such a strong case that everything in the middle is taken for granted and accepted without question.

The Proficience and Advancement of Learning, 1605

JOSEPH ADDISON (1672–1719) was known in his time not only for cofounding the *Spectator* with Richard Steele but also for his Latin verse, his lives of the English poets, his translation of Virgil's *Georgics*, and his tragic play *Cato*, which celebrated individual liberty over governmental tyranny and thus helped to inspire the American Revolution. Though Addison is justly celebrated for creating the persona of a spectator, as well as a cast of characters, to reflect on London society, his *Spectator* pieces are too often classified as essays. For Addison himself thought of his pieces as comprising two distinctly different kinds of writing, as he makes clear in a sustained contrast between "some which are written with regularity and method" and "others that run out into the Wildness of those Compositions, which go by the Name of *Essays*." Thus, in the following passage from the *Spectator,* he clearly conceives of the essay as the antithesis of systematic discourse.

From the *Spectator*

—lucidus Ordo—
[Method gives light]—
Hor. Ars Poet. 41

Among my Daily-Papers which I bestow on the Public, there are some which are written with Regularity and Method, and others that run out into the Wildness of those Compositions which go by the Names of Essays. As for the first, I have the whole Scheme of the Discourse in my Mind before I set Pen to Paper. In the other kind of Writing, it is sufficient that I have several Thoughts on a Subject, without troubling my self to range them in such order, that they may seem to grow out of one another, and be disposed under the proper Heads. Seneca and Montaigne are Patterns for Writing in this last kind, as Tully and Aristotle excel in the other. When I read an Author of Genius who writes without Method, I fancy myself in a Wood that abounds with a great many noble Objects, rising among one another in the greatest Confusion and Disorder. When I read a methodical Discourse, I am in a regular Plantation, and can place my self in its several Centers, so as to take a view of all the Lines and Walks that are struck from them. You may ramble in the one a whole Day together, and every Moment discover something or other that is new to you; but when you have done, you will have but a confused imperfect Notion of the Place: In the other, your Eye commands the whole Prospect, and gives you such an Idea of it, as is not easily worn out of the Memory.

Irregularity and want of Method are only supportable in Men of great Learning or Genius, who are often too full to be exact, and therefore choose to throw down their Pearls in Heaps before the Reader, rather than be at the Pains of stringing them.

Method is of advantage to a Work, both in respect to the Writer and the Reader. In regard to the first, it is a great help to his Invention. When a Man has planned his Discourse, he finds a great many Thoughts rising out of every Head, that do not offer themselves upon the general Survey of a Subject. His Thoughts are at the same time more intelligible, and better discover their Drift and Meaning, when they are placed in their proper Lights, and follow one another in a regular Series, than when they are thrown together without Order and Connection. There is always an Obscurity in Confusion, and the same Sentence that would have enlightened the Reader in one part of a Discourse, perplexes him in another. For the same reason likewise every Thought in a methodical Discourse shows itself in its greatest Beauty, as the several Figures in a piece of Painting receive new Grace from their Disposition in the Picture. The Advantages of a Reader from a methodical Discourse, are correspondent with those of the Writer. He comprehends every thing easily, takes it in with Pleasure, and retains it long.

Spectator, No. 476 (September 5, 1712)

SAMUEL JOHNSON (1709–84) is widely regarded as the most distinguished man of letters in the history of English literature, given the extraordinary range of his achievements in producing the *Dictionary of the English Language, The Lives of the Most Eminent English Poets,* and an annotated edition of Shakespeare, as well as poems, plays, and periodical magazines such as the *Idler* and the *Rambler.* Johnson's neoclassical bias led him, like Addison, to make a clear-cut contrast between the essay and systematic discourse—a contrast reflected in his *Dictionary* definition of it as "a loose sally of the mind; an irregular, indigested piece, not a regular, orderly performance." That contrast is at the heart of his extended reflections on the essay in the following excerpt from the *Rambler.*

From the *Rambler*

As every scheme of life, so every form of writing, has its advantages and inconveniences, though not mingled in the same proportions. The writer of essays escapes many embarrassments to which a large work would have exposed him; he seldom harasses his reason with long trains of consequences, dims his eyes with the perusal of antiquated volumes, or burthens his memory with great accumulations of preparatory knowledge. A careless glance upon a favourite author, or transient survey of the varieties of life, is sufficient to supply the first hint or seminal idea, which, enlarged by the gradual accretion of matter stored in the mind, is by the warmth of fancy easily expanded into flowers, and sometimes ripened into fruit.

The most frequent difficulty by which the authors of these petty compositions are distressed, arises from the perpetual demand of novelty and change. The compiler of a system of science lays his invention at rest, and employs only his judgment, the faculty exerted with least fatigue. Even the relator of feigned adventures, when once the principal characters are established, and the great events regularly connected, finds incidents and episodes crowding upon his mind; every change opens new views, and the latter part of the story grows without labour out of the former. But he that attempts to entertain his reader with unconnected pieces, finds the irksomeness of his task rather increased than lessened by every production. The day calls afresh upon him for a new topick, and he is again obliged to choose, without any principle to regulate his choice.

It is indeed true, that there is seldom any necessity of looking far, or inquiring long for a proper subject. Every diversity of art or nature, every publick blessing or calamity, every domestick pain or gratification, every sally of caprice, blunder of absurdity, or stratagem of affectation, may supply matter to him whose only rule is to avoid uniformity. But it often happens, that the judgment is distracted with boundless multiplicity, the imagination ranges from one design to another, and the hours pass imperceptibly away, till the composition can be no longer delayed, and necessity enforces the use of those thoughts which then happen to be at hand. The mind, rejoicing at deliverance on any terms from perplexity and suspense, applies herself vigorously to the work before her, collects embellishments and illustrations, and sometimes finishes, with great elegance and happiness, what in a state of ease and leisure she never had begun.

Rambler, No. 184 (December 21, 1751)

WILLIAM HAZLITT (1778–1830) attended a Unitarian seminary, where he developed the free-thinking habit of mind that distinguishes most of his writing. Though he first aspired to be a philosopher, expounding the "disinteredness of the human mind," tried his hand as a portrait painter, and then produced an English grammar book, Hazlitt had his first taste of success as a journalist, turning out spirited commentary on a wide range of aesthetic, literary, and political topics. Writing for a variety of newspapers and magazines, Hazlitt developed the outspoken, often abrasive voice that distinguishes most of his collected lectures and essays, particularly his pieces in *Table Talk* (1821–22). Lamb characterized Hazlitt's work as embodying "the style of a discontented man . . . which gives force and life to his writing." But Hazlitt's remarks about Montaigne, in the following excerpt from his piece on the periodical essayists, might also be applied to Hazlitt himself, for he always "had the courage to say as an author what he felt as a man."

From "On the Periodical Essayists"

I now come to speak of that sort of writing which has been so successfully cultivated in this country by our periodical Essayists, and which consists in applying the talents and resources of the mind to all that mixed mass of human affairs, which, though not included under the head of any regular art, science, or profession, falls under the cognizance of the writer, and comes home to the business and bosoms of men.

> Quicquid agunt homines nostri farrago libelli,
> Quotidiana
> [Whate'er men do are the sum of my report.]

is the general motto of this department of literature. It does not treat of minerals or fossils, of the virtues of plants, or the influence of planets;

it does not meddle with forms of belief, or systems of philosophy, nor launch into the world of spiritual existences; but it makes familiar with the world of men and women, records their actions, assigns their motives, exhibits their whims, characterises their pursuits in all their singular and endless variety, ridicules their absurdities, exposes their inconsistencies, "holds the mirror up to nature, and shews the very age and body of the time its form and pressure;" takes minutes of our dress, air, looks, words, thoughts, and actions; shews us what we are, and what we are not; plays the whole game of human life over before us, and by making us enlightened Spectators of its many-coloured scenes, enables us (if possible) to become tolerably reasonable agents in the one in which we have to perform a part. "The act and practice part of life is thus made the mistress of our theorique." It is the best and most natural course of study. It is in morals and manners what the experimental is in natural philosophy, as opposed to the dogmatical method. It does not deal in sweeping clauses of proscription and anathema, but in nice distinctions and liberal constructions. It makes up its general accounts from details, its few theories from many facts. It does not try to prove all black or all white as it wishes, but lays on the intermediate colors, (and most of them not unpleasing ones,) as it finds them blended with "the web of our life, which is of a mingled yarn, good and ill together." It inquires what human life is and has been, to shew what it ought to be. It follows it into courts and camps, into town and country, into rustic sports or learned disputations, into the various shades of prejudice or ignorance, of refinement or barbarism, into its private haunts or public pageants, into its weaknesses and littlenesses, its professions and its practices—before it pretends to distinguish right from wrong, or one thing from another. How, indeed, should it do so otherwise?

> Quid sit pulchrum, quid turpe, quid utile, quid non,
> Plenius et melius Chrysippo et Crantore dicit.

> [Who says, more plainly and better than Chrysippus and Crantor, what is beautiful, what base, what useful, what the opposite of these.—Horace, Epist. I. 2. 4.]

The writers I speak of are, if not moral philosophers, moral historians, and that's better: or if they are both, they found the one character upon the other; their premises precede their conclusions; and we put faith in their testimony, for we know that it is true.

Montaigne was the first person who in his Essays led the way to this kind of writing among the moderns. The great merit of Montaigne then was, that he may be said to have been the first who had the courage to say as an author what he felt as a man. And as courage is generally the effect of conscious strength, he was probably led to do so by the richness, truth, and force of his own observations on books and men. He was, in the truest sense, a man of original mind, that is, he had the power of looking at things for himself, or as they really were, instead of blindly trusting to, and fondly repeating what others told him that they were. He got rid of the go-cart of prejudice and affectation, with the learned lumber that follows at their heels, because he could do without them. In taking up his pen he did not set up for a philosopher, wit, orator, or moralist, but he became all these by merely daring to tell us whatever passed through his mind, in its naked simplicity and force, that he thought any ways worth communicating. He did not, in the abstract character of an author, undertake to say all that could be said upon a subject, but what in his capacity as an inquirer after truth he happened to know about it. He was neither a pedant nor a bigot. He neither supposed that he was bound to know all things, nor that all things were bound to conform to what he had fancied or would have them to be. In treating of men and manners, he spoke of them as he found them, not according to preconceived notions and abstract dogmas; and he began by teaching us what he himself was. In criticizing books he did not compare them with rules and systems, but told us what he saw to like or dislike in them. He did not take his standard of excellence "according to an exact scale" of Aristotle, or fall out with a work that was good for any thing, because "not one of the angles at the four corners was a right one." He was, in a word, the first author who was not a book-maker, and who wrote not to make converts of others to established creeds and prejudices, but to satisfy his own mind of the truth of things. In this respect we know not which to be most charmed with, the author or the man. There is an inexpressible frankness and sincerity, as well as power, in what he writes. There is no attempt at imposition or concealment, no juggling tricks or solemn mouthing, no labored attempts at proving himself always in the right, and everybody else in the wrong; he says what is uppermost, lays open what floats at the top or the bottom of his mind, and deserves Pope's character of him, where he professes to

pour out all as plain
As downright Shippen, or as old Montaigne.

He does not converse with us like a pedagogue with his pupil, whom he wishes to make as great a blockhead as himself, but like a philosopher and friend who has passed through life with thought and observation, and is willing to enable others to pass through it with pleasure and profit. A writer of this stamp, I confess, appears to me as much superior to a common bookworm, as a library of real books is superior to a mere book-case, painted and lettered on the outside with the names of celebrated works. As he was the first to attempt this new way of writing, so the same strong natural impulse which prompted the undertaking, carried him to the end of his career. The same force and honesty of mind which urged him to throw off the shackles of custom and prejudice, would enable him to complete his triumph over them. He has left little for his successors to achieve in the way of just and original speculation on human life. Nearly all the thinking of the two last centuries of that kind which the French denominate morale observatrice, is to be found in Montaigne's Essays: there is the germ, at least, and generally much more. He sowed the seed and cleared away the rubbish, even where others have reaped the fruit, or cultivated and decorated the soil to a greater degree of nicety and perfection. . . .

The ice being thus thawed, and the barrier that kept authors at a distance from common sense and feeling broken through, the transition was not difficult from Montaigne and his imitators, to our Periodical Essayists. These last applied the same unrestrained expression of their thoughts to the more immediate and passing scenes of life, to temporary and local matters; and in order to discharge the invidious office of Censor Morum more freely, and with less responsibility, assumed some fictitious and humorous disguise, which, however, in a great degree corresponded to their own peculiar habits and character. By thus concealing their own name and person under the title of the Tatler, Spectator, &c. they were enabled to inform us more fully of what was passing in the world, while the dramatic contrast and ironical point of view to which the whole is subjected, added a greater liveliness and piquancy to the descriptions. The philosopher and wit here commences news-monger, makes himself master of "the perfect spy o' tie time," and from his various walks and turns through life, brings home little curious specimens of the humors, opinions, and manners of his contemporaries, as the botanist brings home different plants and weeds, or the mineralogist different shells and fossils, to illustrate their several theories, and be useful to mankind.

First published in the *Round Table,* No. 10 (May 5, 1815)

CHARLES LAMB (1775–1834) spent most of his working life as a clerk in the accounting office of the British East India Company, and he devoted most of his private life to the care of his elder sister Mary, after she stabbed their mother to death in a fit of insanity. Despite such burdens and mental problems of his own, Lamb found time to write essays, poems, plays, and literary criticism on Shakespeare, as well as to collaborate with his sister on a popular children's book of tales from Shakespeare. But not until he adopted the complex persona of Elia (1821–25), modeled to some extent on his own whimsical, wistful, witty temperament, did Lamb come into his own as an essayist. Lamb's belief in the importance of a distinctive persona, in the "assumption of a character," is clearly reflected in the following excerpt from his unpublished review of William Hazlitt's *Table Talk*.

From an Unpublished Review of Hazlitt's *Table Talk*

A series of Miscellaneous Essays, however well executed in the parts, if it have not some pervading character to give a unity to it, is ordinarily as tormenting to get through as a set of aphorisms, or a jest-book.—The fathers of Essay writing in ancient and modern times—Plutarch in a measure, and Montaigne without mercy or measure—imparted their own personal peculiarities to their themes. By this balm are they preserved. The Author of the Rambler in a less direct way has attained the same effect. Without professing egotism, his work is as essentially egotistical as theirs. He deals out opinion, which he would have you take for argument; and is perpetually obtruding his own particular views of life for universal truths. This is the charm which binds us to his writing, and not any steady conviction we have of the solidity of his thinking. Possibly some of those Papers, which are generally understood to be failures in the Rambler—its ponderous levities for instance, and unwieldy efforts at being sprightly—

may detract less from the general effect, than if something better in kind, but less in keeping, had been substituted in place of them. If the author had taken his friend Goldsmith into partnership, and they had furnished their quotas for alternate days, the world had been gainer by the arrangement, but what a heterogeneous mass the work itself would have presented!

Another class of Essayists, equally impressed with the advantages of this sort of appeal to the reader, but more dextrous at shifting off the invidiousness of a perpetual self-reference, substituted for themselves an *ideal character*; which left them a still fuller licence in the delivery of their peculiar humours and opinions, under the masqued battery of a fictitious appellation. Truths, which the world would have startled at from the lips of the gay Captain Steele, it readily accepted from the pen of old Isaac Bickerstaff. But the breed of the Bickerstaffs, as it began, so alas! it expired with him. It shewed indeed a few feeble sparks of revival in Nestor Ironside, but soon went out. Addison had stepped in with his wit, his criticism, his morality—the cold generalities which extinguish humour—and the Spectator, and its Successor, were little more than bundles of Essays (valuable indeed, and elegant reading above our praise) but hanging together with very slender principles of bond or union. In fact we use the word Spectator, and mean a Book. At mention of the Tatler we sigh, and think of Isaac Bickerstaff. Sir Roger de Coverly, Will Wimble, Will Honeycomb, live for ever in memory—but who is their *silent Friend*?—Except that he never opens his mouth, we know nothing about him. He writes finely upon all subjects—but himself. He sets every thing in a proper light—but we do not see through his spectacles. He colours nothing with his own hues. The Lucubrations come as from an old man, an old bachelor to boot, and a humourist. The Spectator too, we are told, *is* all this. But a young man, a young married man moreover, or any description of man, or woman, with no sort of character beyond general shrewdness, and a power of observation, might have strung together all that discordant assemblage of Papers, which call the Spectator father. They describe indeed with the utmost felicity all ages & conditions of men, but they themselves smack of no peculiar age or condition. He writes, we are told, because he cannot bring himself to speak, but why he cannot bring himself to speak is the riddle. He is used to good company. Why he should conceal his name, while he lavishly proclaims that of his companions, is equally a secret. Was it to remove him still further from any possibility of our sympathies?—or wherein, we would be informed, lurks the mystery of his short chin?—As a visitor at the Club (a sort of *umbra*) he might have shewn to advantage among those short but masterly sketches—but the mass of matter, spread through eight volumes, is really somewhat too miscellaneous and diffuse, to hang together for identity upon such a shade, such a tenuity!

Since the days of the Spectator and Guardian, Essayists, who have appeared under a fictitious appellation, have for the most part contented themselves with a brief description of their character and story in the opening Paper; after which they dismiss the Phantom of an Editor, and let the work shift for itself, as wisely and wittily as it is able, unsupported by any characteristic pretences, or individual colouring.—In one particular indeed the followers of Addison were long and grievously misled. For many years after the publication of his celebrated "Vision of Mirza," no book of Essays was thought complete without a Vision. It set the world dreaming. Take up any one of the volumes of this description, published in the last century;—you will possibly alight upon two or three successive papers, depicting, with more or less gravity, sober views of life *as it is* —when—pop—you come upon a Vision, which you trembled at beforehand from a glimpse you caught at certain abstractions in Capitals, Fame, Riches, Long Life, Loss of Friends, Punishment by Exile—a set of denominations part simple, part compounded—existing in single, double, and triple hypostases.—You cannot think on their fantastic essences without giddiness, or describe them short of a solecism.—These authors seem not to have been content to entertain you with their day-light fancies, but you *must* share their vacant slumbers & common-place reveries. The humour, thank Heaven, is pretty well past. These Visions, any thing but visionary—(for who ever dreamt of Fame, but by metaphor, some mad Orientalist perhaps excepted?)—so tamely extravagant, so gothically classical—these inspirations by downright malice aforethought—these heartless, bloodless literalities—these "thin consistencies," dependent for their personality upon Great Letters—for write them small, and the tender essences fade into abstractions—have at length happily melted *away* before the progress of good sense; or the absurdity has worn itself out. We might else have still to lament, that the purer taste of their inventor should have so often wandered aside into these caprices; or to wish, if he had chosen to indulge in an imitation of Eastern extravagance, that he had confined himself to that least obnoxious specimen of his skill, the Allegory of Mirza.

The Author before us is, in this respect at least, no visionary. He talks to you in broad day-light. He comes in no imaginary character. He is of the class of Essayists first mentioned. He attracts, or repels, by strong realities of individual observation, humour, and feeling.

The title, which Mr Hazlitt has chosen, is characteristic enough of his Essays. The tone of them is uniformly conversational; and they are not the less entertaining, that they resemble occasionally the *talk* of a very clever person, when he begins to be animated in a convivial party. You fancy that a disputant is always present, and feel a disposition to take up the cudgels yourself [o]n behalf of the other side of the question. Table-Talk is not calculated for cold or squeamish readers. The average thinker will find his common notions a little too roughly disturbed. He must brace up his ears to the reception of some novelties. Strong traits of character stand out in the work; and it is not so much a series of well argued treatises, as a bold confession, or exposition, of Mr Hazlitt's own ways of feeling upon the subjects treated of. It is in fact a piece of Autobiography; and, in our minds, a vigorous & well-executed one. The Writer almost every where adopts the style of a discontented man. This assumption of a character, if it be not truly (as we are inclined to believe) his own, is that which gives force & life to his writing.

First printed in *Lamb as Critic*, ed. Roy Park, London: Routledge and Kegan Paul, 1980

RALPH WALDO EMERSON (1803–82), arguably America's greatest essayist, began his career as a schoolmaster and Unitarian minister. He left the ministry in 1832, a year after his young wife's death, and remade himself as a Transcendentalist, poet, and lecturer. Emerson's essays, which grew out of his journals and lectures, were marked by the aphoristic style displayed in the selections from those journals printed below. In these excerpts one hears him working to resolve the contradictions he felt between his own lofty ambitions and his commitment to democratic egalitarianism and familiar style. For guidance he turns again and again to Montaigne, who was for him a "representative man," representative of the skepticism that lay at the center of essay writing.

From "Montaigne, or the Skeptic"

Over his name he drew an emblematic pair of scales, and wrote "Que scais je?" under it. As I look at his effigy opposite the title-page, I seem to hear him say, "You may play old Poz, if you will; you may rail and exaggerate, —I stand here for truth, and will not, for all the states and churches and revenues and personal reputations of Europe, overstate the dry fact, as I see it; I will rather mumble and prose about what I certainly know,—my house and barns; my father, my wife and my tenants; my old lean bald pate; my knives and forks; what meats I eat and what drinks I prefer, and a hundred straws just as ridiculous,—than I will write, with a fine crow-quill, a fine romance. I like gray days, and autumn and winter weather. I am gray and autumnal myself, and think an undress and old shoes that do not pinch my feet, and old friends who do not constrain me, and plain topics where I do not need to strain myself and pump my brains, the most suitable. Our condition as men is risky and ticklish enough. One cannot be sure of himself and his fortune an hour, but he may be whisked off into some pitiable or ridiculous plight. Why should I vapor and play the philosopher, instead of ballasting, the best I can, this dancing balloon?

So, at least, I live within compass, keep myself ready for action, and can shoot the gulf at last with decency. If there be anything farcical in such a life, the blame is not mine; let it lie at fate's and nature's door."

The Essays, therefore, are an entertaining soliloquy on every random topic that comes into his head; treating every thing without ceremony, yet with masculine sense. There have been men with deeper insight; but, one would say, never a man with such abundance of thoughts: he is never dull, never insincere, and has the genius to make the reader care for all that he cares for.

The sincerity and marrow of the man reaches to his sentences. I know not anywhere the book that seems less written. It is the language of conversation transferred to a book. Cut these words, and they would bleed; they are vascular and alive. One has the same pleasure in it that he feels in listening to the necessary speech of men about their work, when any unusual circumstance gives momentary importance to the dialogue. For blacksmiths and teamsters do not trip in their speech; it is a shower of bullets. It is Cambridge men who correct themselves and begin again at every half sentence, and, moreover, will pun, and refine too much, and swerve from the matter to the expression. Montaigne talks with shrewdness, knows the world and books and himself, and uses the positive degree; never shrieks, or protests, or prays: no weakness, no convulsion, no superlative: does not wish to jump out of his skin, or play any antics, or annihilate space or time, but is stout and solid; tastes every moment of the day; likes pain because it makes him feel himself and realize things; as we pinch ourselves to know that we are awake. He keeps the plain; he rarely mounts or sinks; likes to feel solid ground and the stones underneath. His writing has no enthusiasms, no aspiration; contented, self-respecting and keeping the middle of the road. There is but one exception,—in his love for Socrates. In speaking of him, for once his cheek flushes and his style rises to passion.

Representative Men: Seven Lectures, 1850

ALEXANDER SMITH (1830–67), though born to Scottish parents who could not afford to give him a college education, produced a collection of poetry entitled *Life Drama and Other Poems* (1853) that was initially so well received it went through several editions and led to his appointment as secretary of Edinburgh University. Subsequently, however, Smith's predilection for poetic drama, centering on the inner world of the mind, was derisively referred to as "spasmodic," in mockery of its bombastic self-absorption. After a few other such works, he turned out a collection of essays called *Dreamthorp* (1863) and *A Summer in Skye* (1865), an idealized evocation of life on a Hebridean isle that remains his most successful work. Given the self-absorption of his poetry, it is not entirely surprising that in the following excerpt from his piece on the essay, Smith celebrates the essayist's "egotism, this perpetual reference to self, in which the charm of the essayist resides."

From "On the Writing of Essays"

The essay, as a literary form, resembles the lyric, in so far as it is moulded by some central mood—whimsical, serious, or satirical. Give the mood, and the essay, from the first sentence to the last, grows around it as the cocoon grows around the silkworm. The essay-writer is a chartered libertine, and a law unto himself. A quick ear and eye, an ability to discern the infinite suggestiveness of common things, a brooding meditative spirit, are all that the essayist requires to start business with. Jacques, in "As You Like It," had the makings of a charming essayist. It is not the essayist's duty to inform, to build pathways through metaphysical morasses, to cancel abuses, any more than it is the duty of the poet to do these things. Incidentally he may do something in that way, just as the poet may, but it is not his duty, and should not be expected of him. Skylarks are primarily created to sing, although a whole choir of them may be baked in pies and brought to table; they were born to make music, although they may incidentally stay the pangs of vulgar hunger. The essayist is a kind of poet in prose, and if questioned harshly as to his uses, he might be unable to render a better apology for his existence than a flower might. The essay should be pure literature as the poem is pure literature. The essayist wears a lance, but he cares more for the sharpness of its point than for the pennon that flutters on it, than for the banner of the captain under whom he serves. He plays with death as Hamlet plays with Yorick's skull, and he reads the morals—strangely stern, often, for such fragrant lodging—which are folded up in the bosoms of roses. He has no pride, and is deficient in a sense of the congruity and fitness of things. He lifts a pebble from the ground, and puts it aside more carefully than any gem; and on a nail in a cottage-door he will hang the mantle of his thought, heavily brocaded with the gold of rhetoric. He finds his way into the Elysian fields through portals the most shabby and commonplace.

The essayist plays with his subject, now whimsical, now in grave, now in melancholy mood. He lies upon the idle grassy bank, like Jacques, letting the world flow past him, and from this thing and the other he extracts his mirth and his moralities. His main gift is an eye to discover the suggestiveness of common things; to find a sermon in the most unpromising texts. Beyond the vital hint, the first step, his discourses are not beholden to their titles. Let him take up the most trivial subject, and it will lead him away to the great questions over which the serious imagination loves to brood,—fortune, mutability, death,—just as inevitably as the runnel, trickling among the summer hills, on which sheep are bleating, leads you to the sea; or as, turning down the first street you come to in the city, you are led finally, albeit by many an intricacy, out into the open country, with its waste places and its woods, where you are lost in a sense of strangeness and solitariness. The world is to the meditative man what the mulberry plant is to the silkworm. The essay-writer has no lack of subject-matter. He has the day that is passing over his head; and, if unsatisfied with that, he has the world's six thousand years to depasture his gay or serious humour upon. I idle away my time here, and I am finding new subjects every hour. Everything I see or hear is an essay in bud. The world is everywhere whispering essays, and one need only be the world's amanuensis. The proverbial expression which last evening the clown dropped as he trudged homeward to supper, the light of the setting sun on his face, expands before me to a dozen pages. The coffin of the pauper, which to-day I saw carried carelessly along, is as good a subject as the funeral procession of an emperor. Craped drum and banner add nothing to death; penury and disrespect take nothing away. Incontinently my thought moves like a slow-paced hearse with sable nodding plumes. Two rustic lovers, whispering between the darkening hedges, is as potent to project my mind into the tender passion as if I had seen Romeo touch the cheek of Juliet in the moon-light garden. Seeing a curly-headed child asleep in the sunshine before a cottage door is sufficient excuse for a discourse on childhood; quite as good as if I had seen infant Cain asleep in the lap of Eve with Adam looking on. A lark cannot rise to heaven without raising as many thoughts as there are notes in its song. Dawn cannot pour its white light on my village without starting from their dim lair a hundred reminiscences; nor can sunset burn above yonder trees in the west without attracting to itself the melancholy of a lifetime. When spring unfolds her green leaves I would be provoked to indite an essay on hope and youth, were it not that it is already writ in the carols of the birds; and I might be tempted in autumn to improve the occasion, were it not for the rustle of the withered leaves as I walk through the woods. Compared with that simple music, the saddest-cadenced words have but a shallow meaning.

The essayist who feeds his thoughts upon the segment of the world which surrounds him cannot avoid being an egotist; but then his egotism is not unpleasing. If he be without taint of boastfulness, of self-sufficiency, of hungry vanity, the world will not press the charge home. If a man discourses continually of his wines, his plate, his titled acquaintances, the number and quality of his horses, his men-servants and maid-servants, he must discourse very skilfully indeed if he escapes being called a coxcomb. If a man speaks of death—tells you that the idea of it continually haunts him, that he has the most insatiable curiosity as to death and dying, that his thought mines in churchyards like a "demon-mole"—no one is specially offended, and that this is a dull fellow is the hardest thing likely to be said of him. Only, the egotism that overcrows you is offensive, that exalts trifles and takes pleasure in them, that suggests superiority in matters of equipage and furniture; and the egotism is offensive, because it runs counter to and jostles your self-complacency. The egotism which rises no higher than the grave is of a solitary and a hermit kind—it crosses no man's path, it disturbs no man's *amour propre*. You may offend a man if you say you are as rich as he, as wise as he, as handsome as he. You offend no man if you tell him that, like him, you have to die. The king, in his crown and coronation robes, will allow the beggar to claim that relationship with him. To have to die is a distinction of which no man is proud. The speaking about one's self is not necessarily offensive. A modest, truthful man speaks better about himself than about anything else, and on that subject his speech is likely to be most profitable to his hearers. Certainly, there is no subject with which he is better acquainted, and on which he has a better title to be heard. And it is this egotism, this perpetual reference to self, in which the charm of the essayist resides. If a man is worth knowing at all, he is worth knowing well. The essayist gives you his thoughts, and lets you know, in addition, how he came by them. He has nothing to conceal; he throws open his doors and windows, and lets him enter who will. You like to walk round peculiar or important men as you like to walk round a building, to view it from different points, and in different lights. Of the essayist, when his mood is communicative, you obtain a full picture. You are made his contemporary and familiar friend. You enter into his humours and his seriousness. You are made heir of his whims, prejudices, and playfulness. You walk through the whole nature of him, as you walk through the streets of Pompeii, looking into the interior of stately mansions, reading the satirical scribblings on the walls. And the essayist's habit of not only giving you his thoughts, but telling you how he came by them, is interesting, because it shows you by what alchemy the ruder world becomes transmuted into the finer.

Dreamthorp: A Book of Essays Written in the Country, 1863

WALTER PATER (1839–94) has inspired many an aesthete, epicure, and hedonist with his assertion that "experience itself, is the end," and therefore "To burn always with this hard gem-like flame, to maintain this ecstasy, is success in life." Despite those bold maxims from the conclusion of his *Studies in the History of the Renaissance* (1873), Pater himself was evidently a reclusive scholar and tutor, devoted at first to his studies in art and literature, and then to an ascetic balancing of his often misunderstood aesthetic philosophy in *Marius the Epicurean* (1885) and *Imaginary Portraits* (1887). While Pater's devotion to beauty is often manifest in the elaborate prose style of his essays, his allegiance to more ascetic values can be seen in the following excerpt from *Plato and Platonism* (1893), where he explicitly traces the origins of the essay to the truth-seeking dialectic of the Platonic dialogues.

From "Dialectic"

Three different forms of composition have, under the intellectual conditions of different ages, prevailed–three distinct literary methods, in the presentation of philosophic thought; the metrical form earliest, when philosophy was still a matter of intuition, imaginative, sanguine, often turbid or obscure, and became a *Poem*, Περὶ Φύσεως, "Concerning Nature"; according to the manner of Pythagoras, "his golden verses," of Parmenides or Empedokles, after whom Lucretius in his turn modelled the finest extant illustration of that manner of writing, of thinking.

It was succeeded by precisely the opposite manner, when native intuition had shrunk into dogmatic system, the dry bones of which rattle in one's ears, with Aristotle, or Aquinas, or Spinoza, as a formal treatise; the perfected philosophic temper being situate midway between those opposites, in the third essential form of the literature of philosophy, namely the essay; that characteristic literary type of our own time, a time so rich and various in special apprehensions of truth, so tentative and dubious in its sense of their *ensemble,* and issues. Strictly appropriate form of our modern philosophic literature, the essay came into use at what was really the invention of the relative, or "modern" spirit, in the Renaissance of the sixteenth century.

The poem, the treatise, the essay: you see already that these three methods of writing are no mere literary accidents, dependent on the personal choice of this or that particular writer, but necessities of literary form, determined directly by matter, as corresponding to three essentially different ways in which the human mind relates itself to truth. If oracular verse, stimulant but enigmatic, is the proper vehicle of enthusiastic intuitions; if the treatise, with its ambitious array of premise and conclusion, is the natural out-put of scholastic all-sufficiency; so, the form of the essay, as we have it towards the end of the sixteenth century, most significantly in Montaigne, representative essayist because the representative doubter, inventor of the name as, in essence, of the thing—of the essay, in its seemingly modest aim, its really large and adventurous possibilities—is indicative of Montaigne's peculiar function in regard to his age, as in truth the commencement of our own. It provided him with precisely the literary form necessary to a mind for which truth itself is but a possibility, realisable not as general conclusion, but rather as the elusive effect of a particular personal experience; to a mind which, noting faithfully those random lights that meet it by the way, must needs content itself with suspension of judgment, at the end of the intellectual journey, to the very last asking: *Que scais-je?* Who knows?—in the very spirit of that old Socratic contention, that all true philosophy is but a refined sense of one's ignorance.

And as Aristotle is the inventor of the treatise, so the Platonic Dialogue, in its conception, its peculiar opportunities, is essentially an essay—an essay, now and then passing into the earlier form of philosophic poetry, the prose-poem of Heraclitus. There have been effective writers of dialogue since, Bruno, for instance, Berkeley, Landor, with whom, however, that literary form has had no strictly constitutional propriety to the kind of matter it conveyed, as lending itself (that is to say) structurally to a many-sided but hesitant consciousness of the truth. Thus, with Berkeley, its purpose is but to give a popular turn to certain very dogmatic opinions, about which there is no diffidence, there are no half-lights, in the writer's own mind. With Plato, on the other hand, with Plato least of all is the dialogue—that peculiar modification of the essay—anything less than essential, necessary, organic: the very form belongs to, is of the organism of, the matter which it embodies. For Plato's *Dialogues*, in fact, reflect, they refine upon while they fulfil, they idealise, the actual method, in which, by preference to anything like formal lecturing (the lecture being, so to speak, a treatise in embryo) Socrates conveyed his doctrine to others. We see him in those *Dialogues* of Plato, still loitering in the public places, the open houses, the suburban roads, of Athens, as if seeking truth from others; seeking it, doubtless, from himself, but along with, and by the help of, his supposed scholars, for whom, indeed, he can but bring their own native conceptions of truth to the birth; but always faithfully registering just so much light as is given, and, so to speak, never concluding.

The Platonic Dialogue is the literary transformation, in a word, of what was the intimately home-grown method of Socrates, not only of conveying truth to others, but of coming by it for himself. The essence of that method, of "dialectic" in all its forms, as its very name denotes, is dialogue, the habit of seeking truth by means of question and answer, primarily with one's self.

Plato and Platonism, 1893

Agnes Repplier (1855–1950) was a political conservative and devout Catholic whose pointed, bookish essays were saved from dogmatism by a self-deprecating sense of humor (she poked fun, for instance, at her own spinsterhood and weakness for drink). In her "happy half century" as an essayist, she produced fifteen volumes of essays on subjects ranging from dogs and ale to Christianity and war. She was a classicist and defender of literary traditions who fretted about the effects of modernization and war on the traditional essay. As early as 1894 she engaged in the debates over the "passing of the essay," arguing in the piece that follows that even though the essay had been "warned that it is not in accord with the spirit of the age, and that its day is on the wane," it would survive.

From "The Passing of the Essay"

When I am told, among other prophetic items, that the "light essay" is passing rapidly away, and that, in view of its approaching death-bed, it cannot be safely recommended as "a good opening for enterprise," I am fain, before acquiescing gloomily in such a decree, to take heart of grace, and look a little around me. It is discouraging, doubtless, for the essayist to be suddenly informed that his work is *in articulo mortis*. He feels as a carpenter might feel were he told that chairs and doors and tables are going out of fashion, and that he had better turn his attention to mining, engineering, or a new food for infants. Perhaps he endeavors to explain that a great many chairs were sold in the past week, that they are not without utility, and that they seem to him as much in favor as ever. Such feeble arguments meet with no response. Furniture, he is assured,—on the authority of the speaker,—is distinctly out of date. The spirit of the time calls for something different, and the "best business talent"—delightful phrase, and equally applicable to a window-frame or an epic—is moving in another direction. This is what Mr. Lowell used to call the conclusive style of judgment, "which consists simply in belonging to the other parish;" but parish boundaries are the same convincing things now that they were forty years ago.

Is the essay, then, in such immediate and distressing danger? Is it unwritten, unpublished, or unread? Just ten years have passed since a well-printed little book was offered carelessly to the great English public. It was anonymous. It was hampered by a Latin title which attracted the few and repelled the many. It contained seven of the very lightest essays that ever glided into print. It grappled with no problems, social or spiritual; it touched but one of the vital issues of the day. It was not serious, and it was not written with any very definite view, save to give entertainment and pleasure to its readers. By all the laws of modern mentors, it should have been consigned to speedy and merited oblivion. Yet what happened? I chanced to see that book within a few months of its publication, and sent at once to London for a copy, thinking to easily secure a first edition. I received a fourth, and, with it, the comforting assurance that the first was already commanding a heavy premium. In another week the American reprints of "Obiter Dicta" lay on all the book counters of our land. The author's name was given to the world. A second volume of essays followed the first; a third, the second; a fourth, the third. The last are so exceedingly light as to be little more than brief notices and reviews. All have sold well, and Mr. Birrell has established—surely with no great effort—his reputation as a man of letters. Editors of magazines are glad to print his work; readers of magazines are glad to see it; newspapers are delighted when they have any personal gossip about the author to tell a curious world. This is what "the best business talent" must call success, for these are the tests by which it is accustomed to judge. The light essay has a great deal of hardihood to flaunt and flourish in this shameless manner, when it has been severely warned that it is not in accord with the spirit of the age, and that its day is on the wane.

It is curious, too, to see how new and charming editions of "Virginibus Puerisque" meet with a ready sale. Mr. Stevenson has done better work than in this volume of scattered papers, which are more suggestive than satisfactory; yet there are always readers ready to exult over the valorous "Admirals," or dream away a glad half-hour to the seductive music of "Pan's Pipes." Mr. Lang's "Essays in Little" and "Letters to Dead Authors" have reached thousands of people who have never read his admirable translations from the Greek. Mr. Pater's essays—which, however, are not light—are far better known than his beautiful "Marius the Epicurean." Lamb's "Elia" is more widely read than are his letters, though it would seem a heart-breaking matter to choose between them. Hazlitt's essays are still rich mines of pleasure, as well as fine correctives for much modern nonsense. The first series of Mr. Arnold's "Essays in Criticism" remains his most popular book, and the one which has done more than all the rest to show the great half-educated public what is meant by distinction of mind. Indeed, there never was a day when by-roads to culture were more diligently sought for than now by people disinclined for long travel or much toil, and the essay is the smoothest little path which runs in that direction. It offers no instruction, save through the medium of enjoyment, and one saunters lazily along with a charming unconsciousness of effort. Great results are not to be gained in this fashion, but it should sometimes be play-hour for us all. Moreover, there are still readers keenly alive to the pleasure which literary art can give; and the essayists, from Addison down to Mr. Arnold and Mr. Pater, have recognized the value of form, the powerful and persuasive eloquence of style. Consequently, an appreciation of the essay is the natural result of reading it. Like virtue, it is its own reward. "Culture," says Mr. Addington Symonds, "makes a man to be something. It does not teach him to create anything." Most of us in this busy world are far more interested in what we can learn to do than in what we can hope to become; but it may be that those who content themselves with strengthening their own faculties, and broadening their own sympathies for all that is finest and best, are of greater service to their tired and downcast neighbors than are the unwearied toilers who urge us so relentlessly to the field.

A few critics of an especially judicial turn are wont to assure us now and then that the essay ended with Emerson, or with Sainte-Beuve, or with Addison, or with Montaigne,—a more remote date than this being inaccessible, unless, like Eve in the old riddle, it died before it was born. Montaigne is commonly selected as the idol of this exclusive worship. "I don't care for any essayist later than Montaigne." It has a classic sound, and the same air of intellectual discrimination as another very popular remark: "I don't read any modern novelist, except George Meredith." Hearing these verdicts, one is tempted to say, with Marianne Dashwood, "This is admiration of a very particular kind." To minds of a more commonplace order, it would seem that a love for Montaigne should lead insensibly to an appreciation of Sainte-Beuve; that an appreciation of Sainte-Beuve awakens in turn a sympathy for Mr. Matthew Arnold; that a sympathy for Mr. Arnold paves the way to a keen enjoyment of Mr. Emerson or Mr. Pater. It is a linked chain, and, though all parts are not of equal strength and beauty, all are of service to the whole. "Let neither the peculiar quality of anything nor its value escape thee," counsels Marcus Aurelius; and if we seek our profit wherever it may be found, we insensibly acquire that which is needful for our growth. Under any circumstances, it is seldom wise to confuse the preferences or prejudices of a portion of mankind with the irresistible progress of the ages. Rhymes may go, but they are with us still. Romantic fiction may be submerged, but at present it is well above water. The essay may die, but just now it possesses a lively and encouraging vitality. Whether we regard it as a means of culture or as a field for the "best business talent," we are fain to remark, in the words of Sancho Panza, "This youth, considering his weak state, hath left in him an amazing power of speech."

First published in *Lippincott's Magazine* (June 1894)

William Dean Howells (1837–1920) grew up in Ohio, the son of a newspaper editor. As a young man he wrote a campaign biography of Lincoln that earned him an appointment as United States Consul to Venice and the attention of James Russell Lowell, founding editor of the *Atlantic Monthly*. Picked by Lowell as his successor, Howells served as an editor of the *Atlantic* and then *Harper's* for four decades, writing in his editor's columns about political and literary matters. As a novelist, poet, and essayist, he was especially concerned with issues of justice and the role of the writer in the new world of mass culture. In the piece below he discusses the effects of commercialism on the essay, worrying that the essay had begun "to confuse itself with the article."

From "Editor's Easy Chair"

The old-fashioned essay, as we had it in Montaigne, and almost as we had it in Bacon, obeyed a law as subjective as that of the gypsy music which the Hungarian bands made so popular with us ten or fifteen years ago. Wandering airs of thought strayed through it, owning no allegiance stricter than that which bound the wild chords to a central motive. Often there was apparently no central motive in the essay; it seemed to begin, where it would, and end where it liked. The author was bound to give it a name, but it did not hold him bound otherwise. It could not very well take for title a first line, or part of a first line, like those poems, now rarely written, which opened with some such phrase as, When those bright eyes; or, Had I the wings; or, If yon sweet star. If it could, that would have been the right way of naming most of the essays which have loitered down to us from antiquity, as well as those which help to date the revival of polite learning. Such a custom would have befitted nearly all the papers in the *Spectator* and the *Tatler* and the *Rambler*, and the other periodicals illustrating the heyday of the English essay. These, indeed, preserved an essential liberty by setting out from no subject more severely ascertained than that which lurked in some quotation from the classics, and unless there was an allegory or an apologue in hand, gadded about at their pleasure, and stopped as far from it as they chose. That gave them their charm, and kept them lyrical, far from the dread perhaps of turning out a sermon, when the only duty they had was to turn out a song.

Just how or why the essay should have departed from this elder ideal, and begun to have a conscience about having a beginning, a middle and an ending, like a drama, or a firstly, secondly, and thirdly, like a homily, it would not be easy to say, though we feel pretty sure that it was not from any occasion of Charles Lamb's, or Leigh Hunt's, or William Hazlitt's, or their compeers, in bearing down to our day the graceful tradition which seems now to have been lost. We suspect that the change may have happened through the greater length to which the essay has run in modern times. You may sing a song for a certain period, but if you keep on you have an opera, which you are bound to give obvious form. At any rate, the moment came when the essay began to confuse itself with the article, and to assume an obligation of constancy to premises and conclusions, with the effect of so depraving the general taste that the article is now desired more and more, and the essay less and less. It is doubtful, the corruption has gone so far, whether there is enough of the lyrical sense left in the reader to appreciate the right essay; whether the right essay would now be suffered; whether if any writer indulged its wilding nature, he would not be suspected of an inability to cultivate the growths that perceptibly nourish, not to say fatten, the intellect. We have forgotten, in this matter, that there are senses to which errant odors and flying flavors minister, as grosser succulences satisfy hunger. There is a lyrical sense, as well as a dramatic, an epical, an ethical sense, and it was that which the old-fashioned essay delighted.

First published in *Harper's Magazine* (October 1902)

JOSÉ ORTEGA Y GASSET (1883–1955), a Spanish philosopher and educator, wrote on a wide range of subjects, from aesthetics to politics to metaphysics. He served as a professor at the University of Madrid from 1910 to 1936, when the Spanish civil war forced him to live and teach abroad before returning to Spain after World War II. Ortega is widely known for his cautionary idea in *The Revolt of the Masses* (1929) that democracy can easily lead to the tyranny of an amoral majority, "mass man"; and for his rejection of an ego-centered philosophy ("I think therefore I am") which he countered with his notable belief that "I am myself and my circumstance," and that life therefore embodies an inescapable tension between freedom and fate. Most of Ortega's ideas are contained in collections of essays and lectures that are marked by the clarity of his following reflections on the essay as "science, minus the explicit proof."

From "To the Reader"

These *Meditations*, free from erudition—even in the best sense of the word—are propelled by philosophical desires. Nevertheless I would be grateful if the reader did not expect too much from them. They are not philosophy, which is a science. They are simply essays. The essay is science, minus the explicit proof. For the writer it is a point of intellectual honor not to write anything susceptible of proof without possessing the latter beforehand. But it is permissible for him to eliminate from his work all apodictic appearance, leaving the verifications merely indicated in ellipse, so that he who needs them may find them and so that they do not hinder, on the other hand, the communication of the inner warmth with which the thoughts were conceived. Even books of an exclusively scientific intention are beginning to be written in a less didactic style with fewer labor-saving aids, with footnotes omitted as far as possible and the rigid mechanical apparatus of proof dissolved in a more organic, flowing, and personal discourse.

With greater reason this should be done in essays of this kind, in which, although for the author the doctrines are scientific convictions, he does not expect the reader to accept them as truths. I only offer *modi res considerandi*, possible new ways of looking at things. I invite the reader to test them for himself, to see if, in fact, they provide fertile visions. He, then, by virtue of his intimate and sincere experience, will test their truth or error.

It is my intention that these ideas serve a function much less serious than a scientific one: they will not stubbornly insist on being adopted by others, but merely wish to awaken in kindred minds kindred thoughts, even though they be antagonistic. They are only a pretext and an appeal for a wide ideological collaboration on national themes, and nothing else.

Meditations on Quixote, 1914, reprinted by W. W. Norton, 1961

A[RTHUR] C[HRISTOPHER] BENSON (1862–1925), though reportedly afflicted with a manic-depressive condition, not only served as master of Magdalene College, Cambridge, but also produced more than seventy books, including novels, short-story collections, essay collections, literary biographies, an edition of Queen Victoria's letters, as well as an unpublished diary of more than 4 million words, covering the last twenty-eight years of his life. Benson was best known for his many essays, each typically focused on a single topic, thoughtfully developed in a personable manner that he considered an essential element of the essay, as he makes clear in the following excerpt from "The Art of the Essayist," where he declares that "the charm of the familiar essayist depends upon his power of giving the sense of a good-humoured, gracious and reasonable personality and establishing a sort of pleasant friendship with his reader."

From "The Art of the Essayist"

I have little doubt in my own mind that the charm of the familiar essayist depends upon his power of giving the sense of a good-humoured, gracious and reasonable personality and establishing a sort of pleasant friendship with his reader. One does not go to an essayist with a desire for information, or with an expectation of finding a clear statement of a complicated subject; that is not the mood in which one takes up a volume of essays. What one rather expects to find is a companionable treatment of that vast mass of little problems and floating ideas which are aroused and evoked by our passage through the world, our daily employment, our leisure hours, our amusements and diversions, and above all by our relations with other people—all the unexpected, inconsistent, various simple stuff of life; the essayist ought to be able to impart a certain beauty and order into it, to delineate, let us say, the vague emotions aroused in solitude or in company by the sight of scenery, the aspect of towns, the impressions of art and books, the interplay of human qualities and characteristics, the half-formed hopes and desires and fears and joys that form so large a part of our daily thoughts. The essayist ought to be able to indicate a case or a problem that is apt to occur in ordinary life and suggest the theory of it, to guess what it is that makes our moods resolute or fitful, why we act consistently or inconsistently, what it is that repels or attracts us in our dealings with other people, what our private fancies are. The good essayist is the man who makes a reader say: "Well, I have often thought all those things, but I never discerned before any connection between them, nor got so far as to put them into words." And thus the essayist must have a great and far-reaching curiosity; he must be interested rather than displeased by the differences of human beings and by their varied theories. He must recognize the fact that most people's convictions are not the result of reason, but a mass of associations, traditions, things half-understood, phrases, examples, loyalties, whims. He must care more about the inconsistency of humanity than about its dignity; and he must study more what people actually do think about than what they ought to think about. He must not be ashamed of human weaknesses or shocked by them, and still less disgusted by them; but at the same time he must keep in mind the flashes of fine idealism, the passionate visions, the irresponsible humours, the salient peculiarities, that shoot like sunrays through the dull cloudiness of so many human minds, and make one realize that humanity is at once above itself and in itself, and that we are greater than we know; for the interest of the world to the ardent student of it is that we most of us seem to have got hold of something that is bigger than we quite know how to deal with; something remote and far off, which we have seen in a distant vision, which we cannot always remember or keep clear in our minds. The supreme fact of human nature is its duality, its tendency to pull different ways, the tug-of-war between Devil and Baker which lies inside our restless brains. And the confessed aim of the essayist is to make people interested in life and in themselves and in the part they can take in life; and he does that best if he convinces men and women that life is a fine sort of a game, in which they can take a hand; and that every existence, however confined or restricted, is full of outlets and pulsing channels, and that the interest and joy of it is not confined to the politician or the millionaire, but is pretty fairly distributed, so long as one has time to attend to it, and is not preoccupied in some concrete aim or vulgar ambition.

Because the great secret which the true essayist whispers in our ears is that the worth of experience is not measured by what is called success, but rather resides in a fullness of life: that success tends rather to obscure and to diminish experience, and that we may miss the point of life by being too important, and that the end of it all is the degree in which we give rather than receive.

The poet perhaps is the man who sees the greatness of life best, because he lives most in its beauty and fineness. But my point is that the essayist is really a lesser kind of poet, working in simpler and humbler materials, more in the glow of life perhaps than in the glory of it, and not finding anything common or unclean.

The essayist is the opposite of the romancer, because his one and continuous aim is to keep the homely materials in view; to face actual conditions, not to fly from them. We think meanly of life if we believe that it has no sublime moments; but we think sentimentally of it if we believe that it has nothing but sublime moments. The essayist wants to hold the balance; and if he is apt to neglect the sublimities of life, it is because he is apt to think that they can take care of themselves; and that if there is the joy of adventure, the thrill of the start in the fresh air of the morning, the rapture of ardent companionship, the gladness of the arrival, yet there must be long spaces in between, when the pilgrim jogs steadily along, and seems to come no nearer to the spire on the horizon or to the shining embanked cloudland of the West. He has nothing then but his own thoughts to help him, unless he is alert to see what is happening in hedgerow and copse, and the work of the essayist is to make some-thing rich and strange of those seemingly monotonous spaces, those lengths of level road.

Is, then, the Essay in literature a thing which simply stands outside classification, like Argon among the elements, of which the only thing which can be predicated is that it is there? Or like Justice in Plato's *Republic*, a thing which the talkers set out to define, and which ends by being the one thing left in a state when the definable qualities are taken away? No, it is not that. It is rather like what is called an organ prelude, a little piece with a theme, not very strict perhaps in form, but which can be fancifully treated, modulated from, and coloured at will. It is a little criticism of life at some one point clearly enough defined.

We may follow any mood, we may look at life in fifty different ways—the only thing we must not do is to despise or deride, out of ignorance or prejudice, the influences which affect others; because the essence of all experience is that we should perceive something which we do not begin by knowing, and learn that life has a fullness and a richness in all sorts of diverse ways which we do not at first even dream of suspecting.

The essayist, then, is in his particular fashion an interpreter of life, a critic of life. He does not see life as the historian, or as the philosopher, or as the poet, or as the novelist, and yet he has a touch of all these. He is not concerned with discovering a theory of it all, or fitting the various parts of it into each other. He works rather on what is called the analytic method, observing, recording, interpreting, just as things strike him, and letting his fancy play over their beauty and significance; the end of it all being this: that he is deeply concerned with the charm and quality of things, and desires to put it all in the clearest and gentlest light, so that at least he may make others love life a little better, and prepare them for its infinite variety and alike for its joyful and mournful surprises.

First published in *Modern English Essays*, Vol. 5, 1922

VIRGINIA WOOLF (1882–1941) is best known for her interiorized novels, her feminist projects, her revelatory diaries and letters, but she was also a prolific reviewer, persistently seeking to reform the essay. In one of her earliest pieces on the subject, "The Decay of Essay Writing" (1905), she urged aspiring essayists to "leave the great mysteries of art and literature unassailed" and to "write of themselves" —"that single book to which they alone have the key." In her most ambitious piece on the subject, "The Modern Essay" (1922), excerpted below, she uses a recently published anthology of essays edited by Ernest Rhys as the occasion to offer not only a historical survey but also a virtual poetics of the essay, centered on a paradoxical relationship between essayists and their essayistic personae: "Never to be yourself and yet always—that is the problem."

From "The Modern Essay"

The essay can be short or long, serious or trifling, about God and Spinoza, or about turtles and Cheapside. But as we turn over the pages of these five little volumes, containing essays written between 1870 and 1920, certain principles appear to control the chaos, and we detect in the short period under review something like the progress of history.

Of all forms of literature, however, the essay is the one which least calls for the use of long words. The principle which controls it is simply that it should give pleasure; the desire which impels us when we take it from the shelf is simply to receive pleasure. Everything in an essay must be subdued to that end. It should lay us under a spell with its first word, and we should only wake, refreshed, with its last. In the interval we may pass through the most various experiences of amusement, surprise, interest, indignation; we may soar to the heights of fantasy with Lamb or plunge to the depths of wisdom with Bacon, but we must never be roused. The essay must lap us about and draw its curtain across the world.

So great a feat is seldom accomplished, though the fault may well be as much on the reader's side as on the writer's. Habit and lethargy have dulled his palate. A novel has a story, a poem rhyme; but what art can the essayist use in these short lengths of prose to sting us wide awake and fix us in a trance which is not sleep but rather an intensification of life—a basking, with every faculty alert, in the sun of pleasure? He must know—that is the first essential—how to write. His learning may be as profound as Mark Pattison's, but in an essay it must be so fused by the magic of writing that not a fact juts out, not a dogma tears the surface of the texture. Macaulay in one way, Froude in another, did this superbly over and over again. They have blown more knowledge into us in the course of one essay than the innumerable chapters of a hundred text-books. . . .

But, however much they differ individually, the Victorian essayists yet had something in common. They wrote at greater length than is now usual, and they wrote for a public which had not only time to sit down to its magazine seriously, but a high, if peculiarly Victorian, standard of culture by which to judge it. It was worth while to speak out upon serious matters in an essay; and there was nothing absurd in writing as well as one possibly could when, in a month or two, the same public which had welcomed the essay in a magazine would carefully read it once more in a book. But a change came from a small audience of cultivated people to a larger audience of people who were not quite so cultivated. The change was not altogether for the worse. In volume 3 we find Mr. Birrell and Mr. Beerbohm. It might even be said that there was a reversion to the classic type, and that the essay by losing its size and something of its sonority was approaching more nearly the essay of Addison and Lamb. At any rate, there is a great gulf between Mr. Birrell on Carlyle and the essay which one may suppose that Carlyle would have written upon Mr. Birrell. There is little similarity between "A Cloud of Pinafores," by Max Beerbohm, and "A Cynic's Apology," by Leslie Stephen. But the essay is alive; there is no reason to despair. As the conditions change so the essayist, most sensitive of all plants to public opinion, adapts himself, and if he is good makes the best of the change, and if he is bad the worst. Mr. Birrell is certainly good; and so we find that, though he has dropped a considerable amount of weight, his attack is much more direct and his movement more supple. But what did Mr. Beerbohm give to the essay and what did he take from it? That is a much more complicated question, for here we have an essayist who has concentrated on the work and is without doubt the prince of his profession.

What Mr. Beerbohm gave was, of course, himself. This presence, which has haunted the essay fitfully from the time of Montaigne, had been in exile since the death of Charles Lamb. Matthew Arnold was never to his readers Matt, nor Walter Pater affectionately abbreviated in a thousand homes to Wat. They gave us much, but that they did not give. Thus, some time in the nineties, it must have surprised readers accustomed to exhortation, information, and denunciation to find themselves familiarly addressed by a voice which seemed to belong to a man no larger than themselves. He was affected by private joys and sorrows, and had no gospel to preach and no learning to impart. He was himself, simply and directly, and himself he has remained. Once again we have an essayist capable of using the essayist's most proper but most dangerous and delicate tool. He has brought personality into literature, not unconsciously and impurely, but so consciously and purely that we do not know whether there is any relation between Max the essayist and Mr. Beerbohm the man. We only know that the spirit of personality permeates every word that he writes. The triumph is the triumph of style. For it is only by knowing how to write that you can make use in literature of your self; that self which, while it is essential to literature, is also its most dangerous antagonist. Never to be yourself and yet always—that is the problem. Some of the essayists in Mr. Rhys' collection, to be frank, have not altogether succeeded in solving it. We are nauseated by the sight of trivial personalities decomposing in the eternity of print. As talk, no doubt, it was charming, and certainly the writer is a good fellow to meet over a bottle of beer. But literature is stern; it is no use being charming, virtuous, or even learned and brilliant into the bargain, unless, she seems to reiterate, you fulfil her first condition—to know how to write.

This art is possessed to perfection by Mr. Beerbohm. But he has not searched the dictionary for polysyllables. He has not moulded firm periods or seduced our ears with intricate cadences and strange melodies. Some of his companions—Henley and Stevenson, for example—are momentarily more impressive. But A Cloud of Pinafores has in it that indescribable inequality, stir, and final expressiveness which belong to life and to life alone. You have not finished with it because you have read it, any more than friendship is ended because it is time to part. Life wells up and alters and adds. Even things in a book-case change if they are alive; we find ourselves wanting to meet them again; we find them altered. So we look back upon essay after essay by Mr. Beerbohm, knowing that, come September or May, we shall sit down with them and talk. Yet it is true that the essayist is the most sensitive of all writers to public opinion. The drawing-room is the place where a great deal of reading is done nowadays, and the essays of Mr. Beerbohm lie, with an exquisite appreciation of all that the position exacts, upon the drawing-room table. There is no gin about; no strong tobacco; no puns, drunkenness, or insanity. Ladies and gentlemen talk together, and some things, of course, are not said.

But if it would be foolish to attempt to confine Mr. Beerbohm to one room, it would be still more foolish, unhappily, to make him, the artist, the man who gives us only his best, the representative of our age. There are no essays by Mr. Beerbohm in the fourth or fifth volumes of the present collection. His age seems already a little distant, and the drawing-room table, as it recedes, begins to look rather like an altar where, once upon a time, people deposited offerings—fruit from their own orchards, gifts carved with their own hands. Now once more the conditions have changed. The public needs essays as much as ever, and perhaps even more. The demand for the light middle not exceeding fifteen hundred words, or in special cases seventeen hundred and fifty, much exceeds the supply. Where Lamb wrote one essay and Max perhaps writes two, Mr. Belloc at a rough computation produces three hundred and sixty-five. They are very short, it is true. Yet with what dexterity the practised essayist will utilise his space—beginning as close to the top of the sheet as possible, judging precisely how far to go, when to turn, and how, without sacrificing a hair's-breadth of paper, to wheel about and alight accurately upon the last word his editor allows! As a feat of skill it is well worth watching. But the personality upon which Mr. Belloc, like Mr. Beerbohm, depends suffers in the process. It comes to us not with the natural richness of the speaking voice, but strained and thin and full of mannerisms and affectations, like the voice of a man shouting through a megaphone to a crowd on a windy day.

The Common Reader, 1925

WILLIAM CARLOS WILLIAMS (1883–1963) earned his living as a physician but he also wrote poems, short stories, novels, plays, criticism, an autobiography, and essays. He was an American high modernist who grappled with the problem of America. Williams criticized Eliot and Pound for their European allusions and sought instead to maintain "contact" with what he called "the local." He wrote his epic poem *Paterson* (published between 1946 and 1963) about the New Jersey town in which he lived, half ironically titled one of his novels *The Great American Novel* (1923), and collected a group of essays about American myths and heroes under the title *In the American Grain* (1925). The short piece that follows, entitled "An Essay on Virginia" (1925), is a kind of outtake from *In the American Grain*. It simultaneously advances and enacts a modernist, and more specifically cubist, theory of the essay while also critiquing Virginia, regionalism, and American democracy.

"An Essay on Virginia"

Begin with A to remain intact, redundant not even to the amount of a reflective title. Especially today is it necessary to be academic, the apology for academic precision—which is always essential in realistic ages—being that this has no relation to facts. To essay is to try but not to attempt. It is to establish trial. The essay is the most human literary form in that it is always sure, it remains from the first to last fixed. Nothing affects it. It may stop, but if it stops that is surely the end and so it remains perfect, just as with an infant which fails to continue. It suffers disclosures, up and down, but nothing can affect it. It is as a man: a lunatic or not; no matter. Whatever passes through it, it is never that thing. It remains itself and continues so, pure motion.

Perhaps one should say that it is only an essay when it is wholly uncolored by that which passes through it. Every essay should be, to be human, exactly like another. But the perfect essay should have every word numbered, say as the bones in the body and the thoughts in the mind are fixed, permanent and never vary. Then there could be no confusion, no deception and the pleasure of reading would be increased.

Naturally, that which is sure to remain intact is the only thing to which experience is sufferable. So it is said "to essay" to stand firm, that is, during penetration by a fluid.

"The only thing that changes is man" it is said. This falsehood is true. Its vitality is the same as that of fashions: changelessness. Without one there is not the other. Periods and places by their variety function as do the fashions, to establish man who essays. Geography and history deal wholly with fashion. But the rigidity of the essay is in itself human.

After this description of Virginia it would be impossible to go on were it not for vanity which, the essence of science, enforces accuracy and thoroughness. Not only is it necessary to prove the crystal but the crystal must prove permanent by fracture. This is an essay: the true grace of fashion. The essay must stand while passion and interest pass through. The thing must move to be an engine; this in an essay means the parts are infinitely related to each other—not to "unity" however. It is the crossing of forces that generates interest. The dead centers are incidental. But the sheer centrifugal detail of the essay, its erudition, the scope of its trial, its vanity or love, its force for clarity through change is not understood except as a force that is in its essence centripetal. The motion is from change to the variety of changelessness.

Each essay rings the changes of its range, the breadth, the penetration moving inward about the fashionable brick of all styles, unity. Unity is the shallowest, the cheapest deception of all composition. In nothing is the banality of the intelligence more clearly manifested. There is no less significant matter for the attention. Every piece of writing, it matters not what it is, has unity. Inexpert or bad writing most terribly so. But ability in an essay is multiplicity, infinite fracture, the intercrossing of opposed forces establishing any number of opposed centres of stillness. So the history of Virginia has gone, even more so than in most of the states.

The varied intellectual and moral phases of Virginia are disclosed in a seacoast, a plain and a great valley, taken from east to west. It is covered by holly and wild turkeys. At least there are a few turkeys. You get a turkey dog. He flushes the covey. You then build a blind of brushwood and hide in it, the dog too, since his work is done. Take out the turkey-call and blow it skillfully. The birds will then come creeping in to be killed. Here and there on the old estates there are even a few great holly trees they brought from Carolina. All these things come originally from England. The women are charming. But the men still carry firearms generally and keep the bull in the pasture behind the hill, preferring witticisms with quail or the fox to the sexual breakdown.

The opalescent, sluggish rivers wander indeterminately about the plain. Africans, corn, tobacco, bull-bats, buzzards, rabbits, figs, persimmons are the common accompaniments of these waters. There are no lakes. Oaks and yellow pines are the usual trees. These are essentially the component moments of all essays, hams, anecdotes of battles, broken buildings—the materia are the same. It is their feudal allocation in Virginia that is important. But the essay is essentially modern.

Of Virginia, especially, among the other states, one may say, the older it is the newer it has become. Oaks and women full of mistletoe and men. Hollow trunks for possums and the future. It clings and slips inside. Hunt for it with hounds and lanterns under the "dying moon" crying rebel yells back and forth along the black face of the ridge—from sunset to 1 A.M.: the yelp of the hounds, the shouts, now a horse neighing, now a muffled gunshot. The black women have the faces of statesmen and curiously perfect breasts—no doubt from the natural lives they lead.

Often there will appear some heirloom like the cut-glass jelly stand that Jefferson brought from Paris for his daughter, a branching tree of crystal hung with glass baskets that would be filled with jelly—on occasion. This is the essence of all essays. Or there will be the incident of John Paul, a Scotch gardener's son whom Governor Jones, who owned the most of North Carolina, built into his name. Or there will be an Indian war club; a cylindrical rod of stone encrusted with natural garnets. Or a bronze ax of Spanish make which they found in the hole they dug in removing the old pear tree from the garden. Or, by Willis mountain, a converted Negro cabin: the man who owned the ground on which a great part of Richmond stands—lives here alone a millionaire—on whom the rest draw inexhaustibly. An essay in himself.

In Virginia there is the richest gold mine known to the country before the rush of '49. In the cornfields almost anywhere you'll pick up Indian arrowheads of quartz.

The country is still largely agricultural.

First published in *This Quarter* (Spring 1925)

HILAIRE BELLOC (1870–1953), the son of an English mother and French father, grew up in England, attended Balliol College, Oxford, and became a naturalized British subject in 1902. A devout Catholic and skillful debater, Belloc served from 1906 to 1910 as a Liberal Party Member of Parliament and from 1914 to 1920 as editor of a political journal. He earned his living writing journalism, novels, travel pieces, children's books, and especially essays. Belloc loved to argue. Wells said debating him was "like arguing with a hailstorm," and Woolf likened the voice in his essays to that "of a man shouting through a megaphone to a crowd on a windy day." His iconoclasm and fearless embrace of mass culture come through in the piece that follows, in which he argues, albeit reluctantly, for the modern daily essay of opinion that takes up all the issues of the twentieth century, including religion and Communism.

"An Essay upon Essays upon Essays"

There has been a pretty little quarrel lately—it will probably be forgotten by the time this appears, but no matter—a quarrel between those who write essays and those who have written an essay or two to show that the writing of essays is futile. These last seem to be particularly annoyed by the foison of essays in the present generation. They say it has burst all restraint and is choking us under a flood.

Of old, the essay appeared here and there in some stately weekly paper. Then it dignified once a week some of the more solemn of the daily papers. Then it appeared in another, and another more vulgar. Then, not once a week, but twice a week, in these last: finally, every day. And now (say they) it is everywhere. And the enemies of the essay—or at least of this excess of essays, this spate of essays, this monstrous regiment of essays—are particularly annoyed by the gathering of the same into little books, which they think a further shocking sin against taste. It is bad enough (they say) to drivel away week by week, or even day after day, for your living, but you may be excused (poor devil!), for a living you must get. What is quite unpardonable is to give this drivel the dignity of covers and to place it upon shelves.

The enemies of the modern essay go on to say that it cannot possibly find sufficient subject-matter for so excessive an output. And so on.

Now here let me break modern convention at once, and say that I am a good witness and in a good position also to plead in the matter. I have written this sort of essay for many weary years. I know the motive, I know the method, I know the weakness, but also all that is to be said for it. And I think that, upon the whole, the modern practice is to be supported.

I certainly do not say that with enthusiasm. It would be better for literature, no doubt, and for the casual reader (who reads a great deal too much), if the output were less. It would certainly be better for the writer if he could afford to restrict that output. But I know that, in the first place, the level remains remarkably high in this country (where there are a dozen such things turned out to one in any other), and that it does so remain high is an argument in favour of the medium. For a sufficient standard maintained in any form of writing should be proof that there is material and effort sufficient to that form: that there is a need for that form to supply, and that it is supplied.

These modern essays of ours may be compared to conversation, without which mankind has never been satisfied, which is ever diverse (though continually moving through the same themes), and which finds in the unending multiplicity of the world unending matter for discussion and contemplation. It lacks the chief value of conversation, which is the alternative outlook—the reply. That cannot be helped. But I fancy the reader supplies this somewhat in his own mind, by the movements of appreciation or indignation with which he receives what is put before him. Indeed, sometimes his indignation moves him to provide free copy in protest; though I am afraid that the corresponding pleasure does not get the same chance of expression. I do indeed note, especially in the daily papers nowadays, continual letters from correspondents approving (usually) the more horribly commonplace pronouncements, or those which have been put in to order, as part of some propaganda or other undertaken by the owner of the sheet. These letters I suspect. I believe they are arranged for. But the letters of indignation are certainly genuine, and editors get a good many more than they print. When such letters are written in disapproval of what I myself have written, I nearly always agree with them.

I can also claim to give evidence as a reader of other people's essays.

For I can read this kind of matter with less disgust than any other in the modern press. Yes, I prefer it even to murders. And I cannot tell you how much I prefer it to ignorant comment upon the affairs of Europe or conventional rubbish upon affairs domestic: the presentation of little men as great, of falsehood as truth, of imaginaries as realities.

As for a dearth of subject, I see no sign of it at all. If I consider any one man of that half-dozen or so whom I read regularly, my colleagues in this same trade, I can name no one except myself who tends to repetition. And there is no reason why a fairly well-read man, still active and enjoying occasional travel, let alone the infinite experience of daily life, should lack a subject. Stuff is infinite. The danger lies not in the drying up of matter but in the fossilization of manner. Nor do I find much trace of *that* in my contemporaries.

I have, indeed, the contrary fault to find with the English essay to-day, and that is the restriction of matter. There are whole departments of the highest interest to man which are, by convention, avoided. For instance, until quite lately (when the ice was courageously broken by one group of newspapers), a discussion of the ultimate truths and of whether those truths could be discovered or stated—in other words, a discussion of what is generically called "religion"—was forbidden. Now that the ice *has* been broken, editors have discovered—a little to their astonishment, I think—that the pioneer was right—that there is nothing for which the public has a stronger appetite than theology.

Another form of restriction is the absence of a devil's advocate, and that absence is more clearly marked and of worse effect here than abroad. The *really* unpopular, or the *really* unusual, point of view cannot get stated in pages of general circulation. And that means the absence of creative friction; for conflict is the mother of all things.

The opposition is, indeed, allowed to appear in small, obscure sheets which are devoted to nothing else. But that is of no great public service. What would be of public service would be eager and general discussion, and the perpetual presentation of argument and fact, which the public are not allowed to have.

Take such a simple point as that of Communism. It is a very living issue in our time. It is an active threat in the French commonwealth, a triumphant one in the Russian; it is a subject of immediate anxiety to every government in Europe, and though it has less place here than in any other industrial country, it does indirectly leaven a wide area of thought even here.

But to get it stated—to have said in its favour all that can be said in its favour—one must turn to small publications which are ignored by the principal newspapers and reviews. In these last you never get the Communist position fully and strongly put. You get it vaguely if violently abused—but without definitions and without concrete details; you feel that it is always there in the background, and yet you are never allowed to see it.

Let no one flatter himself that opposition can be heard because certain points of view supposedly unpopular are sometimes put in what are called "daring" or "paradoxical" essays. These are *never* true opposition. They are always either a jest or that worst form of demagogic flattery which consists in telling people what they really think but what they have not hitherto dared to say. Of true opposition in English letters we have to-day none. And English letters are badly the worse for the lack of it.

Written in 1929; published in *One Thing and Another*, 1955

ROBERT MUSIL (1880–1942) grew up the son of an Austrian engineering professor and pursued engineering himself, soon forsaking it for studies in psychology and philosophy. Though he completed a doctorate, he turned down an academic appointment to devote himself to his art. He maintained close but complicated relationships with Kafka, Rilke, and Mann, all of whom admired his fiction. In this selection from his novel *The Man without Qualities* (1930, 1942), Musil ascribes the quality of "essayism" to his protagonist Ulrich. The term (itself an English translation of Musil's word *Essayismus*) turns the essay's passionate skepticism into a way of life, as Musil's narrator makes clear in this question: "A man who wants the truth becomes a scholar; a man who wants to give free range to his subjectivity may become a writer; but what should a man do who wants something in between?" His answer is the balancing act that is essayism, which derives from Emerson (whom Musil admired), is akin to Pater's "unmethodical method," and launches an Austrian-German essayistic tradition that later includes Benjamin, Lukács, and Adorno.

From *The Man without Qualities*

There was something in Ulrich's nature that in a haphazard, paralyzing, disarming way resisted all logical systematizing, the single-minded will, the specifically directed drives of ambition; it was also connected with his chosen term, "essayism," even though it contained the very elements he had gradually and with unconscious care eliminated from that concept. The accepted translation of "essay" as "attempt" contains only vaguely the essential allusion to the literary model, for an essay is not a provisional or incidental expression of a conviction capable of being elevated to truth under more favorable circumstances or of being exposed as an error (the only ones of that kind are those articles or treatises, chips from the scholar's workbench, with which the learned entertain their special public); an essay is rather the unique and unalterable form assumed by a man's inner life in a decisive thought. Nothing is more foreign to it than the irresponsible and half-baked quality of thought known as subjectivity. Terms like true and false, wise and unwise, are equally inapplicable, and yet the essay is subject to laws that are no less strict for appearing to be delicate and ineffable. There have been more than a few such essayists, masters of the inner hovering life, but there would be no point in naming them. Their domain lies between religion and knowledge, between example and doctrine, between *amor intellectualis* and poetry; they are saints with and without religion, and sometimes they are also simply men on an adventure who have gone astray.

Nothing is more revealing, by the way, than one's involuntary experience of learned and sensible efforts to interpret such essayists, to turn their living wisdom into knowledge to live by and thus extract some "content" from the motion of those who were moved: but about as much remains of this as of the delicately opalescent body of a jellyfish when one lifts it out of the water and lays it on the sand.

The Man without Qualities, 1930, modern version trans. Sophie Wilkins, Knopf, 1995

G[ILBERT] K[EITH] CHESTERTON (1874–1936) was a journalist, novelist, playwright, essayist, biographer, historian, religious apologist, mystery writer, and incisive satirist, whom George Bernard Shaw referred to as "a man of colossal genius," in spite of (or perhaps because of) their many disagreements and debates. Though Chesterton reportedly suffered from problems of memory and physical coordination, he produced some eighty books and more than four thousand essays, most of which are marked by a witty style and paradoxical turn of mind, epitomized in the following piece on the "indefinite and indeterminate quality" of the essay—a commonplace of sorts that leads him nonetheless to a striking assertion that "The perfect essay has never been written; for the simple reason that the essay has never really been written."

"The Essay"

The essay is the only literary form which confesses, in its very name, that the rash act known as writing is really a leap in the dark. When men try to write a tragedy, they do not call the tragedy a try-on. Those who have toiled through the twelve books of an epic, writing it with their own hands, have seldom pretended that they have merely tossed off an epic as an experiment. But an essay, by its very name as well as its very nature, really is a try-on and really is an experiment. A man does not really write an essay. He does really essay to write an essay.

One result is that, while there are many famous essays, there is fortunately no model essay. The perfect essay has never been written; for the simple reason that the essay has never really been written. Men have tried to write something, to find out what it was supposed to be. In this respect the essay is a typically modern product, and is full of the future and the praise of experiment and adventure. In other words, like the whole of modern civilization, it does not know what it is trying to find; and therefore does not find it.

It occurs to me here, by the way, that all this applies chiefly to English essayists; and indeed that in this sense the essay is rather an English thing. So far as I remember, English schoolmasters tell a boy to write an essay, but French schoolmasters tell a boy to write a theme. The word theme has a horrid suggestion of relevancy and coherence. The theme is only too near to the thesis. The English schoolmaster profoundly understands his pupils when he assumes that they will not produce a theme but an essay at a theme, or a considerably wild cockshy or pot-shot at a theme. Mr. P. G. Wodehouse (the works of whose imagination do not fall strictly within either the tragic or the epic form) has described how the benevolent nobleman, burdened with a son of the name of Freddie, appealed to that youth to behave, if possible, like a sane and rational human being; to which Freddie replied, with a solemn fervour: "I'll have a jolly good stab at it, Governor." The essayist should be the reasonable human being; the philosopher, the sage with a judgment at once delicate and detached; the thinker considering a theme; the logician expounding a thesis. But England, expecting every man to do his duty, does not expect so much as all this. England knows that her beloved essayists will not be reasonable human beings; but will only have a jolly good stab at it. It is something of a symbol that, for the English schoolboy, an essay is an effort. The whole atmosphere of the thing is full of doubt, experiment and effort. I know not if it is hell, or heaven, or perhaps merely a piece of earth that is for ever England; anyhow all this field is paved with bad essays and good intentions.

Of course there are essays that are really themes and themes that are really theses. They represent what may be called the Extreme Right of rigid right reason and militant purpose, after the Latin model. A model of the militant or controversial essay (and all the more so because there is no mailed fist, but a very iron hand in a very velvet glove) is Alice Meynell's essay in defence of the despised wife of Dr. Johnson. The words are spoken in the softest accent of irony; the mere style preserves all the stylist; special pose of gliding over things easily; but the whole thing is constructed controversially; it is as argumentative as any argument in any law court or debating club. It is also very effective argument, for until it was written, nearly everybody talked exactly that nonsense about poor Mrs. Johnson; and nobody I know of has talked it since. This theme really is a thesis; but when the same writer turns, let us say, to describing in the same elegant English the mere effect of blue twilight glowing in the cracks of the London streets, she is at most concerned with a theme.

Even here a certain Latin logic in her made her stick to the theme. We all know, however, that there are English essays that are very English essays and yet very jolly essays; that are none the less beautiful because they twist and ramble like an English road. Of these are some of Thackeray's *Roundabout Papers* and some of Mr. Belloc's best essays; like that highly unscrupulous dissertation which promises to deal with a particular feature of seventeenth century architecture, proceeds to argue with itself about the respective ages of Charles the Second and Louis the Fourteenth, amplifies itself into a glowing panorama of the landscapes of the Pyrenees, and ends with a Rebuke to His Pen, chiding it for having taken him so far away from the mere title and topic of his essay. People are so prone to say that Mr. Belloc is French that it is worth noting that in this and many other matters he is extraordinarily English. By the true test of literary consistency and conscientiousness, there was much more that was French about Mrs. Meynell. Or perhaps it might be maintained that something of Latin lucidity, which leads the former writer to value the strict form of the sonnet, in itself enables him to perceive the essential formlessness of the essay. Anyhow, except when it is tightened by the militant relevancy of debate or propaganda, the essay does tend to be formless, or at the best to present a very bewildering variety of forms. But I cannot help thinking a man must be as English as Mr. Belloc to enjoy it in its most formless form.

This indefinite and indeterminate quality would at once appear if we tried to classify the subordinate type under the general type of the essay. The types are so many and the tests are so few. There is one kind of essay that consists of staring out of the window at the garden and describing what you see there; but from this I am inhibited by a complete ignorance of the names of all the plants that I see. I have sometimes wondered whether it would be possible to disguise my ignorance under an appearance of abstruse or specialized or purely localized knowledge, as by saying, "That torrid and almost terrible blossom which is called in Persia the Blood of Kings," or: "The shrub which, in spite of its new scientific name, I still love to call *Judæus Esuriens*, as did the dear old naturalists of the later seventeenth century," or: "The little flower that we in Westmoreland have always called Bishop's Buttonhook, though they have another name for it in the South." It is obvious that the same bright and rather breathless enterprise might be applied to another sort of essay; the rambling historical and archæological causerie, in which one name leads to another; and generally to very little else. Would it be safe to begin a paragraph: "I was dipping into Dio Cassius the other day . . . " or to go on: "To find a parallel to this, I imagine we should have to go as far afield as the second period of the Upanishads," and perhaps conclude: "But after all, is not all this to be found in Scotus Erigena?" Very few people have read Dio Cassius or Erigena; and it may be doubted if even the aged Theosophists, who can still be found stranded in drawing-rooms, could pass an examination in the Eastern documents I have named. If done as a skit, it would be a successful skit; for certainly it would expose many before it was itself exposed. If done as the foundation for a solid career of learning, it would be unwise; for though only two people in the world knew it was nonsense, those two would certainly turn up. This covers an excellent sort of essay; the solemn skit, such as Mr. Gilbert Norwood's immortal fancy called *Too Many Books*. Then there is another sort of essay that has lately become fairly common and frequently quite picturesque; that may be called the Historical Glimpse. It will be devoted to describing a day with Moses or an afternoon call on Mahomet or Marat, or a chance meeting with Nero or Mr. Gladstone. The special technique developed for this design generally involves the detailed description of the hero before he is introduced by name, and it ends with: "Fear not, you carry Cæsar," or: "You may be interested to know that you have given a glass of milk to Prince Albert." All these are bold and promising essays at the elusive nature of the essay; but in itself it remains somewhat elusive. And, if I may end this rambling article on the subject of rambling articles, and end it with a personal confession, I will own that I am haunted with a faint suspicion that the essay will probably become rather more cogent and dogmatic, merely because of the deep and deadly divisions which ethical and economic problems may force upon us. But let us hope there will always be a place for the essay that is really an essay. It is an old story that soldiers sing songs round the camp-fire; but I doubt if they are all about soldiering. Indeed they are sometimes so lively in their range over other topics, that respectable patriots have found a difficulty in including them in collections of patriotic songs. St. Thomas Aquinas, with his usual commonsense, said that neither the active nor the contemplative life could be lived without relaxations, in the form of jokes and games. The drama or the epic might be called the active life of literature; the sonnet or the ode the contemplative life. The essay is the joke.

First published as the preface to *Essays of the Year 1931–32*, 1932

KATHARINE FULLERTON GEROULD (1879–1944) thought of herself first of all as a fiction writer, but she was probably best known for her provocative essays on everything from the first Dempsey-Tunney fight to the "plight of the genteel." Politically and culturally she was intensely conservative, and her provocative essays might seem at odds with the argument she makes in the piece that follows —that "the essay is essentially meditative" and not "polemical"—but she is trying to pit Montaignean skepticism against the Leftism of the 1930s, which she saw as universally dogmatic. A year earlier she had called in the pages of the *Saturday Review* for a "plebiscite" on the essay in which she asked readers to choose between "articles" or "essays," "news" or the "truth." Most readers balked at her false either/or and for the next two months they filled the magazine's letters column with complaints.

From "An Essay on Essays"

Though an essay must state a proposition, there are other requirements to be fulfilled. The bones of subject and predicate must be clothed in a certain way. The basis of the essay is meditation, and it must in a measure admit the reader to the meditative process. (This procedure is frankly hinted in all those titles that used to begin with "Of" or "On": "Of Truth," "Of Riches," "On the Graces and Anxieties of Pig-Driving," "On the Knocking at the Gate in 'Macbeth,'" "On the Enjoyment of Unpleasant Places.") An essay, to some extent, thinks aloud; though not in the loose and pointless way to which the "stream of consciousness" addicts have accustomed us. The author must have made up his mind—otherwise, where is his proposition? But the essay, I think, should show how and why he made up his mind as he did; should engagingly rehearse the steps by which he came to his conclusions. ("Francis of Verulam reasoned thus with himself.") Meditation; but an oriented and fruitful meditation.

This is the most intimate of forms, because it permits you to see a mind at work. On the quality and temper of that mind depends the goodness of the production. Now, if the essay is essentially meditative, it cannot be polemical. No one, I think, would call Cicero's first oration against Catiline an essay; or Burke's "Speech on the Conciliation of America"; hardly more could we call Swift's "Modest Proposal" a true essay. The author must have made up his mind, but when he has made it up with a vengeance, he will not produce an essay. Because the process is meditative, the manner should be courteous; he should always, by implication, admit that there are good people who may not agree with him; his irony should never turn to the sardonic. Reasonableness, urbanity (as Matthew Arnold would have said) are prerequisites for a form whose temper is meditative rather than polemical.

We have said that this is the most intimate of forms. Not only for technical reasons, though obviously the essayist is less sharply controlled by his structure than the dramatist or the sonneteer or even the novelist. It is the most intimate because it is the most subjective. When people talk of "creative" and "critical" writing—dividing all literature thus—they always call the essay critical. In spite of Oscar Wilde, to call it critical is probably correct; for creation implies objectivity. The created thing, though the author have torn its raw substance from his very vitals, ends by being separate from its creator. The essay, however, is incurably subjective; even *Wuthering Heights* or *Manfred* is less subjective—strange though it sound—than "The Function of Criticism" or "The Poetic Principle." What Oscar Wilde really meant in "The Critic as Artist"—if, that is, you hold him back from his own perversities—is not that Pater's essay on Leonardo da Vinci was more creative than many a novel, but that it was more subjective than any novel; that Pater, by virtue of his style and his mentality, made of his conception of the Mona Lisa something that we could be interested in, regardless of our opinion of the painting. I do not remember that Pater saw himself as doing more than explain to us what he thought Leonardo had done—Pater, I think, would never have regarded his purple page as other than criticism. I, myself—because I like the fall of Pater's words, and do not much care for Mona Lisa's feline face—prefer Pater's page to Leonardo's portrait; but I am quite aware that I am merely preferring criticism, in this instance, to the thing criticized. I am, if you like, preferring Mr. Pecksniff's drunken dream—"Mrs. Todgers's idea of a wooden leg"—to the wooden leg itself. Anything (I say to myself) rather than a wooden leg!

A lot of nineteenth century "impressionistic" criticism—Jules Lemaître, Anatole France, etc.—is more delightful than the prose or verse that is being criticized. It is none the less criticism. The famous definition of "the adventures of a soul among the masterpieces" does not put those adventures into the "creative" category; it merely stresses their subjectivity. Wilde is to some extent right when he says that criticism is the only civilized form of autobiography; but he is not so right when he says that the highest criticism is more creative than creation. No one would deny that the purple page Wilde quotes tells us more about Pater than it does about Leonardo, or even about Mona Lisa—as Macaulay's "Essay on Milton" conceivably tells us more about Macaulay than about the author of *Paradise Lost*. All Bacon's essays together but build up a portrait of Bacon—Francis of Verulam reasoning with himself; and what is the substance of the *Essays of Elia*, but Elia? "Subjective" is the word, however, rather than "creative."

It is this subjectivity—Montaigne's first of all, perhaps—that has confused many minds. It is subjectivity run wild that has tempted many people to believe that the familiar essay alone *is* the essay; which would make some people contend that an essay does not necessarily state a proposition. But we are talking of the essay itself; not of those bits of whimsical prose which are to the true essay what expanded anecdote is to the short story.

The essay, then, having persuasion for its object, states a proposition; its method is meditation; it is subjective rather than objective, critical rather than creative. It can never be a mere marshalling of facts; for it struggles, in one way or another, for truth; and truth is something one arrives at by the help of facts, not the facts themselves. Meditating on facts may bring one to truth; facts alone will not. Nor can there be an essay without a point of view and a personality. A geometrical proposition cannot be an essay, since, though it arranges facts in a certain pattern, there is involved no personal meditative process, conditioned by the individuality of the author. A geometrical proposition is not subjective. One is even tempted to say that its tone is not urbane!

Perhaps—with the essay thus defined—we shall understand without effort why it is being so little written at present. Dorothy Thompson has said that Germany is living in a state of war. The whole world is living more or less in a state of war; and a state of war produces any literary form more easily than the essay. It is not hard to see why. People in a state of war, whether the war be military or economic, express themselves polemically. A wise man said to me, many years ago, that, in his opinion, the worst by-product of the World War was propaganda. Many times, in the course of the years, I have had occasion to recall that statement. There are perhaps times and places where propaganda is justified—it is not for me to say. But I think we should all agree that the increasing habit of using the technique of propaganda is corrupting the human mind in its most secret and delicate processes. Propaganda has, in common with all other expression, the object of persuasion; but it pursues that legitimate object by illegitimate means—by *suggestio falsi* and *suppressio veri*; by the *argumentum ad hominem* and hitting below the belt; by demagogic appeal and the disregard of right reason. The victim of propaganda is not intellectually persuaded, but intellectually—if not emotionally—coerced. The essayist, whatever the limitations of his intelligence, is bound over to be honest; the propagandist is always dishonest.

First published in the *North American Review* (December 1935)

WALTER MURDOCH (1874–1970) was the youngest of fourteen children born to a Scottish minister and his wife. The family moved to Melbourne, Australia, when Walter was ten, and he was educated there. Murdoch spent his life as an academic but always reached beyond the classroom for a larger audience, writing regular book reviews and "Answers" columns for various Australian newspapers, lecturing to clubs, and speaking on radio about cultural and political issues. He advocated for women's rights, was against outlawing the Communist Party, and argued that Australia should not secede from the Commonwealth. In the piece that follows, his sure but measured, friendly tone is on display as he argues that the essay's main tradition is Montaignean and personal rather than Baconian and formal. According to Murdoch, "The essay is to prose what the lyric is to poetry; it is intensely personal. It is not a statement of facts, it is not a cold, abstract argument, it is not an inflammatory harangue; it is a quiet talk, reflecting the personal likes and dislikes of the author."

From "The Essay"

I have been reading the excellent little volume of *Selected Modern English Essays* which the Oxford University Press has added to its "World's Classics" series—a collection of cheap books for which we ought to give thanks twice a day. The essays selected are modern with a vengeance; most of the authors are still alive; those who are not are among them that died o' Wednesday; and the later essays in the volume are by men considerably younger than he who now writes. And the subjects cover a wide range—from Walt Whitman to the House of Commons, from "A Medieval Girl School" to "Cockney Humour," from Judas Iscariot to Alphonse Daudet; very fine mixed feeding. And as I read essay after essay (they are all readable), I asked myself:—What is the bond between all these pieces of writing, so different in manner, and in matter so various? and why do we call them all essays? Essays they are—genuine essays, not chapters of books, not sermons, not newspaper articles, not harangues, but essays.

What then is an essay? And I came to the conclusion that a good essay is the best substitute that literature has to offer us for a good talk. The word "essay" has, of course, been terribly misused. Bacon's bundles of wise saws are not essays—nobody ever talked like that. Macaulay's narratives are little histories or little biographies, but they are not essays. Locke's *Essay Concerning Human Understanding* is not an essay, but a treatise. Pope's *Essay on Man* is a piece of didactic verse, whereas a real essay is never didactic and never verse. Emerson's *Essays* are not essays, but sermons. Half the things that masquerade as essays are really dissertations. But the real essay—the art whose patron saint is Montaigne—is quite distinct from any other form of literature. It began, in England, with Cowley; flowered in the days of Addison and Steele; faded; revived a little in Goldsmith's time; faded again; flowered again, gorgeously, in the days of Lamb and Hazlitt and Leigh Hunt; faded once more, this time so completely that it might have been thought to be dead. The Victorians—whose virtues I have so often praised—could not write essays. In a sense, it was their very virtue that disqualified them; they were too earnest. It is the mark of the Victorian that when you sit down for a cosy chat with him, before you know where you are you find that he is "holding forth." Now an essayist never holds forth. I have sometimes thought we might define by saying, "Have you read Ruskin? Well, an essayist is the opposite of Ruskin."

And now it has revived a little; and it is delightful to run through this little Oxford volume and see how many genuine essayists are among us, excellent practitioners of this most delicate and difficult and beautiful art. And what is more, the essay has actually become popular again, more popular than at any time since the days of the *Spectator*. The essay is, in fact, the one kind of writing that can at present hold up its head and look the popular novel in the face, and say, "I, too, have a public." I do not mean, of course, that a volume of essays can hope for the kind of resounding success that a bad novel can command; but I mean that with discriminating readers who know a good thing when they see it the essay has come to its own again. The publishers' lists prove this. Mr E. V. Lucas and Mr Max Beerbohm, Mr Chesterton and Mr Belloc, all genuine essayists, are popular in a sense in which no essayist was popular twenty years ago.

The essay is to prose what the lyric is to poetry; it is intensely personal. It is not a statement of facts, it is not a cold, abstract argument, it is not an inflammatory harangue; it is a quiet talk, reflecting the personal likes and dislikes of the author. It never pretends to treat a subject exhaustively; it is brief, informal, modest. The style of an essayist must be, as Sir Edmund Gosse has said, "confidential," and "a model of current cultivated ease of expression and a mirror of the best conversation." It must have a certain dignity; it must be familiar—not high-faluting—but not too familiar. There are some authors who seem continually, as they write, to be winking at you, and calling you "old chap," and pointing their jokes by digging you playfully in the ribs. I do not like being called "old chap," and I am sensitive in the region of the ribs. The essayist must behave himself like a gentleman; good manners are more essential to him than to any other kind of writer. He must have a sense of humour, but he must not be a buffoon. He must be wise, too; but with all his wisdom he must never forget that he is talking to the reader, not instructing him. Whatever he talks about—and his range is infinite, from the philosophy of Hegel to the habits of cats—he must touch it lightly; that is essential. If for a moment he becomes heavy or pompous or pontifical, the charm is snapped, the spell dissolved. It is, as I have said, a most delicate art; it looks so extremely easy and is really so difficult. We have a hundred good lyrics, in English, for one good essay; as good singers are a hundred times more plentiful than good talkers. The editor of this little anthology has chosen some of the best talkers of our time, and has caught them at their happiest moments. I cannot imagine a better book to slip into your pocket when you are setting out upon a walking tour or a finer companion for a railway journey. . . . If the essay should come to displace the novel in popular favour, it would be a clear sign of an advance in civilization. When we are prepared to sit down and listen to an easy, informal talk by a wise, humorous, kindly observer of life, without demanding that he shall tell us a story, we show that we are growing up.

First published in *Collected Essays*, 1938

ENRIQUE ANDERSON IMBERT (1910–2000), an Argentinian journalist, literary critic, and fiction writer, known as one of the early practitioners of "magic realism," spent most of his early years writing and teaching in Argentina, until the dictatorship of Juan Peron compelled him to leave in 1947. Taking up residence in the United States, Anderson Imbert devoted himself primarily to pathbreaking historical and critical studies of Spanish-American literature. As a professor at the University of Michigan, then at Harvard, he was known for an intensely personal classroom style that once led him to teach a work dressed in the garb of a gaucho. Anderson Imbert's intense style can also be heard throughout his defense of the essay, reprinted below, a highlight of which is his spirited assertion that "I do not believe a systematic treatise, constructed with methods and bibliographies, like those that arouse professors, is worth more, necessarily, than a personal essay, spontaneous and audacious, on the same theme."

From "In Defense of the Essay"

I do not believe that a systematic treatise, constructed with methods and bibliographies, like those that arouse professors, is worth more, necessarily, than a personal essay, spontaneous and audacious, on the same theme. Everything depends on the author and his fruit.

It is clear that the fanatics of philosophy will say that a philosophical system—above all if it is German—has more rigor, dignity, and hierarchy than an essay—above all if it is English. But, people, let us not talk about philosophy, first as if it monopolizes all offices of intelligence; and second as if it truly exists! I lament emphasizing philosophy, but I have no other choice: philosophy professors are those I have seen—with their very high eyebrows—disdaining essayists. Professionals of the concept, it would not be at all strange if they were to think that written genres have greater objectivity than writers.

The belief that concepts can become independent of the psychological process that elaborates them, substantiate themselves like the spiritualists' ectoplasm, convert themselves into "objective spirit," and resent the men who gave them life has always seemed a manifestation of madness to me. It was in a rage of sensibility that Aristotle elaborated his concept of poetic genres; but it was in a prolonged span of madness—from the Renaissance to Romanticism—that those genres were hypostatized into rhetorical realities and began to exercise an insulting power upon poets themselves. I respect the theoretical investigations of many sincere and original men whose work I envision as the concept of philosophy; but if they tell me, with the defiant air of a Quixote, that philosophy (from Toboso or wherever) demands something greater than respect, since it is the unparalleled queen of all intellectual disciplines, and I should obey it or die, then I rebel and swear I do not know that lady named Philosophy.

I am not absolute enough in my idealism to suppose that everything, even the elephant, is an illusion of my conscience. No. I believe in the heavy elephant. At least I believe that outside my being there is something that, upon entering my conscience, is represented to me as an image I call "elephant." But I refuse to believe that there is something called Philosophy, and much less that this Philosophy obliges me to be ashamed of my essays or to comply with academic methods. I do not know what an elephant is in itself, but it is enough for me to know that if that piece of noumenon puts a foot on me (or what I imagine is a foot) the noumenal foot will crush me. On the other hand, in the dominion of my conscience I am free, and there is nothing spiritual from the outside that can crush me. There are two elephants: the illusory and the other, which crushes me; but there is only one Philosophy, the illusory one, which cannot harm me.

I am skeptical, therefore, of the prejudice that an essay is less worthy than a philosophical treatise. The pellet is as round as the moon.

What happens is that many suppose that an essay is a rehearsal in something that one does not know well. A certain university professor (Argentine, of course) was upset because a colleague had published an essay. It seemed a trifling thing. "Why not rehearse at home," he exclaimed, "instead of rehearsing in public?" It seemed to him that to express oneself in informal, quick, and pleasant pages was to squander the theme and probably the brain!

But essays are not mumblings in an unlearned language; they are not the first steps on a path that others—the authors of treatises, theses, dissertations, and discourses—have already traveled to its end. Neither mumblings nor first steps were the pages by Montaigne, "the father of the essay." The history of the essay does not show us a limbo of indecisive people or apprentices, but of an emphatic assembly of spirits who felt confident, ingenious, and aware.

The essay's discredit in Argentina is due to snobs who have suddenly begun to make usurious calculations: if instead of being generous with periodicals—they say—they were to commit themselves to writing more extensive and systematic works, the country would grow in cultural import. Why? English literature is among the finest in the world thanks, in part, to the essay: Bacon, Cowley, Steele, Addison, Swift, Johnson, Goldsmith, Lamb, Hazlitt, Coleridge, Ruskin, Pater, Stevenson, Shaw, Chesterton, Woolf, Huxley, etc., are presences entirely on the face of a great literature, not loose threads hanging off the back of the tapestry. The essay is not always more humble than other literary genres. Who doubts that an essay by Addison is worth more than a tragedy by Addison? The essay is not always more ephemeral than a treatise. Great *Summae* have disappeared in the abyss and—as Paul Valéry says of the ancient empires—they have left us only their beautiful names. The word *Thomism*, for example; doesn't it sound beautifully phantom like the word *Babylonia*?

As I do not believe in genres, I do not believe in definitions either. A scholarly approximation would be this: the essay is a composition in prose, discursive but artistic through its richness in anecdotes and descriptions, brief enough that we can read it in one sitting, with an unlimited register of themes interpreted in all tones and with total liberty from a very personal point of view. If one considers this more or less current definition, one will see that the essay's very noble function consists of poeticizing the plain exercise of the writer's intelligence and fantasy, in prose. The essay is a conceptually constructed work of art; it is a logical structure, but one where logic begins to sing. I know that Croce would reject these opinions: he, who in one of his theoretical abuses arrived at denying poetic worth even to Dante's allegories, would not admit that there could be lyricism in an essay. "Where there is concept there is no poetry!" But conferring unity to something is already a poeticizing act. Any construction is animated with a touch of poetry when its interior unity has become visible, easy, and pleasant. There are philosophical systems, mathematical theories, scientific hypotheses, and historical characterizations that are converted into poems by the work and grace of a unifying spirit. And the essay is, above all else, a minimal unity, delicate and vivacious, wherein concepts may shine.

From *The Oxford Book of Latin American Essays*, translated by Jesse H. Lytle

MAX BENSE (1910–1990), a German philosopher of science and aesthetics, spent most of his teaching career as a professor of the philosophy of technology at the University of Stuttgart. In his teaching and in numerous books, Bense sought to promote a rational, scientific, even mathematical approach to the analysis of art and literature, as in *Mathematics and Beauty* (1960). Bense was particularly interested in using such an approach to explain the communicative nature of signs and symbols, images and texts—an approach that he set forth in *An Introduction to Information Theoretical Aesthetics* (1969). Bense's scientific orientation to writing is reflected in the following excerpt from his piece "On the Essay and Experimentation," in which he asserts that "the essay is an experimental method; it is about writing experimentally, and one needs write about it in the same sense that one speaks of experimental physics, which distinguishes itself from theoretical physics rather cleanly."

From "On the Essay and Its Prose"

"Essay" means in German: *Versuch*—attempt and experiment. This poses the question of whether the expression means that an enlightened literary person is "attempting" to write about something, or whether writing about a defined or half-defined subject has the character of an experiment, an experiment on that subject. We are convinced that the essay is an experimental method; it is about writing experimentally, and one needs write about it in the same sense that one speaks of experimental physics, which distinguishes itself from theoretical physics rather cleanly. In experimental physics, to stay with our metaphor, one poses a question to nature, expects an answer, examines it and quantifies; theoretical physics describes nature by demonstrating analytically, axiomatically, and deductively its adherence to its laws due to mathematic necessity. This is the difference between an essay and a treatise. Composing experimentally, pushing an object of study here and there, interrogating, prodding, examining, thoroughly reflecting on it, tackling subject matter from different sides and gathering what is seen in mental purview and giving name to what the subject matter makes visible under the conditions produced by writing: That is essay writing. The writing subject at work in the essay is not "attempting" anything; rather, he produces the conditions under which subject matter is brought into the context of a literary configuration. There is no attempt at writing, there is no attempt at knowing; the attempt is at how subject matter behaves literarily; thus a question is posed, subject matter is experimented with. We can see that the character of essay writing does not simply reside in the literary form in which something is composed. The content, the subject matter treated, appears "essayistic" because it appears under conditions. In this respect a capacity for perspective as in Leibniz, Dilthey, Nietzsche and Ortega y Gasset is inherent to every essay. They advance a philosophical perspectivalism to the extent that in their meditations they exert a certain thinking and knowing which are based on point of view. Even those who have read only a small portion of the writings of these men will not fail to recognize the mastery of their abilities in the essay. If this mastery is concealed in Leibniz's epistolary form, it is obvious in Dilthey; if, as with Nietzsche, it dresses up in the ability to write aphorisms, in Ortega's case the essay is the intended form.

At this point I must emphasize that in every essay those wonderful sentences show up which are like the seeds of the whole thing, from which the essay can replenish itself again and again. I mean those enticing prose sentences, in which one can see that there is no perfect border to poetry here. These are, so to speak, the elementary sentences of an essay, which belong to prose and poetry alike. They are fragments of a "perfected speech of sense," that is, fragments of a linguistic body which touch us like part of nature, and they are fragments of a bluntly expressed thought, that is, fragments of a completed deduction, which touch us like a part of a Platonic idea. One must take it upon himself to read in both languages if one wants to partake in the full satisfaction of an essay . . . or one transforms the essay before realizing it into a series of aphorisms which all pointedly express a thought, as can be seen in Lichtenberg, Novalis, and Goethe, or perhaps into a series of very compressed images, something like Rimbaud's "Illuminations," whose torn parts present an almost perfect unending lyric.

And with that we confront a further point of definition in our meditation. Is it not striking that all great essayists are critics? Is it not striking that all historical periods, which are distinguished by the essay, are ultimately periods of criticism? What does that imply?

To dissect the thought: In France the essay developed in relation to the sober, critical works of Montaigne. His advice for living and dying, thinking and working, enjoyment and lamentation are the fruits of a critical spirit. The element within which these reflections operate is the element of the grand French moralists and doubters. He is a spiritual source of his time, the beginning of a protesting critical context of spirit, which goes on to influence in full the seventeenth and eighteenth centuries. A lineage runs from Montaigne to Gide, Valéry and Camus. Bacon developed the essay in England. Bacon—who in every respect wrote his essays with cunningly moral, skeptical, enlightened, and succinctly critical ulterior motives. At bottom he was the great precursor of Swift, Defoe, Hume, W. G. Hamilton, De Quincey and Poe, as well as the others who came later: Chesterton, T. S. Eliot, Strachey, et cetera. In Germany Lessing, Möser and Herder—whose inexhaustible "Letters for the Advancement of Humanity" stand out as the most significant collection of German essays—initiate and at the same time master our form of experimental literature. Everyone knows the critical depths their works contain. Friedrich Schlegel, himself a master critic and essayist, describes Herder as a pure manifestation of the critic and identifies in him the man of protest in the fullest sense, while Adam Müller calls the Lessing of his lecture on the origin of German criticism and the essay "one of the most influential spiritual sources." And we have furthermore already mentioned Dilthey, Nietzsche, and Ortega y Gasset. More recent authors follow them: Gottfried Benn, who came out of expressionism; Hofmiller, one of our first literary critics; Karl Hillebrand and Ernst Robert Curtius, who succeeded in making an analyst's penetrating take on the world sparkle out of moments from the present day. Ernst Jünger, whose essays experiment with things in Montaigne's calm, half cynical, half skeptical manner; Rudolf Kassner, who tirelessly seeks to preserve the world-historical conditions for analytical understanding; Thomas Mann, who pours the breath of the epic into prolonged expressions, doing so with a diversity of theme that encompasses art, historiography, psychology, history, and politics; finally the Austrian essayists from Kürenberger and Speidel to Karl Kraus, Hofmannsthal and Stoessl, who even honored this literary form with a theory stating that "the instinctual and the known" are "equally" at work in the essay.

This much is clear: the essay originates from the critical essence of our intellect, whose desire for experimentation is simply a necessity of its manner of being, its method.

First published in *Merkur* (1947), translated here by Eugene Sampson

MARIANO PICÓN-SALAS (1901–65) was a Venezuelan diplomat, historian, and essayist, who lived in Chile and elsewhere during brutal dictatorships in Venezuela but always returned to his native country. Throughout his career, Picón-Salas devoted himself to interpreting the varied culture, history, and literature of South America; like others of his time, known as *mundonovistas* (that is, "newworldists" or Latin Americanists), he sought to overcome the elitist influence of Spain. In a wide-ranging series of books and essays, he contributed to the definition and celebration of a South American identity by writing not only about specific personages and countries but also about the entire continent, as in *A Cultural History of Spanish America, from Conquest to Independence* (1944). Though the following excerpt from "On the Essay" resonates with a concern for social justice, born no doubt of his experience in Venezuela, Picón-Salas ultimately seems most concerned that essayists express themselves in "a language so personal and appropriate that it is recognized as one's own."

From "On the Essay"

The function of the essayist—one like Carlyle, Emerson, Santayana, or Unamuno—would seem to be to reconcile poetry and philosophy, to offer a strange bridge between the world of images and that of concepts, warning the reader of the dark turns of the labyrinth and hoping to help him seek an opening through which to pass. The essayist doesn't pretend like a philosopher to offer a systematic understanding of the world universally valid but works from and within the immediate situation or conflict. For isn't it the case that Plato and St. Augustine participate similarly in joining the world of ideas and the world of interior subjectivity? This explains the final inadequacy and artificiality of the literary genres since, for example, the Platonic *Dialogues* and the *Confessions* of St. Augustine draw simultaneously upon the nature of philosophy and upon the essay.

The essay's primary insistence on the concrete, a vision of the universe not only intellectual but physical and plastic, marks a permeable frontier between its territory and philosophy. Probably on that English autumn afternoon when the physicist Isaac Newton saw an apple fall, the essayist would have been content to describe the event and leave to the good Isaac all its fine calculations; perhaps he would venture—if it were no anachronism—to announce to the *Edinburgh Review* that something of supreme importance was on the verge of being understood about the physical world. Meanwhile the philosopher would not have left it to Newton to formulate the laws of gravitation in language clear and distinct. By this pathway we can say, metaphorically, that the essayist writes when an apple has fallen at his feet and when, with the fine senses of a hunter and a poet, he detects that something is happening or is going to happen.

An essayist like Erasmus seems to say to the Roman Catholic Church, be careful or a Luther will appear, and one like Carlyle to the English liberals, don't give in too much to their cries and demands or there may arise an avenger of the working class. Perhaps the essayist does not dare convert into law a whole series of symptoms as a philosopher may, but he will profile and describe them. And this description, for its part, is not that of the novelist who would resolve it in the relations of John, James, and Maria (for there are no novels without women and even in the narratives considered the most misogynist there is always a woman hidden), but he would write in such a way that, while feeling intensely personal, aspires also to what we call realism.

In its own nature, the essay develops by preference in epochs of crisis, when humans feel most confounded and, threatened, are expressing with alarm—before new ones emerge—the values of an older culture. Plato, Lucian, and St. Augustine testified successively to crises of the ancient soul; they saw gods be born and die in order to draw out clarity and certainty from the general turbulence. In the same manner, our good neighbor from Bordeaux, Michel de Montaigne, who did not aspire to be a hero but to be an enlightened man, benevolent and sensitive, advanced modern philosophy and the thought of future ages by epitomizing in himself the confusion of his time. It is terrible that the Catholics slaughter the Huguenots and the Huguenots the Catholics since no religion should be wiped out is the simple truth he deduced when, returning to his chateau, burdened with the tragic news of the street and feeling once again the discomforting pain of his kidney stones, he sat in his study, reread Tacitus—who saw similar butcheries and violence—and laid out a higher standard to which humans could aspire.

Considering the matter this way, everyone could write essays since everyone has contemplated injustices; but apart from the fact that the field of the essay is not exclusively that of ethics, nor would the most ambitious association of essayists aspire to the immediate correction of the multiple griefs and errors of humankind, the problem becomes, as always, the larger one of literature. Many young men have been lost to the streets of Carthage, loving the prostitutes, adoring false gods, and receiving later—like an extraordinary light in the dark—the message of the new religion of Christ; but only St. Augustine could write the *Confessions.* In the same manner, among all the letters and testimonies that would have passed between Paris and Bordeaux during the religious wars of the late sixteenth century, we preserve, above all, the words of the author of the *Essays,* not only because they teach tolerance and justice, but because they were written in that language which their author himself called "succulent and nervous, short and concise, less delicate and decked out than vehement and brusque," the language that signals the unmistakable personality of Montaigne as the father of all essayists.

The formula of the essay—how simple this seems to affirm—is that of all literature: have something to say, say it in a manner that excites the conscience and awakens the emotions of other persons, in a language so personal and appropriate that it is recognized as one's own. So we speak of the prose of Plato, of Voltaire, of Cervantes, of Unamuno. All the rest is but the confetti of rhetoric that not even the greatest writers avoid entirely so as to make more social, easy, and approachable the explosive and cathartic effect of their greatest ideas and most authentic books. Literature, too, like all human products, dons a mask, which in our age could be a mask of vapors.

First published in *Cuadernos* 8 (1954), translated here by David Hamilton

GERMÁN ARCINIEGAS (1900–99) was a Colombian journalist, historian, educator, diplomat, and political activist, who devoted much of his career to speaking out against the brutality and oppression of military governments throughout South America. In *The State of Latin America* (1952), he chronicled the tortures so extensively and vividly that a concern for his safety compelled him to emigrate to the United States, where he taught at Columbia University before returning to Colombia. In numerous books and essays, Arciniegas also sought to challenge a Eurocentric view of South America with a celebration of its multicultural heritage, as he makes clear in asserting that "In our America, from Indian copper, African ebony, and Iberian olive has come an infinite range of hues." Here as elsewhere in "The Essay in Our America," excerpted below, Arciniegas conceives of the South American essay as inextricably bound up with the complex cultural history of the continent itself.

From "The Essay in Our America"

In this America of ours, which is *mestizo*, not Latin, the novel arrives late, the theater does not mature, but the essay flourishes. Because we are problematic, we must interpret ourselves. In a certain sense, we are the most difficult and complicated people in all the world. When in the field of letters an essayist appears who discovers a new angle on the problem that grips us—that of knowing who we are and where we are going—he is called "*Maestro.*" It is the only occasion when we use that term with respect, almost with veneration. Otherwise we use it ironically and call the shoemaker a maestro or the musician who plays the guitar in the square in the middle of the night. But it is another matter when we speak of Justo Sierra, of Hostos or Rodó, or more recently of Alfonso Reyes or Sanín Cano.

America is the only continent to have appeared recently, the only one to have sprung out of what was totally unknown. Some dreamers had premonitions of its existence but only as an exercise of the imagination, and even then the best they could do was invent and then destroy an image, create a fantasy of Atlantis then tell of its immediate disappearance. When Toscanelli and Columbus insisted on the roundness of the earth, the one by way of simple calculation the other by daring to demonstrate the fact, they imagined only the coasts of Asia on the far side of the Atlantic, the islands of Japan. The revelation that Amérigo Vespucci made of discovering a new continent produced such stupefaction in Europe that geographers felt compelled to ask that he give his name to the new world. Asia and Africa had been explored centuries earlier. The spirit of Asia and Africa had long been flowing in the European bloodstream, their sources no more than journeys clouded by distance and by the difficulty of travel. But there had been Marco Polos, and they knew the color of those peoples, what they thought, and what they produced. America erupted like the provocation for an essay. It is the ultimate subject. It was not mere coincidence or by caprice that Montaigne, the creator of the modern essay, preoccupied himself with a man from America. That good savage of whom he spoke would remain alive in the minds of Europeans until travelers of the age of Bougainville, La Condamine, and Humboldt refreshed their memories of him and so the outpouring of romantic literature burst forth by which Europeans understood America in the eighteenth century.

In truth, the essay on the New World began to be written in the first decade of the sixteenth century by the explorers themselves. Amérigo Vespucci discussed fully the problem of the color of American people just as he discussed all the geographical theories that stood between what men saw with their own eyes in the new world and what they had glimpsed in books. From the work of Las Casas or of Sahagún, one can extract independent essays in which it is wonderful to see how currents of medieval thought and humanism cross. Of everything said later in essays of the nineteenth century, there are adumbrations not at all negligible in those primitive texts born of the surprise of discovery.

Moreover, it is our America that stands almost alone in modern times for forming the grand hybridization of race. It is a hybridization that remains green and fresh for sociological study. Europe is certainly a continent of mixed breeding, but the Asian invasion is so distant from us that it has evaporated as a point of memory, similar to the mixing of Africans with the people of Mediterranean Europe, and no one concerns himself with a process that remote. Here on the contrary we have a Babel not of languages but of colors. And we bear it with relative ease. In the United States, which must only combine black with white, the partisans of segregation still fight to the death and the Supreme Court must endure their arrogant defiance. In our America, from Indian copper, African ebony, and Iberian olive has come an infinite range of hues, and when José Vasconcelos suggests the possibility that a cosmic race could have established in our land all those colors and then tied them to the other three continents with strings now lost, he is called by that name that we honor most, *Maestro.*

In another sense, too, our America is unique. It is unstable, chaotic, and anarchic, but it minds a different theory on the issue that, perhaps, has most concerned European history in the modern period: the manner in which some people murder others. Three centuries of continual peace offer something Europeans have never known. It is true that in the nineteenth century we practiced the exercise of civil war, but the total number of dead in those wars does not reach that of a major battle on the old continent. There have been no wars of conquest. No armies have been formed to invade one's neighbors. The only large-scale invasion one remembers is that of Mexico by the United States. The War of the Pacific involving Chile, Peru, and Bolivia and the alliance of Brazil and Argentina against Paraguay are episodes that one cannot compare with the constant warfare of Europe. The system of the American states has frozen international war. But our America is unstable. In every country, constitutions change with feverish frequency. Dictatorships and revolutions alternate without respite or truce. Our collective passions contrast with the mechanical precision of the imperturbable growth of the United States before and after the Civil War.

There is one situation evident in the contrasting histories of the United States and of Latin America that explains this phenomenon. In the United States, independence was no more than the natural development and political evolution of the colonies. There a democratic government, liberal and representative, was being practiced in separate regions that already had the experience of self-governing. Those bodies corresponded to populations from all over Europe that had been drawn to America by a democratic vocation. The English, German, French, Russian, and Dutch colonies that had begun to function as business enterprises were formed by those who needed to find freedom for themselves in the practice of their religion. They emigrated from Europe with the plan of achieving an independent life. In Latin America the opposite occurred. There one lived under the absolute power of an empire governed on the one hand by Roman ideas of a central power and on the other by the strong arm of the Catholic Church. The Church saw in the slightest gesture of independence an ideology that suggested Lutheranism, Judaism, or Calvinism and smothered it with evident efficiency. Because of these circumstances, the essay in the United States becomes an optimistic synthesis of its own progress; it is a philosophy in which one sees the complacency of a healthy organism that develops industries, cities, farms and ranches across the width of a republic unburdened by the green infernos of our furious and deadly geography.

In contrast, the Latin American essay is a passage along the edge of an abyss. Among our themes is the temptation that one feels only along the precipices of death. One of our first great essays, "The Letter of Jamaica" by Bolivar, illustrates this dramatic element of our being. You look in vain in the writings of Washington for a comparable page. The deeds that the hero of the north needed to consider during his campaigns or after his triumph never formed in him the urgency of reflections so profound. While the United States, rich and arrogant, emboldened by its successes and with a big game hunter at its head, coins the happy and oblivious expression, "Manifest Destiny," which presumes to include half the Caribbean, Alcides Arguedas speaks, in Hispanic America, of a diseased people, our people, and Francisco García Calderón tries in vain, with his elegant and Francophile rhetoric, to imagine the creation of a continent born from the actions he himself presents in macabre parade.

It is obvious that the natural resources of our America and its human reserves of communities formed in battles most anguished and unequal allow us to consider a future of extraordinary influence. But the depths from which we emerge place us in a tragic landscape. One cannot find as a theme for the essay anything more rich of contrasts, with more melancholy shadows, recondite secrets, and sharper crises—and with more hymns of hope and life.

First published in *Cuadernos* 19 (1956), translated here by David Hamilton

THEODOR W. ADORNO (1903–69) was born Theodor Ludwig Wiesengrund in Frankfurt am Main, the only child of a wealthy German-Jewish wine merchant and Corsican-Catholic singer and musician. Displaced by the Nazis, he spent 1934 to 1949 in Oxford, New York, and Los Angeles, during which time he became a naturalized American citizen and adopted his mother's name. Adorno, an accomplished pianist, composer, and music critic, did not join the Institute of Social Research (or Frankfurt School) until 1938 but is usually associated with the school's Marxian critique of the culture industry and collaborated often with its director Max Horkheimer. In an excerpt from his "The Essay as Form" (1958), Adorno argues that because it is a kind of antigenre, the essay promotes skepticism and independent thought, a view that dates to Pater but that Adorno finds in conversation with Lukács and Musil. When Adorno claims, "The essay shys away from the violence of dogma," his use of "shys away" wisely suggests that it would be dogmatic to hold that any form is inherently, always, and definitely *not* dogmatic.

From "The Essay as Form"

With regard to scientific procedure and its philosophic grounding as method, the essay, in accordance with its idea, draws the fullest consequences from the critique of the system. Even the empiricist doctrines that grant priority to open, unanticipated experience over firm, conceptual ordering remain systematic to the extent that they investigate what they hold to be the more or less constant pre-conditions of knowledge and develop them in as continuous a context as possible. Since the time of Bacon, who was himself an essayist, empiricism—no less than rationalism—has been "method." Doubt about the unconditional priority of method was raised, in the actual process of thought, almost exclusively by the essay. It does justice to the consciousness of non-identity, without needing to say so, radically un-radical in refraining from any reduction to a principle, in accentuating the fragmentary, the partial rather than the total. "Perhaps the great Sieur de Montaigne felt something like this when he gave his writings the wonderfully elegant and apt title of *Essays*. The simple modesty of this word is an arrogant courtesy. The essayist dismisses his own proud hopes which sometimes lead him to believe that he has come close to the ultimate: he has, after all, no more to offer than explanations of the poems of others, or at best of his own ideas. But he ironically adapts himself to this smallness—the eternal smallness of the most profound work of the intellect in face of life—and even emphasizes it with ironic modesty." The essay does not obey the rules of the game of organized science and theory that, following Spinoza's principle, the order of things is identical with that of ideas. Since the airtight order of concepts is not identical with existence, the essay does not strive for closed, deductive or inductive, construction. It revolts above all against the doctrine—deeply rooted since Plato—that the changing and ephemeral is unworthy of philosophy; against that ancient injustice toward the transitory, by which it is once more anathematized, conceptually. The essay shys away from the violence of dogma, from the notion that the result of abstraction, the temporally invariable concept indifferent to the individual phenomenon grasped by it, deserves ontological dignity. The delusion that the *ordo idearum* (order of ideas) should be the *ordo rerum* (order of things) is based on the insinuation that the mediated is unmediated. Just as little as a simple fact can be thought without a concept, because to think it always already means to conceptualize it, it is equally impossible to think the purest concept without reference to the factual. Even the creations of phantasy that are supposedly independent of space and time, point toward individual existence—however far they may be removed from it. Therefore the essay is not intimidated by the depraved profundity which claims that truth and history are incompatible. If truth has in fact a temporal core, then the full historical content becomes an integral moment in truth; the *a posteriori* becomes concretely the *a priori*, as only generally stipulated by Fichte and his followers. The relation to experience—and from it the essay takes as much substance as does traditional theory from its categories—is a relation to all of history; merely individual experience, in which consciousness begins with what is nearest to it, is itself mediated by the all-encompassing experience of historical humanity; the claim that social-historical contents are nevertheless supposed to be only indirectly important compared with the immediate life of the individual is a simple self-delusion of an individualistic society and ideology. The depreciation of the historically produced, as an object of theory, is therefore corrected by the essay. There is no salvaging the distinction of a first philosophy from a mere philosophy of culture that assumes the former and builds on it, a distinction with which the taboo on the essay is rationalized theoretically. The intellectual process which canonizes a distinction between the temporal and the timeless is losing its authority. Higher levels of abstraction invest thought neither with a greater sanctity nor with metaphysical content; rather, the metaphysical content evaporates with the progress of abstraction, for which the essay attempts to make reparation. The usual reproach against the essay, that it is fragmentary and random, itself assumes the giveness [sic] of totality and thereby the identity of subject and object, and it suggests that man is in control of totality. But the desire of the essay is not to seek and filter the eternal out of the transitory; it wants, rather, to make the transitory eternal. Its weakness testifies to the non-identity that it has to express, as well as to that excess of intention over its object, and thereby it points to that utopia which is blocked out by the classification of the world into the eternal and the transitory. In the emphatic essay, thought gets rid of the traditional idea of truth.

The essay simultaneously suspends the traditional concept of method. Thought acquires its depth from penetrating deeply into a matter, not from referring it back to something else. In this the essay becomes polemical by treating what is normally held to be derived, without however pursuing its ultimate derivation. The essay freely associates what can be found associated in the freely chosen object. It does not insist stubbornly on a realm transcending all mediations—and they are the historical ones in which the whole of society is sedimented—rather the essay seeks truth contents as being historical in themselves. It does not concern itself with any supposed primeval condition in order to contravene society's false sociality, which, just because it tolerates nothing not stamped by it, ultimately tolerates nothing indicative of its own omnipresence and necessarily cites, as its ideological complement, that nature which its own praxis eliminates. The essay silently abandons the illusion that thought can break out of *thesis* into *physis*, out of culture into nature. Spellbound by what is fixed and admittedly deduced, by artifacts, the essay honors nature by confirming that it no longer exists for human beings. The essay's Alexandrianism replies to the fact that by their very existence the lilac and the nightingale, wherever the universal net allows them to survive, only want to delude us that life still lives. The essay abandons the main road to the origins, the road leading to the most derivative, to being, the ideology that simply doubles that which already exists; at the same time the essay does not allow the idea of immediacy, postulated by the very concept of mediation, to disappear entirely. All levels of the mediated are immediate to the essay, before its reflection begins.

As the essay denies any primeval givens, so it refuses any definition of its concepts. Philosophy has completed the fullest critique of definition from the most diverse perspectives, including those of Kant, Hegel and Nietzsche. But science has never adopted this critique. While the movement beginning with Kant, a movement against the scholastic residues in modern thought, replaces verbal definition with an understanding of concepts as part of the process in which they are temporally embodied, the individual sciences insist stubbornly on the pre-critical job of definition—and do so for the sake of the undisturbed security of their operation. In this regard the neopositivists, who identify philosophy with scientific method, agree with Scholasticism. The essay, in contrast, takes the anti-systematic impulse into its own procedure, and introduces concepts directly, "immediately," as it receives them. They gain their precision only through their relation to one another. In this, however, the essay gets some support from the concepts themselves. For it is a mere superstition of a science exclusively concerned with the appropriation of raw materials to believe that concepts are in themselves undetermined, that they are first determined by their definition. Science requires the image of the concept as a *tabula rasa*, in order to secure its claim to domination; the claim to be the sole power at the head of the table. Actually, all concepts are already implicitly concretized through the language in which they stand. The essay begins with such meanings and, itself being essentially language, it forces these meanings on farther; it wants to help language, in its relation to concepts, to grasp these concepts reflectively in the way that they are already unconsciously named in language. That effort is already envisaged by the procedure of meaning-analysis in phenomenology; only there the relation of concepts to language is fetishized. The essay remains as skeptical of this as it is of definition. Without apology the essay draws on itself the reproach that it does not know beyond a doubt just what is to be understood as the real content of concepts. For the essay perceives that the longing for strict definitions has long offered, through fixating manipulations of the meanings of concepts, to eliminate the irritating and dangerous elements of things that live within concepts. Yet the essay can neither do without general concepts—even language that does not fetishize the concept cannot do without concepts—nor does it treat them arbitrarily. It therefore takes the matter of presentation more seriously than do those procedures that separate out method from material and are indifferent to the way they represent their objectified contents. The *how* of expression should rescue, in precision, what the refusal to outline sacrifices, without, however, betraying the intended matter to the arbitrariness of previously decreed significations. In this Benjamin was an unequaled master. Such precision, however, cannot remain atomistic. Not less, but more than the process of defining, the essay urges the reciprocal interaction of its concepts in the process of intellectual experience. In the essay, concepts do not build a continuum of operations, thought does not advance in a single direction, rather the aspects of the argument interweave as in a carpet. The fruitfulness of the thoughts depends on the density of this texture. Actually, the thinker does not think, but rather transforms himself into an arena of intellectual experience, without simplifying it. While even traditional thought draws its impulses from such experience, such thought by its form eliminates the remembrance of these impulses. The essay, on the other hand, takes them as its model, without simply imitating them as reflected form; it mediates them through its own conceptual organization; it proceeds, so to speak, methodically unmethodically.

The way in which the essay appropriates concepts is most easily comparable to the behavior of a man who is obliged, in a foreign country, to speak that country's language instead of patching it together from its elements, as he did in school. He will read without a dictionary. If he has looked at the same word thirty times, in constantly changing contexts, he has a clearer grasp of it than he would if he looked up all the word's meanings; meanings that are generally too narrow, considering they change depending on the context, and too vague in view of the nuances that the context establishes in every individual case. Just as such learning remains exposed to error, so does the essay as form; it must pay for its affinity with open intellectual experience by the lack of security, a lack which the norm of established thought fears like death. It is not so much that the essay ignores indisputable certainty, as that it abrogates the ideal. The essay becomes true in its progress, which drives it beyond itself, and not in a hoarding obsession with fundamentals. Its concepts receive their light from a *terminus ad quem* hidden to the essay itself, and not from an obvious *terminus a quo*. In this the very method of the essay expresses the utopian intention. All of its concepts are presentable in such a way that they support one another, that each one articulates itself according to the configuration that it forms with the others. In the essay discreetly separated elements enter into a readable context; it erects no scaffolding, no edifice. Through their own movement the elements crystallize into a configuration. It is a force field, just as under the essay's glance every intellectual artifact must transform itself into a force field.

First published in *Noten zur Literatur*, 1958, translated by Bob Hullot-Kentor and Frederic Will

Aldous Huxley (1894–1963) was born into a family of prominent British intellectuals. His grandfather Thomas was a colleague of Darwin's and his mother was the niece of Matthew Arnold. His own circle of friends included D. H. Lawrence, George Orwell, the Bloomsbury writers, and, after moving to Southern California, Ray Bradbury and Anita Loos. Best known for his dystopian novel *Brave New World* (1932) and his memoir about using hallucinogenic drugs *The Doors of Perception* (1954), Huxley also wrote plays, poetry, screenplays, travel books, and many collections of essays. The taxonomy that follows comes from the preface to his 1960 *Collected Essays*. In it, Huxley suggests "a three-poled frame of reference" for thinking about the essay: the "personal," "objective," and "universal."

From the Preface to *Collected Essays*

What is true of the novel is only a little less true of the essay. For, like the novel, the essay is a literary device for saying almost everything about almost anything. By tradition, almost by definition, the essay is a short piece, and it is therefore impossible to give all things full play within the limits of a single essay. But a collection of essays can cover almost as much ground, and cover it almost as thoroughly as can a long novel. Montaigne's Third Book is the equivalent, very nearly, of a good slice of the *Comédie Humaine*.

Essays belong to a literary species whose extreme variability can be studied most effectively within a three-poled frame of reference. There is the pole of the personal and the autobiographical; there is the pole of the objective, the factual, the concrete-particular; and there is the pole of the abstract-universal. Most essayists are at home and at their best in the neighborhood of only one of the essay's three poles, or at the most only in the neighborhood of two of them. There are the predominantly personal essayists, who write fragments of reflective autobiography and who look at the world through the keyhole of anecdote and description. There are the predominantly objective essayists who do not speak directly of themselves, but turn their attention outward to some literary or scientific or political theme. Their art consists in setting forth, passing judgment upon, and drawing general conclusions from, the relevant data. In a third group we find those essayists who do their work in the world of high abstractions, who never condescend to be personal and who hardly deign to take notice of the particular facts, from which their generalizations were originally drawn. Each kind of essay has its special merits and defects. The personal essayists may be as good as Charles Lamb at his best, or as bad as Mr. X at his cutest and most self-consciously whimsical. The objective essay may be as lively, as brassily contentious as a piece by Macaulay; but it may also, with fatal ease, degenerate into something merely informative or, if it be critical, into something merely learned and academic. And how splendid, how truly oracular are the utterances of the great generalizers! "He that hath wife and children hath given hostages to fortune; for they are impediments to great enterprises, either of virtue or mischief." And from Bacon we pass to Emerson. "All men plume themselves on the improvement of society, and no man improves. Society never advances. It recedes as fast on one side as it gains on the other. For everything that is given, something is taken." Even a Baltasar Gracián, that briefest of essayists who writes as though he were cabling his wisdom, at two dollars a word, to the Antipodes, sometimes achieves a certain magnificence. "Things have their period; even excellences are subject to fashion. The sage has one advantage: he is immortal. If *this* is not his century, many others will be." But the medal of solemn and lapidary generalization has its reverse. The constantly abstract, constantly impersonal essayist is apt to give us not oracles but algebra. As an example of such algebraic writing, let me quote a short passage from the English translation of Paul Valéry's *Dialogues*. It is worth remarking that French literature has a tradition of high and sustained abstraction; English literature has not. Works that in French are not at all out of the common seem, when translated, strange almost to the point of absurdity. But even when made acceptable by tradition and a great talent, the algebraic style strikes us as being very remote from the living reality of our immediate experience. Here, in the words of an imaginary Socrates, is Valéry's description of the kind of language in which (as I think, unfortunately) he liked to write. "What is more mysterious than clarity? what more capricious than the way in which light and shade are distributed over the hours and over men? Certain peoples lose themselves in their thoughts, but for the Greeks all things are forms. We retain only their relations and, enclosed, as it were, in the limpid day, Orpheus-like we build, by means of the word, temples of wisdom and science that may suffice for all reasonable creatures. This great art requires of us an admirably exact language. The very word that signifies language is also the name, with us, for reason and calculation; the same word says these three things." In the stratosphere of abstract notions this elegant algebra is all very well; but a completely bodiless language can never do justice to the data of immediate experience, nor can it contribute anything to our understanding of the "capricious lights and shades" in the midst of which, whether we like it or not, we must perforce live out our lives.

The most richly satisfying essays are those which make the best not of one, not of two, but of all the three worlds in which it is possible for the essay to exist. Freely, effortlessly, thought and feeling move in these consummate works of art, hither and thither between the essay's three poles—from the personal to the universal, from the abstract back to the concrete, from the objective datum to the inner experience.

The perfection of any artistic form is rarely achieved by its first inventor. To this rule Montaigne is the great and marvelous exception. By the time he had written his way into the Third Book, he had reached the limits of his newly discovered art. "What are these essays," he had asked at the beginning of his career, "but grotesque bodies pieced together of different members, without any definite shape, without any order, coherence, or proportion, except they be accidental." But a few years later the patchwork grotesques had turned into living organisms, into multiform hybrids like those beautiful monsters of the old mythologies, the mermaids, the man-headed bulls with wings, the centaurs, the Anubises, the seraphim—impossibilities compounded of incompatibles, but compounded from within, by a process akin to growth, so that the human trunk seems to spring quite naturally from between the horse's shoulders, the fish modulates into the full-breasted Siren as easily and inevitably as a musical theme modulates from one key to another. Free association artistically controlled—this is the paradoxical secret of Montaigne's best essays. One damned thing after another—but in a sequence that in some almost miraculous way develops a central theme and relates it to the rest of human experience. And how beautifully Montaigne combines the generalization with the anecdote, the homily with the autobiographical reminiscence! How skilfully he makes use of the concrete particular, the *chose vue*, to express some universal truth, and to express it more powerfully and penetratingly than it can be expressed by even the most oracular of the dealers in generalities!

Collected Essays, 1960

MICHAEL HAMBURGER (1924–2007) was born in Berlin. His father was a Jewish pediatrician, his mother a Polish Quaker. When Hitler became chancellor in 1933, the family moved to England, where Hamburger earned a degree at Christ Church, Oxford. After marrying the poet, actress, and broadcaster Anne Beresford in 1951 and beginning a family, he taught at a number of universities in England and the United States. Hamburger thought of himself first as a poet and published more than twenty volumes of verse, but he earned a steady living and many awards as a translator, introducing English readers to Friedrich Holderlin and Paul Celan, and providing definitive translations of many others, including his friend W. G. Sebald. He also wrote criticism, autobiography, and journalism. In "An Essay on the Essay," Hamburger uses the metaphor of the essay as a walk to digress upon many of the form's traits, worrying all the while that our automobile- and results-centered modern culture may not be hospitable to a genre more concerned with the journey than with the destination.

"An Essay on the Essay"

Even that isn't quite right: an essay really ought not to be on anything, to deal with anything, to define anything. An essay is a walk, an excursion, not a business trip. So if the title says "on" that can only mean that this essay passes over a certain field—but with no intention of surveying it. This field will not be ploughed or cultivated. It will remain a meadow, wild. One walker is interested in wild flowers, another in the view, a third collects insects. Hunting butterflies is permitted. Everything is permitted —everything except the intentions of surveyors, farmers, speculators. And each walker is allowed to report whatever he happens to have observed about the field—even if that was no more than the birds that flew over it, the clouds that have still less to do with it, or only the transmutations of birds or clouds in his own head. But the person who drove there, sat there inside his car and then says he was there is no essayist. That's why the essay is an outmoded genre. ("Form" is what I almost wrote, but the essay is not a form, has no form; it is a game that creates its own rules.)

The essay is just as outmoded as the art of letter-writing, the art of conversation, the art of walking for pleasure. Ever since Montaigne the essay has been highly individualistic, but at the same time it presupposes a society that not only tolerates individualism but enjoys it—a society leisured and cultivated enough to do without information. The whole spirit of essay-writing is contained in the first sentence of the first great collection of English essays—Francis Bacon's of 1597: "What is *Truth*; said jesting *Pilate*; And would not stay for an Answer." A jesting Pilate who asks questions but doesn't wait for answers is the archetypal personification of the essay, of essay-writing and essayists. The English essay flourished for three centuries, even when the earnestness of the Victorian age had begun to question its peculiar relation to truth. Only the totalitarian systems of this century turned walking without a purpose into a crime. Since the time of G. K. Chesterton and Virginia Woolf the essay has been a dead genre. Needless to say, people continued—and still continue—to write prose pieces which they call essays; but already George Orwell was too "committed," too puritanical, too much aware of a crisis to take walks without a bad conscience.

The essay is not a form, but a style above all. Its individualism distinguishes it from pure, absolute or autonomous art. The point of an essay, like its justification and its style, always lies in the author's personality and always leads back to it. The essayist is as little concerned with pure, impersonal art as with his subject. Since the vast majority of so-called critical essays attaches primary importance to subjects, that is, to answers and judgments, the perpetuation of that genre does not prove that the essay has survived. Most critical essays are short treatises. With a genuine essay it makes no difference whether its title refers to a literary theme, whether to the origin of tragedy or the origin of roast pig.

But since the essay is not a form the spirit of essay-writing can assert itself outside the genre. Where confidence in his readership was lacking, for instance, the essayist often changed into an aphorist. Lichtenberg, Friedrich Schlegel and Friedrich Nietzsche were laconic, partly repressed essayists. Essay-writing insinuated itself even into poetry: a pseudo-epic like Byron's *Don Juan* or Heine's *Atta Troll*, whose wit always points back to the personalities of their authors, whose plots are interrupted again and again by their narrators' peripatetic arbitrariness. Story-telling and essay-writing were inseparable in the prose pieces of Robert Walser, and it was no accident that one of them, an outstanding one, was called "The Walk." It was the spirit of essay-writing that drove Walser the storyteller into self-destructive parody: "In Thuringia, at Eisenach if you like, there lived a so-called beetleologist, who once again had a niece. When shall I have done with nieces and the like? Perhaps never. In that case, woe is me! Grievously the girl in the house next door suffered under learned surveillance."

Some of the digressions in Musil's *The Man without Qualities*, too, are genuinely essayistic, because Musil was a seeker, a man without designs who asked questions that he couldn't answer. So are the *Ficciones* of Jorge Luis Borges. So are many of the shorter writings of Ernst Bloch, Walter Benjamin and Th. W. Adorno—however weighty their themes.

The spirit of essay-writing walks on irresistibly, even over the corpse of the essay, and is glimpsed now here, now there, in novels, stories, poems or articles, from time to time in the very parkland of philosophy, formidably walled and strictly guarded though it may seem, the parkland from which it escaped centuries ago to wander about in the wild meadow. But it is never glimpsed where that wild meadow has been banned from human consciousness even as a memory or possibility, where walls have become absolute and walking itself has become a round of compulsion and routine. It has come to terms with the overcrowded streets of large cities, but hardly with factories, barracks, offices, not at all with prison yards and extermination camps. Anyone who can never get these out of his mind cannot tolerate the aimlessness and evasiveness of essay-writing, but calls it shameless, egotistic and insolent. But somewhere or other the spirit of essay-writing is walking on; and no one knows where it will turn up. Perhaps in the essay again, one day?

First published in *Akzente* 12 (1965)

FERNAND OUELLETTE (1930–) is one of Canada's most renowned writers and intellectuals. Though known for his passionate, mystical poetry, Ouellette has also been a fierce advocate for Quebec independence. He cofounded the magazine *Liberté* in 1959 (which his friend André Belleau also helped edit), produced radio essays for Radio-Canada, and has taught at several universities. He has won the Governor General's Award three times, accepting it twice: in 1985, for his novel *Lucie ou un midi en novembre*, and in 1987, for the collection of poetry *Les Heures*. In 1970, after winning the award for *Les actes retrouvés*, a collection of essays, he refused it in protest against the government's actions during the October Crisis, when the War Measures Act was used to arrest 497 people and to hold them without charges or bail. Ouellette's poetic inclinations (and learning) are on display in "Ramblings on the Essay," where he argues for a lyrical essay, one that "can only be flashes of lightning, fragments from a strange time, desperate leaps out of its own form."

"Ramblings on the Essay"

Longing is the umbilical cord of the highest life. — Kierkegaard

All of this is, yet again, only a story of ecstasy and disappointment.
— Mallarmé

Criticism seemed to us to be a path of sorts, not a view or a position.
—Jean-Pierre Richard

What seems to most to be a work devoted to "weighing" the souls of memory is for me essentially a "trial," a "struggle," a "glance," the unloading of what has been shaped or lived. A specific form of being, of action, and of purpose is answered by the epiphany of another form. The essay shakes the foundation of memory by proposing a plan of the whole based on one or several parts of a whole. So it seems to me like one of the privileged forms of desire, of aspiration, of the "unhoped for." It is moved more by "the imagination of desire," by the possible, than by the volition to create a synthesis, by seizing what *is*. In this respect, Northrop Frye was correct to write that " . . . in essays and in lyrics the primary interest is in *dianoïa* or poetic thought . . . that the reader gets from the writer" [from *Anatomy of Criticism*, 52]. And on the other hand, young Lukács is not far off the mark in *Soul and Form*, when he offers a definition of the essay as an autonomous "form" situated between literature and philosophy, between "imaginative creation" and "conceptual creation."

I should make clear that when I think of the form or genre of the *essay*, I am not referring to the elaborate work of a Camus but rather to *assertion* [in *affirmation*], to a fabric of leaps and "sallies." To me, the essay seems a melting pot of "verbal combustion," a melting pot of prose that will not allow itself to be depleted, prose that refuses to "perish." The essayist holds on to traces of brilliance the way a feline tracks a moving shape. He desires so ardently that he runs the risk of "blinding his soul to everything else" (Democritus). I'm not interested in finding a global answer, when I let myself be so fascinated by the swelling of the irreducible, by projecting on a screen the leaps of my imagination, by my thoughtful reflections. Forms, characters, aspects, and essences are, certainly, chosen by those who are completely devoted, but they are also filtered and distilled to the oneness of the person who posits ideas, who only knows how to do so by projecting a beam of light straight into the eyes of those who approach him. Achim von Arnim was right to observe that "judgments are quite insignificant things; each should do what he must for his own salvation." This does not seem very far from Heraclitus's "I searched for myself." Therefore, for me the essay is like a trial, a precipitation of the human, a fragment of confession: a concentrated fragment of imagination, of awareness, and of writing. (How this would have appalled the great classical minds of the seventeenth century, especially Pascal, who rejected the imagination as "a teacher of error and falsity!") This is why I spoke of a melting pot above, because it truly is really about transmutation, since all that remains of the encounter between the "self" and the other when the writing is done is a complete transformation of the self. The other is in a way invaded then transmuted within the self. The essayist rivets himself to the essence of a Hölderlin, for example, but what remains of the man-poet afterwards? What remains of the crystallized dazzle and sound of his poems if they can only be returned to us through a self, a self who, we can only hope, does not turn away from the "divine"? How can the essayist claim to be objective? Isn't he wearing a mask? How radical has he become? To what extent does he consume the object of his essay? Those who do not instigate, do not create, but conceive of the essay as an ideological category are undoubtedly better off to think with a critical approach. For if, as is claimed, it is within criticism that the crisis in writing is ending, one could on the contrary speak of an increasing tension within the essay. The essayist who does not claim to be a critic—I set aside critical essays here—is a strange being who, without becoming overwhelmed, only feeds off the insights of his fellow-man. He is not likely to dominate from the summit of his structural reading or to produce, like a scholar, a socio-historical synthesis of what he perceives around him. The essayist communes with what could undo him. He desires "to think with his entire body." He throws himself into the volcano, hoping that the volcano will liquefy in his veins.

It's clear that he hardly cares about pondering the multiple forms of memory. And it is even clearer that he acts as a counter-memory, that the essay does not let itself be stripped down to an abstract idea. Contemplating the substance of memory, or its acts, seems more comforting to me. It is not a question, moreover, of denying the usefulness of such work. But I feel that the essayist is someone who mourns the loss of the great flashes of insight into what was clearly a path toward accomplishment or pathetic disaster. He agrees to the work of mourning. He insists on setting a few lights out in the dark, to follow their path, where to try to fully embrace certain forms or events might well reduce everything to ashes. Notice how Simone Weil exposes the illusion of strength, how she reveals the quality of her soul by uncovering the moments in which soul itself is revealed in *The Iliad* . . . Notice how Bonnefoy immerses himself in the stones of Ravenna . . . I could easily provide countless examples . . . Of course, it isn't a matter of claiming some praxis, like Novalis, some "magical idealism" where a thought provides the means of changing the world. This does not mean that I completely deny the efficacy of the essay—on the contrary. However, the essayist is not a wizard. He doesn't have "magical powers." Moreover, unlike the scientist, he doesn't aspire to *power*. His strength comes to him from his concentration, from his meditation, even from the effectiveness of his speech. His effect is not significantly different from the poet's. A reversal of sorts takes place in the verbal realm when moving from the poem to the essay: a sliding from one pole to the other in an attempt to find a delicate balance between the concept and the "sound-sense." Essays like poems are *creations* and, consequently, *acts*. From this standpoint, Baudelaire was right to assert that only the poet could be a true critic. For isn't it necessary "to face poetry in order to write good prose"? Or, in another sense, isn't it a matter of "the quest for a style," as Mallarmé said? Is it possible that they were speaking of the person whom I conceive of as an essayist? That person seems to me like a creature who spins and leaps. And without renouncing the essayist, wouldn't he be somewhat antithetical to Montaigne, who dedicated himself to making detailed portraits of his self, by means of concentrating on his memories? Wasn't it as an essayist that Pascal pitted himself against Montaigne? Even considering Heraclitus, Lao Tzu, Saint Augustine and many others, it still seems to me that a certain kind of thought and writing were toppled by the great Pascal. But we had to wait for Hölderlin, Novalis, Baudelaire, Rimbaud, Mallarmé, and Nietzsche to be truly convinced of this. After all, isn't *A Season in Hell* a prime example of a radiant essay?

Of course, I'm not categorizing the numerous forms of the essay according to the standards that academics give them. I'm not proposing any models to anyone. My essayist is someone who prefers to sally forth, to indulge in "verbal combustion," and essentially chooses to accept *wandering* absolutely—a being who, as Chestov has hoped, proceeds at things "haphazardly, eyes closed," a rambling and playful spirit. Didn't Mallarmé present himself as a "man accustomed to dreaming" in order to *gaze at* Villiers de l'Isle-Adam? Can it be said of the essayist, as Aristotle said of "the poet" Homer, that he *lies a lot*? One of the critic's roles is, doubtlessly, to point out the inanity of the leaps that the reckless essayist takes in the "course" of his writings and the impotence of his "gaze" of things—or even to extract from it the kinds of shifting that it would be useful to submit to memory. Couldn't a dialectical relationship be established between the essayist and the critic, like the interplay of shapes in the sand and the movement of the tide?

Thus, the essay can only be a *work* or, according to Valéry's expression, the state that results from a series of internal transformations. We are not far removed from the situation of poetry. For a poet, an essay must have the characteristics of poetry, of *poesis*. Isn't this the sense in which it was said that as a critic Baudelaire was never wrong?

To summarize—in taking a bit of a detour toward a lovely expression drawn from Valery's *Dance and the Soul*—I could almost say that the essay, by definition, can only be flashes of lightning, fragments from a strange time, desperate leaps out of its own form. Undoubtedly, this may all seem "ridiculous," especially compared to the attempts at synthesis of critics, philosophers, and sociologists. But to follow the essayist is to venture onto quicksand or to leap from the top of a tower. And no one is obliged to ramble. No one is obliged to welcome the brilliance and follow it along the wandering path on a quest for oneness, a quest for Being.

Here is the poet who has not yet sung.
But soon he will sing,
And by the end of his song
He will know the science of the stars.
—Taliesin

First published in *Etudes Litteraires* 5 (1972), translated here by Carl Klaus, Ned Stuckey-French, and Lindsey Scott

GUILLERMO DÍAZ-PLAJA (1909–84) was a member of a noted Spanish literary family. One brother wrote children's books, another was a journalist. A professor at important Spanish universities, including Instituto del Teatro de Barcelona and Universidad de Barcelona, Díaz-Plaja was extremely prolific, publishing over two hundred books, including more than two dozen collections of essays. He also edited anthologies and textbooks, and wrote poetry, cultural history, literary criticism, travel narratives, autobiography, and journalism. In the following piece, this noted professor, having recently judged a student essay contest, concludes that the essay is an "adult genre," one that requires "discreetly" hidden erudition and a willingness to remain in "permanent doubt"—traits that come only with age, if at all.

"The Limits of the Essay"

I have been asked once again to take on the bittersweet role of judging the Young Essayist Competition of the Spanish Editorial Press, and the experience has been rich in suggestions, which, as I will explain, take the form of questions.

I have asked myself, in fact, whether a competition for a young essayist (by which we mean a writer under forty) is not a contradiction in terms. I believe it is. If, in contrast, we connect poetry with youth, why not then connect similarly the essay? Simply put, it is because the essay is an unequivocal symptom of maturity.

An essayist is produced when the period of acquiring information is allowed to develop into a personal understanding. Like wine left in a cask to acquire its appropriate character, the essay is the product of a long distillation of mental juices. It is the result of data received then analyzed at length from the sovereign vantage of a thinker.

The essay, then, is a difficult genre because it is an adult genre. Because it is an essence, the fruit of a passion meditated upon to the point of transcending premature expression since, as Dante put it in a verse that pleased Montaigne—"doubting pleases me as much as knowing" (*Che non men que saper dubbiar l'agrata*)—it does not matter to the essayist that he remains in doubt. From doubt comes the enormous freedom that the essay possesses as a genre.

These thoughts come together because, given the presentations at the competition mentioned, one notices the gross error of mistaking the essay for an investigation. A doctoral thesis is not an essay; a scientific treatise is not an essay. Each of those literary genres embodies erudite learning and systematic exposition. The essay possesses neither of those characteristics. Erudition, which it hides discreetly, it leaves as a supporting substructure. "The essay is learning without explicit proof," said Ortega. Consequently, the essayist remains free of the need of footnotes at the bottom of every page, and its suggestions gain support through an understanding with the reader to accept the essayist himself as his own authority, freely expressed.

With regard to methodology, the essayist remains free of the systematic demonstration of a treatise—or of pure investigation in the form of a thesis. The essayist, really, is an arbitrary wanderer over a theme that remains hidden. One recognizes in him the ability of ordering his ideas capriciously, hovering over a line of thought like bees around their hive. He is permitted even to surprise us, to deceive us, to snatch away an anticipated vantage and reveal a profile unexpressed and more suggestive concerning the theme in question.

But, beware. The essay is no superficial game. It demands depth, penetration, and novelty of perspective. The mere gloss (in the epigrammatic sense of Orsiano) does not reach that level, nor does the journalistic article, which can place itself in contrast at the opposite generic extreme.

And so we can say that the essay negotiates exactly the middle of the road that goes from airy glossing to the solid doctoral thesis.

First published in *La Estafeta Literaria* 582 (February 15, 1976), translated here by David Hamilton

EDWARD HOAGLAND (1932–) began his writing career as a novelist in the mid-1950s and 1960s, but most of his work since then has been devoted to nonfiction, particularly nature writing and travel writing, based on numerous expeditions in Alaska, British Columbia, and Africa, as well as wide-ranging essays in a Montaignean manner, often about his life in New York City or his home in Vermont, which led John Updike to speak of him as "the best essayist of my generation." Hoagland's allegiance to Montaigne is reflected in the title of the following piece on the essay, "What I Think, What I Am," as well as in its ultimate concern with the essay as the embodiment of authorial consciousness: "the very freedom the mind possesses is bestowed on this branch of literature, and the fascination of the mind is the fascination of the essay."

"What I Think, What I Am"

Our loneliness makes us avid column readers these days. The personalities in the San Francisco *Chronicle*, Chicago *Daily News*, New York *Post* constitute our neighbors now, some of them local characters but also the opinionated national stars. And movie reviewers thrive on our yearning for somebody emotional who is willing to pay attention to us and return week after week, year after year, through all the to-and-fro of other friends, to flatter us by pouring out his/her heart. They are essayists of a type, as Elizabeth Hardwick is, James Baldwin was.

We sometimes hear that essays are an old-fashioned form, that so-and-so is the "last essayist," but the facts of the marketplace argue quite otherwise. Essays of nearly any kind are so much easier than short stories for a writer to sell, so many more see print, it's strange that though two fine anthologies remain that publish the year's best stories, no comparable collection exists for essays. Such changes in the reading public's taste aren't always to the good, needless to say. The art of telling stories predated even cave painting, surely; and if we ever find ourselves living in caves again, it (with painting and drumming) will be the only art left, after movies, novels, photography, essays, biography, and all the rest have gone down the drain—the art to build from.

One has the sense with the short story as a form that while everything may have been done, nothing has been overdone; it has a permanence. Essays, if a comparison is to be made, although they go back four hundred years to Montaigne, seem a mercurial, newfangled, sometimes hokey affair that has lent itself to many of the excesses of the age, from spurious autobiography to spurious hallucination, as well as to the shabby careerism of traditional journalism. It's a greased pig. Essays are associated with the way young writers fashion a name—on plain, crowded newsprint in hybrid vehicles like the *Village Voice*, *Rolling Stone*, the *New York Review of Books*, instead of the thick paper stock and thin readership of *Partisan Review*.

Essays, however, hang somewhere on a line between two sturdy poles: this is what I think, and this is what I am. Autobiographies which aren't novels are generally extended essays, indeed. A personal essay is like the human voice talking, its order the mind's natural flow, instead of a systematized outline of ideas. Though more wayward or informal than an article or treatise, somewhere it contains a point which is its real center, even if the point couldn't be uttered in fewer words than the essayist has used. Essays don't usually boil down to a summary, as articles do, and the style of the writer has a "nap" to it, a combination of personality and originality and energetic loose ends that stand up like the nap on a piece of wool and can't be brushed flat. Essays belong to the animal kingdom, with a surface that generates sparks, like a coat of fur, compared with the flat, conventional cotton of the magazine article writer, who works in the vegetable kingdom, instead. But essays, on the other hand, may have fewer "levels" than fiction, because we are not supposed to argue much about their meaning. In the old distinction between teaching and storytelling, the essayist, however cleverly he camouflages his intentions, is a bit of a teacher or reformer, and an essay is intended to convey the same point to each of us.

This emphasis upon mind speaking to mind is what makes essays less universal in their appeal than stories. They are addressed to an educated, perhaps a middle-class, reader, with certain presuppositions, a frame of reference, even a commitment to civility that is shared—not the grand and golden empathy inherent in every man or woman that a storyteller has a chance to tap.

Nevertheless, the artful "I" of an essay can be as chameleon as any narrator in fiction; and essays do tell a story quite as often as a short story stakes a claim to a particular viewpoint. Mark Twain's piece called "Corn-pone Opinions," for example, which is about public opinion, begins with a vignette as vivid as any in *Huckleberry Finn*. Twain says that when he was a boy of fifteen, he used to hang out a back window and listen to the sermons preached by a neighbor's slave standing on top of a woodpile: "He imitated the pulpit style of the several clergymen of the village, and did it well and with fine passion and energy. To me he was a wonder. I believed he was the greatest orator in the United States and would some day be heard from. But it did not happen; in the distribution of rewards he was overlooked. . . . He interrupted his preaching now and then to saw a stick of wood, but the sawing was a pretense—he did it with his mouth, exactly imitating the sound the bucksaw makes in shrieking its way through the wood. But it served its purpose, it kept his master from coming out to see how the work was getting along."

A novel would go on and tell us what happened next in the life of the slave—and we miss that. But the extraordinary flexibility of essays is what has enabled them to ride out rough weather and hybridize into forms that suit the times. And just as one of the first things a fiction writer learns is that he needn't actually be writing fiction to write a short story—that he can tell his own history or anybody else's as exactly as he remembers it and it will be "fiction" if it remains primarily a story—an essayist soon discovers that he doesn't have to tell the whole truth and nothing but the truth; he can shape or shave his memories, as long as the purpose is served of elucidating a truthful point. A personal essay frequently is not autobiographical at all, but what it does keep in common with autobiography is that, through its tone and tumbling progression, it conveys the quality of the author's mind. Nothing gets in the way. Because essays are directly concerned with the mind and the mind's idiosyncrasy, the very freedom the mind possesses is bestowed on this branch of literature that does honor to it, and the fascination of the mind is the fascination of the essay.

First published in the *New York Times Book Review* (June 27, 1976)

E[LWYN] B[ROOKS] WHITE (1899–1985) is best known for his children's books *Stuart Little*, *Charlotte's Web*, and *The Trumpet of the Swan*, in addition to *The Elements of Style* (with William Strunk Jr.), which have sold tens of millions of copies, but his essays for the *New Yorker* and *Harper's* were some of the best of the twentieth century. Even as an essayist, he is often characterized as a humorist, but again he was more than this. Though he never abandoned his sense of humor and genial tone, he wrote important essays about the natural world and the need for a world government, and took strong stands against fascism, nuclear testing, and the anticommunist witch-hunts of the 1950s. In the piece that follows, White acknowledges the essayist's "self-imposed role of second-class citizen," but also revels in the essayist's freedom to adopt a variety of personas, including "philosopher, scold, jester, raconteur, confidant, pundit, devil's advocate, [and] enthusiast."

From the Foreword to *Essays of E. B. White*

The essayist is a self-liberated man, sustained by the childish belief that everything he thinks about, everything that happens to him, is of general interest. He is a fellow who thoroughly enjoys his work, just as people who take bird walks enjoy theirs. Each new excursion of the essayist, each new "attempt," differs from the last and takes him into new country. This delights him. Only a person who is congenitally self-centered has the effrontery and the stamina to write essays.

There are as many kinds of essays as there are human attitudes or poses, as many essay flavors as there are Howard Johnson ice creams. The essayist arises in the morning and, if he has work to do, selects his garb from an unusually extensive wardrobe: he can pull on any sort of shirt, be any sort of person, according to his mood or his subject matter—philosopher, scold, jester, raconteur, confidant, pundit, devil's advocate, enthusiast. I like the essay, have always liked it, and even as a child was at work, attempting to inflict my young thoughts and experiences on others by putting them on paper. I early broke into print in the pages of *St. Nicholas*. I tend still to fall back on the essay form (or lack of form) when an idea strikes me, but I am not fooled about the place of the essay in twentieth-century American letters—it stands a short distance down the line. The essayist, unlike the novelist, the poet, and the playwright, must be content in his self-imposed role of second-class citizen. A writer who has his sights trained on the Nobel Prize or other earthly triumphs had best write a novel, a poem, or a play, and leave the essayist to ramble about, content with living a free life and enjoying the satisfactions of a somewhat undisciplined existence. (Dr. Johnson called the essay "an irregular, undigested piece"; this happy practitioner has no wish to quarrel with the good doctor's characterization.)

There is one thing the essayist cannot do, though—he cannot indulge himself in deceit or in concealment, for he will be found out in no time. Desmond MacCarthy, in his introductory remarks to the 1928 E. P. Dutton & Company edition of Montaigne, observes that Montaigne "had the gift of natural candour. . . . " It is the basic ingredient. And even the essayist's escape from discipline is only a partial escape: the essay, although a relaxed form, imposes its own disciplines, raises its own problems, and these disciplines and problems soon become apparent and (we all hope) act as a deterrent to anyone wielding a pen merely because he entertains random thoughts or is in a happy or wandering mood.

I think some people find the essay the last resort of the egoist, a much too self-conscious and self-serving form for their taste; they feel that it is presumptuous of a writer to assume that his little excursions or his small observations will interest the reader. There is some justice in their complaint. I have always been aware that I am by nature self-absorbed and egoistical; to write of myself to the extent I have done indicates a too great attention to my own life, not enough to the lives of others. I have worn many shirts, and not all of them have been a good fit. But when I am discouraged or downcast I need only fling open the door of my closet, and there, hidden behind everything else, hangs the mantle of Michel de Montaigne, smelling slightly of camphor.

Essays of E. B. White, 1977

WILLIAM H. GASS (1924–) is an American fiction writer and professor of philosophy best known for his literary essays. His erudite, richly rhetorical, and sometimes personal essays have been occasioned by invitations to symposia or to deliver commencement addresses, or have begun as book reviews or introductions to new editions, but they invariably turn round to discussions of Gass's theory of art and his philosophy of language. The excerpt that follows is taken from a longer meditation on Emerson and his career as an essayist. In it, Gass discusses Emerson in detail, but also advances his own formalist concerns, displays his love of figurative language, and fiercely defends the essay (and imaginative literature more broadly) against the slick, the commercial, and the merely scholarly.

From "Emerson and the Essay"

The essayist is an amateur, a Virginia Woolf who has merely done a little reading up; he is not out for profit (even when paid), or promotion (even if it occurs); but is interested solely in the essay's special *art*. Meditation is the essence of it; it measures meanings; makes maps; exfoliates. The essay is unhurried (although Bacon's aren't); it browses among books; it enjoys an idea like a fine wine; it thumbs through things. It turns round and round upon its topic, exposing this aspect and then that; proposing possibilities, reciting opinions, disposing of prejudice and even of the simple truth itself—as too undeveloped, not yet of an interesting age.

The essay is obviously the opposite of that awful object, "the article," which, like items picked up in shops during one's lunch hour, represents itself as the latest cleverness, a novel consequence of thought, skill, labor, and free enterprise; but never as an activity—the process, the working, the wondering. As an article, it should be striking of course, original of course, important naturally, yet without possessing either grace or charm or elegance, since these qualities will interfere with the impression of seriousness which it wishes to maintain; rather its polish is like that of the scrubbed step; but it must appear complete and straightforward and footnoted and useful and certain and is very likely a veritable Michelin of misdirection; for the article pretends that everything is clear, that its argument is unassailable, that there are no soggy patches, no illicit inferences, no illegitimate connections; it furnishes seals of approval and underwriters' guarantees; its manners are starched, stuffy, it would wear a dress suit to a barbecue, silk pajamas to the shower; it knows, with respect to every subject and point of view it is ever likely to entertain, what words to use, what form to follow, what authorities to respect; it is the careful product of a professional, and therefore it is written as only writing can be written, even if, at various times, versions have been given a dry dull voice at a conference, because, spoken aloud, it still sounds like writing written down, writing born for its immediate burial in a Journal. It is a relatively recent invention, this result of scholarly diligence, and its appearance is proof of the presence, nearby, of the Professor, the way one might, perceiving a certain sort of speckled egg, infer that its mother was a certain sort of speckled bird. It is, after all, like the essay, modest, avoiding the vices and commitments of the lengthy volume. Articles are to be worn; they make up one's dossier the way uniforms make up a wardrobe, and it is not known—nor is it clear about uniforms either—whether the article has ever contained anything of lasting value.

Like the article, the essay is born of books, as Benjamin's essay, "Unpacking My Library," points out about itself; and for every essay inspired by an event, emotion, bit of landscape, work of plastic art, there are a hundred (such as Montaigne's famous "On Some Lines of Virgil") which frankly admit it—to having an affair; because it is the words of others which most often bring the essay into being. "I myself am neither a king nor a shepherd," Hazlitt writes apropos a speech from Henry VI he's cited, "books have been my fleecy charge, and my thoughts have been my subjects." Hence the essayist is in a feminine mood at first, receptive to and fertilized by texts, hungry to quote, eager to reproduce; and often, before the essay itself is well underway in the reader's eye, its father will be briefly introduced, a little like the way a woman introduces her fiancé to her friends, confident and proud of the good impression he will make. Thus Lukács begins "Longing and Form" with a quote from *La vita nuova*, and Roland Barthes, to outdo all, opens *The Pleasures of the Text* with one in the Latin of Thomas Hobbes. It is the habit of Emerson to add these mottoes later, and to compose them himself, which is not surprising, for we do find Emerson moved by his own hand more than most.

Born of books, nourished by books, a book for its body, another for its head and hair, its syllable-filled spirit, the essay is more often than not a confluence of such little blocks and strips of text. Let me tell you, it says, what I have just read, looked up, or remembered of my reading. Horace, Virgil, Ovid, Cicero, Lucretius meet on a page of Montaigne. Emerson allows Othello and Emilia words, but in a moment asks of Jacobi, an obscure reformer and now no more than a note, a bigger speech. A strange thing occurs. Hazlitt does not quote Shakespeare but Henry VI, whose voice is then lined up to sing in concert with the rest: the living and the dead, the real and the fictitious, each has a part and a place. Virginia Woolf writes of Addison by writing of Macaulay writing of Addison, of whom Pope and Johnson and Thackeray have also written. On and On. In this way the essay confirms the continuity, the contemporaneity, the reality of writing. The words of Flaubert (in a letter), those of Madame Bovary (in her novel), the opinions of Gide (in his *Journal*), of Roger Fry, of Gertrude Stein, of Rilke, of Baudelaire (one can almost imagine the essay's subject and slant from this racy cast of characters), they form a new milieu—the context of citation. And what is citation but an attempt to use a phrase, a line, a paragraph, like a word, and lend it further uses, another identity, apart from the hometown it hails from?

It was inevitable that a compilation should be made of them. In my edition (the second) of the *Oxford Dictionary of Quotations*, there are 104 from Emerson, one of which is "I hate quotations," while another states that "Next to the originator of a good sentence is the first quoter of it." (Have I just now quoted Emerson, or have I quoted the *Oxford Dictionary of Quotations*?) Occasions call for quotations, qualify them, sanctify them somewhat as the Bible was—that book from which the habit stems and still draws sustenance, since the essay is, after all, a sort of secular sermon, inducing skepticism, and written by the snake.

And how they dispose themselves, these voices: inside the writer's sentences like an unbroken thread; in an isolated block upon the page, a lawn of white space around them like a house in a clearing; or in a note dropped out of the text like a piece of loose change from the author's pocket. Sometimes they stand alone like inscriptions on gates or conclude like epitaphs on tombs; they filter through a text like light through leaves or are enclosed like a hand in loving hands. Emerson's own essay "Quotation and Originality" permits me to make another point: that the essayist's subjects—in a sense always the same: other books, loneliness, love and friendship, human frailty—constantly provide a fresh challenge to thought, for if I were to write on quotation now, I should have to take into account a whole history since, not only Herman Meyer's *The Poetics of Quotation in the European Novel*, for example, but certainly Beckett's *How It Is*, which is mainly a buried quotation:

> how it was I quote before Pim with Pim after Pim how it is three parts I say it as I hear it

The essay convokes a community of writers, then. It uses any and each and all of them like instruments in an orchestra. It both composes and conducts. Texts are plundered precisely because they are sacred, but the method, we are essay-bound to observe, is quite different from that of the Scholastics, who quoted authorities in order to acquire their imprimaturs, or from that of the scholar, who quoted in order to provide himself with a set of subjects, problems, object lessons, and other people's errors, convenient examples, confirming facts, and laboratory data. However, in the essay, most often passages are repeated out of pleasure and for praise; because the great essayist is not merely a sour quince making a face at the ideas of others, but a big belly-bumper and exclaimer aloud; the sort who is always saying, "Listen to this! Look there! Feel this touchstone! Hear that!" "By necessity, by proclivity,—and by delight, we all quote," Emerson says. You can be assured you are reading an excellent essay when you find yourself relishing the quotations as much as the text that contains them, as one welcomes the chips of chocolate in those overcelebrated cookies. The apt quotation is one of the essayist's greatest gifts, and, like the good gift, congratulates the giver.

Yale Review 71.3 (Spring 1982)

JEAN STAROBINSKI (1920–) is a Swiss literary critic, historian of ideas, and scholar of French literature, who holds not only a PhD but also an MD. During his early career, he worked as an assistant in psychiatry and internal medicine at the University of Geneva, and subsequently taught both French literature and the history of medicine in American, French, and Swiss universities. He is known for his book-length studies of Montaigne and of Rousseau, as well as for his works on melancholia and his semantic history of key scientific terms. His wide-ranging interests have also led to studies of European clothing, art, and revolution in the eighteenth century and of the morality of evil. Starobinski's interest in the semantic history of words (and in Montaigne) is fully on display in the following reflections on the problem of defining the essay.

From "Can One Define the Essay?"

Receiving the European Essay Prize forced me to ask: can one define the *essay*, once accepting the assumption that the essay does not submit to any convention? What power does one attribute to this form of writing, what are, all things considered, the essay's conditions, responsibilities, and challenges?

What is important is the present effectiveness that one can ascribe to the essay, which is the future works that one will invent following from this form. But it is not pointless to take a look back in the direction of etymologies and origins. And primarily, where does the word itself come from? Its history consists of too many remarkable aspects to not be recalled. (I will only examine the word *essay*,[1] and I will neglect, not without regret, the Latin words that Montaigne's contemporaries used to translate the title of his book; *conatus*, *tentamina*, etc.)

Essay, known in French since the twelfth century, stems from the Latin base *exagium*, the scale; to try[2] derives from *exagiare*, which signifies to weigh. In proximity to this term we find *examen*: needle, long narrow strip on the beam of the scale, thus follows, weighed consideration, control. But another meaning of *examen* designates a swarm of bees, a flock of birds. The common etymology would be the verb *exigo*, to push out, to chase, then to demand. How enticing if the nuclear meaning of today's words had to result from their meanings in a distant past! The *essay* might as well be the *demanding weighing*, the *thoughtful examination*, but also the *verbal swarm*[3] from which one liberates development. By which singular intuition did the author of *The Essays* strike a balance on his work, by adding for a motto the famous *What do I know*? This emblem—doubtlessly destined, when the trays are at equal heights, to represent the suspense of the spirit—also represented the act of the essay itself, the examination of the position of the beam. It is in resorting to the same weight metaphor that Galileo, founder of experimental physics, calls the work that he published in 1623 "*Il saggiatore.*" . . . If we continue to examine the lexicons, they will teach us that *to try* was rivaled by *to prove, to test* in the speakers of the east and the south, an enriching rivalry that makes the essay the synonym of a *testing* of a *search for proof.* These are, admittedly, true letters of semantic nobility that make us admit that the best philosophy manifests itself in the form of the essay.

Let us pursue again for a moment the history of the word. Its fortune will extend outside of France. *The Essays*[4] of Montaigne have the good fortune of being translated and published in English by John Florio in 1603 and they will impose in England their title, if not their style. Starting with Sir Francis Bacon, people set to writing *Essays* across the Channel. When Locke publishes his *Essay concerning Human Understanding*, the word "essay" does not announce the spontaneous prose of Montaigne, it signals a book where new ideas are proposed, an original interpretation of a controversial problem. And it's in this *value* that the word will be often used. It alerts the reader and makes him wait for a renewal of perspectives, or at least the statement of the fundamental principles from which a new idea will be possible. Voltaire dramatically changes the approach to historical facts in his *Essay on the Manners of Nations*; the inaugural act of Bergson's philosophy is entitled *Essay on the Immediate Data of Consciousness*.[5]

Nevertheless, we must be careful not to believe that the history of the word *essay* and its derivatives is a uniformly triumphant progress. I have celebrated until the present the eminent dignity of the essay. I must however admit that this is not universally recognized. The essay also has, at least to certain eyes, its stains, its indignity, and the word itself, in one of its meanings, is responsible for this. The essay, the *first essay*, is only a preliminary approach. He who wants to *succeed*, doesn't he have to do more?

It is not French, but English that, at the beginning of the seventeenth century, invented the word *essayist*. And this word, since its first appearances, is not exempt from a pejorative nuance. One reads from the quill of Ben Jonson: *Mere essayists, a few loose sentences, and that's all!* It seems that the word *essayist* was not transplanted into France until later. We find it in 1845 in the work of Théophile Gautier meaning "of an author of non-detailed works." Let us notice that a suspicion of superficiality could attach itself to the essay. Montaigne himself offers weapons to detractors of the essay. He is ironic, or feigns to be ironic, about his book (because Montaigne's strategies are subtle) in declaring that he is only claiming *to touch upon and to nip at the head* of his chosen subject matter: so that one does not take him for a learned man, for a miracle worker of the system, for an author of massive treaties. The *head* is the flower, not the roots. There are specialists, *artists* to trace back to the roots. Montaigne, he only writes for pleasure, without looking to fill his work with citations and commentaries. But it is necessary to note: the learned men who had well-scorned him, or rather, they took to noticing the difference in genres and to defending the professionalism of knowledge of which Montaigne, perhaps by nobiliary pride, did not intend to be suspected. The University, at the peak of his positivist period, having fixed the rules and the canons of serious exhaustive research, rejected the essay and *essayism* to foreign darkness, at the risk of banishing at the same time the splendor of style and the audacities of thought. Seen from the classroom, evaluated by the dissertation committee, the essayist is a likeable amateur departing to rejoin the impressionist critic in the suspicious non-scientific area. And it is true that, losing sometimes its substance; the essay could transform itself into a journal column, a polemic pamphlet, and chatter about this and that. Still, none of these sub-genres of the essay merits being criticized in itself! The column can become *a short poem in prose*; the pamphlet, if written by Constant, can be titled *Of the Spirit of Conquest*; the chatter can speak with the voice of Mallarmé. A certain ambiguity, nevertheless, persists. Let us say it plainly, if one declared that I practice essayism, I would be slightly hurt, and I would take it as a reproach.

Let us imagine that we are looking at the title page of the book, such as it reads in 1580: *Essays of Messire Michel, Lord of Montaigne, Knight of the Order of the King, and Ordinary Gentleman of his Chamber*. Montaigne displays all of his names and *titles* and recommends himself. *Messire Michel* appears in many more characters than the little word *Essays* that is isolated on the upper line. This title reveals at the same time an evasion and a provocation: an evasion, because, in this intolerant time, it is not good to give foothold, in arguments that are too affirmative, to the accusation of heresy and of impiety. The cataloging was thus postponed by several decades. What pretext can be offered to religious censure by a thought of which the products define themselves, in their apparently disparate plurality, as drafts, attempts, fantasies, *indecisive* imaginations? To say that one goes no further than thinking in the essay or again: *I go inquiring and not knowing*, or again: *I do not teach at all, I narrate*, is to announce that we must not look for, in this volume, material of doctrinal disputation. This humility, entirely visible, is nothing but a show. Montaigne knows very well that one calls *essay* the use of a touchstone that allows a determination without fail of the nature and the name of a metal. And in declaring himself the author of essays, Montaigne presents another challenge. He leads us to believe that a book warrants being published, even if it remains open, if it achieves no essence, if it only offers an unfinished experience, if it only consists of preliminary work,—for as much as he relates closely to an existence, to the singular existence of Messire Michel, Lord of Montaigne. I am not the first to highlight this: the importance of the individual, of the *person* (saying it with the word that Denis de Rougemont has charged so much with meaning), must have become considerable, outside of all religious consecration, historic or poetic, so that the first gentleman would come to decide to give us his *essays*, to reveal to us his *conditions* and his *humors*.

From what objects and from what realities did Montaigne make the essay and how did he do it? Such is the question that we must post with insistence if we want to understand the challenges of the essay. Let us notice right away that the peculiarity of the essay is plural, multiple, which legitimizes the plural of the title *Essays*. It is not only about *repeated tentatives*, resumed *ponderings*, *first essays* at the same time partial and untiring: this allure of beginning, this *inchoative* aspect of the essay, are surely key, since he implies the abundance of joyous energy that never exhausts itself in his game. But moreover, his scope is unlimited, and the diversity, to which measures the wingspan of Montaigne's work and activity, gives us since the creation of the genre an exact insight into the rights and the privileges of the essay.

At first glance, let us say that we can discern two sides of the essay: one objective, the other subjective. And let us add straight away that the work of the essay aims at establishing between these two sides, an indissoluble relationship. The domain of experience, for Montaigne, is first the *world* that resists him: these are the objects that the world offers to his clutches; it is fortune that is making light work out of him. Such is the experimented material, the substance submitted to his weighing, to a weighing which for him, despite the emblem of the scale, is less the instrumental act practiced literally by Galileo, than a weighting in naked hands, a shaping, a handling. "Think with your hands," Montaigne heard himself in that phrase, him whose hands were always moving, although he declared himself unfit for all manual labor; it is necessary to know how to both *meditate* and *handle* life....

But that is not yet where the domain of the essay ends. What is principally put to the test is the power to try and to test, the ability to judge and to observe. To fully satisfy the law of the essay, "the essayer" must have a go at himself. In each essay directed towards the external reality, or towards his body, Montaigne experiments with his own intellectual forces, their strengths and their insufficiencies: such are the reflexive aspect, the subjective side of the essay, where self-consciousness begins to develop as a new authority of the individual, authority that judges the act of judging, that observes the ability of the observer. From his foreword *To the Reader*, declarations are not lacking where Montaigne assigns the primordial role to self-study, self-comprehension, as if the "benefit" for which the conscience searches was to shed light on the self, for the self. In the history of mentalities, innovation is so important that one was pleased to salute in the *Essays* the advent of the *portrayal* of the *self*, at the very least in Vulgar language. (Montaigne had been preceded by religious autobiographers, by Petrarch, but in Latin.) One saw in them their principal merit, their novelty the most striking. But it is important to remark that Montaigne offers us neither a diary, nor an autobiography. He depicts himself while looking at himself in the mirror, certainly: but, even more often, he defines himself indirectly, as though leaving himself out—in expressing his opinion: he depicts himself with scattered brushstrokes, for general interest questions: presumption, vanity, repentance, experience. He depicts himself speaking of friendship and education; he depicts himself meditating on state policy, evoking the massacre of the Indians, challenging confessions obtained by torture in criminal interrogations. In the essay according to Montaigne, the practice of internal reflection is inseparable from the inspection of exterior reality. It is after tackling the great moral questions, after listening to the maxims of the classic authors, after facing the rifts of the present-day world, that in looking to communicate his *cogitations* he finds himself *consubstantial to his book*, offering of himself an indirect representation, that only looks to complement and to enrich itself: *I am myself the matter of my book.*

1. It will be important to note here that the French for essay, *essai*, holds two meanings in English, that of the *essay*, as well as that of *a try* or *an attempt*: the latter being the original meaning, while the former has developed as a direct result of Montaigne's work in question here.

2. In French, *essayer*, follows a more obvious etymological link.

3. In French, *essaim*.

4. NB. Montaigne's writing has been modernized.

5. Diderot, whose thought is quite often the tuning fork for Montaigne's, brings confirmation: "I prefer an essay to a treaty: an essay where one throws me some genius ideas that are almost isolated, to a treaty where these precious seeds are suffocated under a heap of repetition." *On the Diversity of our Judgments*, in *Complete Works*, (Club Français du Livre, t. 13, 1972, 874.)

First published in *La Revue de Belles-lettres* (1983), translated here by Lindsey Scott

André Belleau (1930–86), born and raised in Montreal, spent much of his early career as a civil servant for the Canadian government. But in mid-life he left governmental work, returned to college, earned a doctorate, and became a literature professor and theorist of literary texts. Belleau was especially interested in the problem of how a writer can give voice to the numerous voices that inhabit and surround him, a problem he set forth in his second collection of essays *To Catch the Voices* (1986). This notable collection contains short pieces that he wrote between 1959 and 1986, focusing on his fascination with the wide-ranging idioms of journalism, television, public officials, and the street. In the following piece, Belleau bears witness to the complex way in which an essay evolves, given the interplay between language and thought within an essayist's head and the language of the culture for which he writes.

"Little Essayistic"

Let us start with a banality: the novelist and the poet are no more original writers than the essayist (or the critic). One hears occasionally in our milieu: "We, the poets and the novelists, we work with life while you, poor essayists, you work with what we make." But what one forgets is that novelists also work with what has been said and written before them, so much so that they do not enjoy a sort of metaphysical presence or an entitlement towards what one could call life or art or the primary substance of art. Most critics and essayists—at least as I imagine—are conscious of the necessarily secondary character of their venture. But to say to one or another of our local novelists: "Your novel presents itself as the rearrangement of a particular type of writing and of some themes of which the prototypes appeared ten, twenty, or thirty years ago," is to seriously risk becoming the object of physical abuse. We must forgive them. They do not know or they pretend not to know.

A writer is always first and foremost a rewriter. There is no indignity in that. Authors never hid from this fact until recently. That is not the essential. What is essential is the assuming the esthetic function. That is not nothing.

Therefore, to finish with this banality, the distinction between "creator," on one hand, and critic, on the other, shows itself now to be completely obsolete and tacky, since the modern novel has evolved to include a more and more critical dimension, and critique has also evolved to become an endeavor of writing, it proves quite difficult to separate the two. In this way, today, an essayist is an artist of the narrativity of ideas and a novelist, an essayist of the artistic plurality of language. The novel is eaten by the essay (*Sophie's Choice* by Styron, *La mort vive* by Ouellette), the essay overturns fiction (Vadeboncoeur, Borges).

There is a story; I would say even an intrigue in the essay, in the sense that one gives these words when one speaks of the story or the intrigue of a novel or a short story. The triggers that launch the activity of the essayist are sometimes cultural events, sometimes emerging ideas from the cultural domain. But so that they may enter into the transforming space of writing, these ideas and events must be swept-up in a space of movement that includes campaigns, roadblocks, issues, divisions, junctions, attractions, and repulsions. And the next thing you know they drive themselves to the heart of fictional characters and they fuel between them relationships of love, of hate, of opposition, of aid, etc. They produce a real dramatization of the cultural world and I would bet that at the end, there are both winning and losing ideas. An idea sparks the taste for writing, an idea makes, in a way, the desire to write for the essayist more strong than not writing, and this idea will encounter all sorts of obstacles like the hero of the novel. Idea or hero problematic . . .

Which event? Which idea? Let us here think about a real or possible cultural event, about a current or new idea that pops up all of the sudden in the essayist's mind. They are not immaterial. They have a color, a heat, an outline, almost a physical weight. The most abstract idea, for the writer impassioned for abstraction, becomes alive just from this abstraction. It can also happen that the essayist begins with a title that attracts him, solicits him in the same way as a color for the painter or a chord for the musician. The whole essay will consist precisely in allowing the pleasure of a desired title (the reader does not realize this). One will say that here the essay will find itself in words and ideas.

(I came across some time ago a title that much pleased me: "On an Adage of Erasmus." I am counting on soon writing an essay in order to be able to use it.)

Let us admit, thus, that it consists in eroticized ideas operating on the essayist in the manner of fantasies. They come back, they haunt him. He guards the idea in himself as if in a sort of elementary magnetic field where he feels the circuits take shape, possibilities that have the idea to orient them, to connect them to other ideas. During this period of maturation, attentive to the trips, to the journeys, to the openings and closings, the essayist will decide if all of this is vivid enough, fast enough, plentiful enough, unexpected enough, and complex enough to give place to the form of an essay, or moreover to the course of an essay. One will recall the Latin etymology of the word "essay,"[1] *exagium*, itself derived from the verb *exigere*, which has two meanings: *to weigh* (the essay "weighs" ideas; the *examination*, scholarly form of *exagium*, "weighs" the merits of candidates) and *to chase out of a place* (from where the *swarm*,[2] not a scholarly form, but popular form of *exagium*). The essay is not a weighing, an evaluation of ideas; it is a swarm of ideas-words.

Everyone knows it: writers make new work with the discourse of their society. It is the indispensable environment of language without which we would not be able to even begin to write the start of a sentence. But the apparition of essayists in literature supposes another condition: that the cultural content of social discourse is not situated below a certain threshold. Because the essayist works more specifically with the language of the culture. And to me it seems evident that a society where the signs of culture are made scarce will produce few essayists. It would be easy to imagine culture as a rare gas in a society that is saturated with sports talk, publicity, etc.

The formation of an essayist demands much more time than that of a poet or of a novelist. I say this without sarcasm. At eighteen, one can be Rimbaud, one cannot be an essayist. The reason for this is simple. I repeat: the essayist works in the cultural domain with the signs of culture. He has the pleasure to live in the semiosphere. And yet the knowledge and the mastery of language that make up the cultural world turn out to be an endeavor that is infinitely longer than the knowledge and mastery of fictional forms that are destined to represent social languages of existence. That is why, often, the essayist only begins to feel like a writer later in life.

The essayist sometimes likes to take questions which are complicated in appearance and give them another kind of confusion than the received confusion. But inversely, he may find himself possessed by the demon of clarity, of logic, of the demonstrable. We should not hesitate to here speak of obsessions. There are desires or what is clear and perfectly articulated. They are the triggers and motors of writing. One must respect them on the same level as the taste for the color mauve in Flaubert writing *Madame Bovary*. We have here phenomenon of the same order. That which is of the order of the fantastic is anchored in the most material and profound realities of our lives. According to certain viewpoints, which are short sighted and superficial, the passion for clarity found in essayists would have an ideological vector, would reveal a Cartesian spirit, reactionary, tinted with "male chauvinism." And if the essayist who seems to battle against confusion would himself impose this confusion to feel the pleasure of dispelling it? In fact, the essay is a research tool. He who has practiced it knows that it allows him to discover.

1. The French for essay, "essai" has a double sense in English: essay, and a try or an attempt.

2. In the original French *essaim*.

First published in *Liberté* 150 (December 1983), translated here by Lindsey Scott

ELIZABETH HARDWICK (1916–2007) grew up in Kentucky, the eighth of eleven children. After graduating from the University of Kentucky in 1939, she moved to New York to pursue graduate studies at Columbia University but left two years later to write fiction. Her first novel caught the eye of Philip Rahv, coeditor of *Partisan Review*, who asked her to contribute. At Rahv's magazine and others, she began to write very personal review essays about a wide range of cultural and political issues. "I have always written essays as if they were examples of imaginative writing, as I believe them to be," she later said. In 1963, Hardwick, her husband the poet Robert Lowell, and a small group of friends launched the *New York Review of Books*, which would become a center of American intellectual debate and her literary home. In the piece that follows, Hardwick uses the task at hand—in this instance, writing an introduction to an anthology of the year's best essays—to explore the history of the essay, first-person narration, and the relationship between the article and the essay.

From the Introduction to *The Best American Essays, 1986*

The essay? Thousands of pages of prose are published each month and not many of them are given to fiction. Perhaps most of the pages are information about the events of the day or the week and are not to be thought of as essays. What is this thunder and hail of newsprint felling the forests of the world? Journalism? Not quite, not nowadays. The knowing would not restrict the word *journalism* to mere information, if information can be thought of as *mere*. Nowadays journalism is a restless and predatory engagement, having established its imperial mandate under the phrase *new journalism*, established its claim with such occupying force that the phrase itself is no longer needed, no longer defining.

If we cannot be sure we are reading journalism according to the rules of the professional schools, we are even less certain that we are reading the elevated essay. Still, there is something called the essay, and volumes by individual writers are published under the title. Even then the term does not provide a serenity of precision; it is not altogether genuine in its shape, like fiction or poetry. It does not even have the advantage of pointing to scale since some essays are short and many are long and most incline to a condition of unexpressed hyphenation: the critical essay, the autobiographical essay, the travel essay, the political—and so on and so on.

There is a self-congratulatory sense in the word *essay*. It wants to signify that what has been offered is not a lesser offering, not just a review, a sketch, a "piece"—odd, useful word—summoned to feed the hungry space of periodicals. Sometimes the vagrant coinage *essayistic* appears in the press, and this is bad news for the language since it indicates an extension of murky similarity to what is itself more than a little cloudy. Of course, we always know what a barbarism is trying to say; its nature is to indicate the struggle for definition.

To be like an essay, if not quite the real thing, means that, in a practical bit of prose, attention has been paid to expressiveness and that to gain expressiveness certain freedoms have been exercised, freedoms illicit in the minds of some readers, freedoms not so much exercised as seized over the border. Essays are aggressive even if the mind from which they come is fair, humane, and, when it is to the point, disinterested. Hazlitt, in an essay on the poets living in his own time, writes: "Mrs. Hannah More is another celebrated modern poetess, and I believe still living. She has written a great deal which I have never read." It might take Mrs. More, if indeed she lived still, some time to figure out just what was being said.

The aggressiveness of the essay is the assumption of the authority to speak in one's own voice and usually the authority is earned by previous performance. We see a name on the cover or inside the pages and we submit to the reading with some eagerness, which may be friendly eagerness or not. One of the assumptions of the essayist is the right to make his own mistakes, since he speaks only for himself, allowing for the philosopher's cunning observation that "in my opinion" actually asserts "all reasonable men will agree." This claim is sometimes disputed by an elected authority, the editor, who may think too many villages have been overrun by the marauder. Since the freedom of the open spaces is the condition of the essay, too much correction and surgical intervention turns the composition into something else, perhaps an article, that fertile source of profit and sometimes pleasure in the cultural landscape.

William Gass, in what must be called an essay, a brilliant one, about Emerson, an essayist destined from the cradle, makes a distinction between the article and the essay. Having been employed by the university and having heard so many of his colleagues "doing an article on," Gass has come to think of the article as "that awful object" because it is under the command of defensiveness in footnote, reference, coverage, and would also pretend that all must be useful and certain, even if it is "very likely a veritable Michelin of misdirection." If the article has a certain sheen and professional polish, it is the polish of "the scrubbed step"—practical economy and neatness. The essay, in Gass's view, is a great meadow of style and personal manner, freed from the need for defense except that provided by an individual intelligence and sparkle. We consent to watch a mind at work, without agreement often, but only for pleasure. Knowledge hereby attained, great indeed, is again wanted for the pleasure of itself.

We would not want to think of the essay as the country of old men, but it is doubtful that the slithery form, wearisomely vague and as chancy as trying to catch a fish in the open hand, can be taught. Already existing knowledge is so often required. Having had mothers and fathers and the usual miserable battering of the sense of self by life may arouse the emotional pulsations of a story or a poem; but feeling is not sufficient for the essay. Comparisons roam about it, familiarity with those who have plowed the field before, shrewdness concerning the little corner or big corner that may remain for the intrusion of one's own thoughts. Tact and appropriateness play a part. How often we read a beginner's review that compares a thin thing to a fat one. "John Smith, like Tolstoy, is very interested in the way men interact under the conditions of battle." Well, no.

Fortunately, the essay is not a closed shop, and the pages do vibrate again and again with the appearance of a new name with no credentials admired or despised. An unknown practitioner of the peculiar animation of the prose of an essay takes up the cause. It is an occasion for happiness since it is always astonishing that anyone will write an essay. Some write them not once but more or less regularly. To wake up in the morning under a command to animate the stones of an idea, the clods of research, the uncertainty of memory, is the punishment of the vocation. And all to be done without the aid of end-rhyme and off-rhyme and buried assonance; without an imagined character putting on a hat and going into the street.

Those with the least gift are most anxious to receive a commission. It seems to them that there lies waiting a topic, a new book, a performance, and that this is known as material. The true prose writer knows there is nothing given, no idea, no text or play seen last evening until an assault has taken place, the forced domination that we call "putting it in your own words." Talking about, thinking about a project bears little relation to the composition; enthusiasm boils down with distressing speed to a paragraph, often one of mischievous banality. To proceed from musing to writing is to feel a robbery has taken place. And certainly there has been a loss; the loss of the smiles and ramblings and discussions so much friendlier to ambition than the cold hardship of writing.

Essays are addressed to a public in which some degree of equity exists between the writer and the reader. Shared knowledge is a necessity, although the information need not be concrete. Perhaps it is more to be thought of as a sharing of the experience of reading certain kinds of texts, texts with omissions and elisions, leaps. The essayist does not stop to identify the common ground; he will not write, "Picasso, the great Spanish painter who lived long in France." On the other hand, essays are about something, something we may not have had reason to study and master, often matters about which we are quite ignorant. Elegance of presentation, reflection made interesting and significant, easily lead us to engage our reading minds with Zulus, herbaceous borders in the English garden, marriage records in eighteenth-century France, Japanese scrolls. . . .

So there is no end to the essay, and no beginning. Walter Benjamin makes a visit to Moscow: "Each thought, each day, each life lies here as on a laboratory table." The poet, Jules Laforgue, goes to Berlin to be in the service of the Empress: "She has been bored, she is still bored, and she still dreams." Joan Didion has been to Alcatraz Island in California: "Alcatraz Island is covered with flowers now: orange and yellow nasturtiums, geraniums, sweet grass, blue iris, black-eyed Susans. Candytuft springs up through the cracked concrete in the exercise yard."

The essay, at least in reduction, is to be thought of as popular. Think of the number published. In the lightest examples—short sentences, short altogether, with photographs surrounding the shortness—it appears that words here and there about celebrities are gratifying in the gross. This cannot be the search for information, since there is little information in them. Libel is the handmaiden of information about the living. The appeal of celebrity journalism seems to rest upon a promise and to accept the fact that the promise will again and again be unfilled. To know the sanitized items, in almost infinite repetition, about the famous indicates an overwhelming appetite. Born somewhere, lives somewhere, may have a "wonderful" child, possibly a mate to whom, for the time being, everything is owed. Parents somewhere and, nearer, the career itself. "I want to improve my acting." All of this is prose of some kind, a commission arranged and concluded.

The true essay, making as it does a contribution to the cultural life, is not so simple. Its celebrities are likely to be long-dead painters, writers, and thinkers; living ones not memorable in photographs, and not a synopsis. Insofar as essays give information, and of course they do in their way, a peculiar condition of reciprocity, reader participation, prevails. Wit, the abrupt reversal, needs to strike a receptive ear or eye or else the surprise is erased, struck down. Expressiveness is an addition to statement, and hidden in its clauses is an intelligence uncomfortable with dogmatism, wanting to make allowances for the otherwise case, the emendation.

A well-filled mind itself makes the composition of essays more thorny rather than more smooth, with everything readily available. There is seldom absolute true assertion unless one is unaware. Words and phrases, ideas and opinions, invading the vast area of even the narrowest topic must fall back on a fluency of reference, reference sometimes merely hinted, if the convincing is to be achieved. Conviction itself is partial and the case is never decided. The essay is not the ground of verdicts. It rests on singularity rather than consensus.

The Best American Essays, 1986

GABRIEL ZAID (1934–) is a native of Monterrey, Mexico's second-largest city. Trained as an engineer, he became a poet and essayist. He has written for many magazines but is most often associated with *Vuelta*, which he launched with Octavio Paz in 1976. A reclusive figure who grants no photographs or interviews, Zaid is an independent, even iconoclastic thinker who criticizes armchair Marxists as *rábanos*, or radishes (red on the outside, white on the inside), and the Mexican bourgeoisie as slavish imitators of their counterparts to the north. He is best known in the United States for *So Many Books* (2003), which dismisses "the death of the book" and focuses instead on the fact that books remain cheap, plentiful, and diverse. In the following piece, Zaid describes the essay as a kind of stealth genre—a centaur that is both man and horse, but recognized as neither, or a kind of wheelbarrow foolishly valued for its contents rather than for its ability to carry those contents.

From "Alfonso Reyes' Wheelbarrow"

Among industrial folklore's stories and legends, there is the one about the guy who was carting construction materials in a wheelbarrow in a suspicious manner. The inspectors checked his papers over and over again, but everything was fine; they went through the materials to see if something was hidden there, but to no avail. The man would walk away smiling, like a triumphant prankster, while the inspectors remained perplexed, defeated at a game they didn't comprehend. It took them a long time to figure out that he was stealing wheelbarrows.

Alfonso Reyes's inspectors seem more fortunate, but they are not. They miss the essays while checking their content. An essay is not a report of research conducted in a laboratory: it is the laboratory itself, where life is put to the test in a text, where the author's imagination, creativity, experimentation, critical sensitivity are displayed. To essay is just that: to try, to probe new wordings to live with, new possibilities of being by reading. The misunderstanding arises when the essay instead of referring, for instance, to "The Traveler's Melancholy" (*Calendario*), refers to issues that could or should (in the eyes of the narrow-minded reader) be considered academic. It arises when the reader focuses solely on the improvable data rather than on the unbeatable prose. Similarly, the inspector can grow indignant with the actor who plays marvelously the evil character, instead of admiring him. Or with Shakespeare because he penned the play using someone else's plot. Or with the painter who considers his own the copy he made in a museum of a painting that he found interesting, so that he could observe it and take pleasure in recreating it (like Reyes who rewrote and published in his *Archivo* a book that had interested him). Or with the audience who listens to Bach's *St Matthew's Passion* without knowing any German, even if what matters in this work are not the words, but the music.

Reyes was aware of this problem and he helped us understand it through a memorable metaphor: the essay is the centaur of literary genres. An inspector of centaurs will not be able to understand the game if he believes that a centaur is a man on a horse; if he believes that the horse is simply a means of transportation. The essay is both art and science, but its science is not in the content it conveys, but in the wheelbarrow; it is not the professor's science (even if it takes advantage of it, illustrates it, or opens new venues for it). Its science is that of the artist, who experiments, combines, searches, imagines, builds, criticizes what he wants to say, before knowing it. In an essay, the knowledge that matters is the one achieved by virtue of writing it; the knowledge that did not exist before, even if the author knew many things, both from his own experience and from that of others, that helped him in his essay.

The essayist may advance on both paths, because that's what the centaur calls for. He may not only bring to light important original texts, which spring from his being, his mind, his hands, but also things that the experts had not discovered, and that they should take advantage of. Unfortunately, they cannot do so without risking their reputation. The assumption being that there cannot be valid discoveries outside the trade. That's why the chicanery of borrowing without acknowledgment is so common: it would be frowned upon to quote an essayist in an academic work. Which shows pettiness, but is without literary consequence, unless the essayists allowed themselves to be intimidated and acted as if creation were less important or any less research than academic work.

Reyes was not intimidated. In his early twenties he wrote reviews admirable for the quality of their prose, verve, and precision for the *Revista de Filología Española* (collected in *Entre libros*). He wrote like a philologist who masters his technique, in the double sense of being a professional and of writing way above his profession: like a true writer. He recalled it, thirty years later in Monterrey ("Mi idea de la historia," *Marginalia*, second series): "I complied from research to publication with all of its critical apparatus. However, I would not mistake those preparatory disciplines with the actual exegesis and cultural evaluation that I was aspiring to do. You see, learned tricks can be narrowed down to easy to teach automatic rules, which, once learned, are applied with monotonous impersonality. That is not the case with the arts of interpretation and narration, where the technique hinges upon being talented." The importance of this distinction and, especially, of the hierarchy it establishes, is obvious in the reviews found in *Entre libros*, which have retained all their flavor despite being written between 1912 and 1923. It doesn't matter that the books and facts they refer to are outdated. The true novelty, what is still news, as Pound would say (*poetry is news that stays news*), is the prose worked on like poetry. Facts grow old, the wheelbarrow doesn't.

It is possible and desirable, as Reyes shows, that the expert be much more than a specialist: an essaying mind, a true writer. It has happened with philosophers, historians, lawyers, physicians. But with the rise of the university as training center for technocrats, free culture (as opposed to wage-earning culture), authorial culture (as opposed to culture authorized by proceedings and credentials), the creation of ideas, metaphors, points of view, ways of seeing things, look like nothing compared with sound academic work. The correct hierarchy is the opposite one. Writing essays is so difficult that mediocre writers should not try it: they should limit themselves to academic work.

It is only natural that the experts, especially when science necessitates large budgets, be aware of the importance of public relations. That they engage in two complementary forms of social communication: the publication of findings formally addressed to their colleagues in specialized periodicals and in popular science magazines aimed at the general public. For them an essay is popular science. They even hire writers to present their work for them. But the essay is a literary genre of the creative intellect, not the news broadcast of layman science. The ancillary function (that is how Reyes calls it in *El deslinde*) uses prose as an ancilla, a maid, a slave, a servant of the material being conveyed; a wheelbarrow subservient to the specialist's laboratory. The essay, on the contrary, subjects data (specialized or otherwise) to the laboratory of prose, to the laboratory of learning sought in original formulations, to the laboratory of being that is questioned, criticized and recreated in a text.

The reader incapable of refreshing, restoring, or reorganizing himself when reading an essay that is truly essaying, is a reader impoverished by technocratic culture. He doesn't know that his wheelbarrow has been stolen.

First published as "La carretilla alfonsina" in *Proceso* 583 (January 4, 1988), translated here by Maria Willstedt and Gabriel Zaid

SCOTT RUSSELL SANDERS (1945–) is a literary critic, fiction writer, and essayist who taught at Indiana University from 1971 until his retirement in 2009. He is an environmentalist and peace activist and has focused often in his essays on the geography—spiritual and political—of his native Midwest. Though he has written movingly about public issues, his work has achieved perhaps its most powerful effects when confronting dark, personal themes that are at once both private and universal. In essays about his father's death and alcoholism, for instance, Sanders infuses his careful, polished style with the details of memory and the energy of emotion. In the piece reprinted below, Sanders states that his intention as an essayist is to "pay my respects to a minor passage of history in an out-of-the-way place" and to "speak directly out of my life into the lives of others."

From "The Singular First Person"

In this era of prepackaged thought, the essay is the closest thing we have, on paper, to a record of the individual mind at work and at play. It is an amateur's raid in a world of specialists. Feeling overwhelmed by data, random information, and the flotsam and jetsam of mass culture, we relish the spectacle of a single consciousness making sense of a portion of the chaos. We are grateful to Lewis Thomas for shining his light into the dark corners of biology, to John McPhee for laying bare the geology beneath our landscape, to Annie Dillard for showing us the universal fire blazing in the branches of a cedar, to Peter Matthiessen for chasing after snow leopards and mystical insights in the Himalayas. No matter if they are sketchy, these maps of meaning are still welcome. As Joan Didion observes in her own collection of essays, *The White Album*, "We live entirely, especially if we are writers, by the imposition of a narrative line upon disparate images, by the 'ideas' with which we have learned to freeze the shifting phantasmagoria which is our actual experience" (Didion, 11). Dizzy from a dance that seems to accelerate hour by hour, we cling to the narrative line, even though it may be as pure an invention as the shapes drawn by Greeks to identify the constellations.

The essay is a haven for the private, idiosyncratic voice in an era of anonymous babble. Like the blandburgers served in their millions along our highways, most language served up in public these days is textureless, tasteless mush. On television, over the phone, in the newspaper, wherever humans bandy words about, we encounter more and more abstractions, more empty formulas. Think of the pablum ladled out by politicians. Think of the fluffy white bread of advertising. Think, Lord help us, of committee reports. In contrast, the essay remains stubbornly concrete and particular: it confronts you with an oil-smeared toilet at the Sunoco station, a red vinyl purse shaped like a valentine heart, a bow-legged dentist hunting deer with an elephant gun. As Orwell forcefully argued, and as dictators seem to agree, such a bypassing of abstractions, such an insistence on the concrete, is a politically subversive act. Clinging to this door, that child, this grief, following the zigzag motions of an inquisitive mind, the essay renews language and clears trash from the springs of thought. A century and a half ago, Emerson called on a new generation of writers to cast off the hand-me-down rhetoric of the day, to "pierce this rotten diction and fasten words again to visible things" (Emerson, 30). The essayist aspires to do just that.

As if all these virtues were not enough to account for a renaissance of this protean genre, the essay has also taken over some of the territory abdicated by contemporary fiction. Pared down to the brittle bones of plot, camouflaged with irony, muttering in brief sentences and gradeschool vocabulary, today's fashionable fiction avoids disclosing where the author stands on anything. Most of the trends in the novel and short story over the past twenty years have led away from candor—toward satire, artsy jokes, close-lipped coyness, metafictional hocus-pocus, anything but a direct statement of what the author thinks and feels. If you hide behind enough screens, no one will ever hold you to an opinion or demand from you a coherent vision or take you for a charlatan.

The essay is not fenced round by these literary inhibitions. You may speak without disguise of what moves and worries and excites you. In fact, you had better speak from a region pretty close to the heart, or the reader will detect the wind of phoniness whistling through your hollow phrases. In the essay you may be caught with your pants down, your ignorance and sentimentality showing, while you trot recklessly about on one of your hobbyhorses. You cannot stand back from the action, as Joyce instructed us to do, and pare your fingernails. You cannot palm off your cockamamie notions on some hapless character. If the words you put down are foolish, everyone knows precisely who the fool is.

To our list of the essay's contemporary attractions we should add the perennial ones of verbal play, mental adventure, and sheer anarchic high spirits. The writing of an essay is like finding one's way through a forest without being quite sure what game you are chasing, what landmark you are seeking. You sniff down one path until some heady smell tugs you in a new direction, and then off you go, dodging and circling, lured on by the songs of unfamiliar birds, puzzled by the tracks of strange beasts, leaping from stone to stone across rivers, barking up one tree after another. Much of the pleasure in writing an essay—and, when the writing is any good, the pleasure in reading it—comes from this dodging and leaping, this movement of the mind. It must not be idle movement, however, if the essay is to hold up; it must be driven by deep concerns. The surface of a river is alive with lights and reflections, the breaking of foam over rocks, but beneath that dazzle it is going somewhere. We should expect as much from an essay: the shimmer and play of mind on the surface and in the depths a strong current.

Works Cited

Didion, Joan. *The White Album*. New York: Simon and Schuster, 1979.

Emerson, Ralph Waldo. *Nature*. Vol. 1 of *The Complete Works of Ralph Waldo Emerson*. Boston: Houghton Mifflin, 1903.

First published in the *Sewanee Review* 96.4 (1988)

PHILLIP LOPATE (1943–) is a distinguished American essayist, film critic, cultural commentator, and educator, who currently holds an endowed professorship at Hofstra University. A versatile author, Lopate has produced two poetry collections, three novels, a collection of film criticism, a book about the Manhattan waterfront, and the award-winning memoir *Being With Children* (1975), based on his twelve years as a "writer-in-the-schools." He is perhaps best known for three collections of wide-ranging and candid personal essays, *Bachelorhood* (1981), *Portrait of My Body* (1986), and *Against Joie de Vivre* (1989), as well as for his pathbreaking anthology *The Art of the Personal Essay* (1994). Lopate's devotion to the essay is reflected in the following piece that features a sweeping history of it together with an exploration of where it stands in contemporary writing.

"What Happened to the Personal Essay?"

The personal or familiar essay is a wonderfully tolerant form, able to accommodate rumination, memoir, anecdote, diatribe, scholarship, fantasy, and moral philosophy. It can follow a rigorously elegant design, or—held together by little more than the author's voice—assume an amoebic shapelessness. Working in it liberates a writer from the structure of the well-made, epiphanous short story and allows one to ramble in a way that more truly reflects the mind at work. At this historical moment the essayist has an added freedom: no one is looking over his or her shoulder. No one much cares. Commercially, essay volumes rank even lower than poetry.

I know; when my first essay collection, *Bachelorhood*, came out, booksellers had trouble figuring out where to stock it. Autobiography? Self-help? Short stories? I felt like saying, "Hey, this category has been around for a long time; what's the big deal?" Yet, realistically, they were right: what had once been a thriving popular tradition had ceased being so. Readers who enjoyed the book often told me so with some surprise, because they hadn't thought they would like "essays." For them, the word conjured up those dreaded weekly compositions they were forced to write on the gasoline tax or the draft.

Essays are usually taught all wrong, they are harnessed to rhetoric and composition, in a two-birds-with-one-stone approach designed to sharpen freshman students' skills at argumentation. While it is true that historically the essay is related to rhetoric, it in fact seeks to persuade more by the delights of literary style than anything else. Elizabeth Hardwick, one of our best essayists, makes this point tellingly when she says, "The mastery of expository prose, the rhythm of sentences, the pacing, the sudden flash of unexpected vocabulary, redeem polemic. . . . The essay . . . is a great meadow of style and personal manner, freed from the need for defense except that provided by an individual intelligence and sparkle. We consent to watch a mind at work, without agreement often, but only for pleasure."

Equally questionable in teaching essays is the anthology approach, which assigns an essay apiece by a dozen writers according to our latest notions of a demographically representative and content-relevant sampling. It would be more instructive to read six pieces each by two writers, since the essay (particularly the familiar essay) is so rich a vehicle for displaying personality in all its willfully changing aspects.

Essays go back at least to classical Greece and Rome but it was Michel de Montaigne, generally considered the "father of the essay," who first matched the word to the form around 1580. Reading this contemporary of Shakespeare (thought to have influenced the Bard himself), we are reminded of the original, pristine meaning of the word, from the French verb *essayer*, to attempt, to try, to leap experimentally into the unknown. Montaigne understood that, in an essay, the track of a person's thoughts struggling to achieve some understanding of a problem *is* the plot. The essayist must be willing to contradict himself (for which reason an essay is not a legal brief), to digress, even to risk ending up in a terrain very different from the one he embarked on. Particularly in Montaigne's magnificent late essays, free-falls that sometimes go on for a hundred pages or more, it is possible for the reader to lose all contact with the ostensible subject, bearings, top, bottom, until there is nothing to do but surrender to this companionable voice, thinking alone in the dark. Eventually, one begins to share Montaigne's confidence that "all subjects are linked to one another," which makes any topic, however small or far from the center, equally fertile.

It was Montaigne's peculiar project, which he claimed rightly or wrongly was original, to write about the one subject he knew best: himself. As with all succeeding literary self-portraits—or all succeeding stream-of-consciousness, for that matter—success depended on having an interesting consciousness, and Montaigne was blessed with an undulatingly supple, learned, skeptical, deep, sane, and candid one. In point of fact, he frequently strayed to worldly subjects, giving his opinion on everything from cannibals to coaches, but we do learn a large number of intimate and odd details about the man, down to his bowels and kidney stones. "Sometimes there comes to me a feeling that I should not betray the story of my life," he writes. On the other hand, "No pleasure has any meaning for me without communication."

A modern reader may come away thinking that the old fox still kept a good deal of himself to himself. This is partly because we have upped the ante on autobiographical revelation, but also because Montaigne was writing essays, not confessional memoirs, and in an essay it is as permissible, as honest, to chase down a reflection to its source as to admit some past shame. In any case, having decided that "the most barbarous of our maladies is to despise our being," Montaigne did succeed, via the proto-psychoanalytic method of the *Essais*, in making friends with his mind.

Having taken the essay form to its very limits at the outset, Montaigne's dauntingly generous example was followed by an inevitable specialization, which included the un-Montaignean split between formal and informal essays. The formal essay derived from Francis Bacon; it is said to be "dogmatic, impersonal, systematic, and expository," written in a "stately" language, while the informal essay is "personal, intimate, relaxed, conversational, and frequently humorous" (*New Columbia Encyclopedia*). Never mind that most of the great essayists were adept at both modes, including Bacon (see, for example, his wonderful "Of Friendship"), it remains a helpful distinction.

Informal, familiar essays tend to seize on the parade and minutiae of daily life: vanities, fashions, oddballs, seasonal rituals, love and disappointment, the pleasures of solitude, reading, going to plays, walking in the street. It is a very urban form, enjoying a spectacular vogue in eighteenth- and early nineteenth-century London, when it enlisted the talents of such stylists as Swift, Dr. Johnson, Addison and Steele, Charles Lamb, William Hazlitt, and a visiting American, Washington Irving. The familiar essay was given a boost by the phenomenal growth of newspapers and magazines, all of which needed smart copy (such as that found in the *Spectator*) to help instruct their largely middleclass, *parvenu* readership on the manners of the class to which it aspired.

Although most of the *feuilletonistes* of this period were cynical hacks, the journalistic situation was still fluid enough to allow original thinkers a platform. The British tolerance for eccentricity seemed to encourage commentators to develop idiosyncratic voices. No one was as cantankerously marginal in his way, or as willing to write against the grain of community feeling, as William Hazlitt. His energetic prose style registered a temperament that passionately, moodily swung between sympathy and scorn. Anyone capable of writing so bracingly frank an essay as "The Pleasures of Hating" could not—as W. C. Fields would say—be all bad. At the same time, Hazlitt's enthusiasms could transform the humblest topic, such as going on a country walk or seeing a prizefight, into a description of visionary wholeness.

What many of the best essayists have had—what Hazlitt had in abundance—was quick access to their blood reactions so that the merest flash of a prejudice or opinion might be dragged into the open and defended. Hazlitt's readiness to entertain opinions, coupled with his openness to new impressions, made him a fine critic of painting and the theater, but in his contrariness he ended by antagonizing all of his friends, even the benign, forgiving Charles Lamb. Not that Lamb did not have *his* contrary side. He, too, was singled out for a "perverse habit of contradiction," which helped give his "Elia" essays, among the quirkiest and most charming in the English language, their peculiar bite.

How I envy readers of *London* magazine, who might have picked up an issue in 1820 and encountered a new, high-spirited essay by Hazlitt, Lamb, or both! After their deaths, the familiar essay continued to attract brilliant practitioners such as Stevenson, De Quincey, and Emerson. But subsequently, a little of the vitality seeped out of it. "Though we are mighty fine fellows nowadays, we cannot write like Hazlitt," Stevenson confessed. And by the turn of the century, it seemed rather played out and toothless.

The modernist aesthetic was also not particularly kind to this type of writing, relegating it to a genteel, antiquated nook, belles lettres—a phrase increasingly spoken with a sneer, as though implying a sauce without the meat. If "meat" is taken to mean the atrocities of life, it is true that the familiar essay has something obstinately nonapocalyptic about it. The very act of composing such an essay seems to implicate the writer in humanist-individualist assumptions that have come to appear suspect under the modernist critique.

Still it would be unfair to pin the rap on modernism, which Lord knows gets blamed for everything else. One might as well "blame" the decline of the conversational style of writing. Familiar essays were fundamentally, even self-consciously, conversational: it is no surprise that Swift wrote one of his best short pieces on "Hints Toward an Essay on Conversation"; that Montaigne tackled "Of the Art of Discussion"; that Addison and Steele extensively analyzed true and false wit; that Hazlitt titled his books *Table Talk*, *Plain Speaker*, and *The Round Table*, or that Oliver Wendell Holmes actually cast his familiar essays in the form of mealtime dialogues. Why would a book like Holmes's *The Autocrat At the Breakfast Table*, a celebration of good talk that was so popular in its time, be so unlikely today? I cannot go along with those who say "The art of conversation has died, television killed it," since conversation grows and changes as inevitably as language. No, what has departed is not conversation but conversation-flavored writing, which implies a speaking relationship between writer and reader. How many readers today would sit still for a direct address by the author? To be called "gentle reader" or "*hypocrite lecteur*," to have one's arm pinched while dozing off, to be called to attention, flattered, kidded like a real person instead of a privileged fly on the wall—wouldn't most readers today find such devices archaic, intrusive, even impudent? Oh, you wouldn't? Good, we can go back to the old style, which I much prefer.

Maybe what has collapsed is the very fiction of "the educated reader," whom the old essayists seemed to be addressing in their conversational remarks. From Montaigne onward, essayists until this century have invoked a shared literary culture, the Greek and Latin authors and the best of their national poetry. The whole modern essay tradition sprang from quotation. Montaigne's *Essais* and Burton's *Anatomy of Melancholy* were essentially outgrowths of the "commonplace book," a personal journal in which quotable passages, literary excerpts, and comments were written. Though the early essayists' habit of quotation may seem excessive to a modern taste, it was this display of learning that linked them to their educated reading public and ultimately gave them the authority to speak so personally about themselves. Such a universal literary culture no longer exists; we have only popular culture to fall back on. While it is true that the old high culture was never really "universal"—excluding as it did a good deal of humanity—it is also true that without it, personal discourse has become more hard-pressed. What many modern essayists have tried to do is to replace that shared literary culture with more and more personal experience. It is a brave effort and an intriguing supposition, this notion that individual experience alone can constitute the universal text that all may dip into with enlightenment. But there are pitfalls: on the one hand, it may lead to cannibalizing oneself and one's privacy; on the other hand, much more common (and to my mind, worse) is the assertion of an earnestly honest or "vulnerable" manner without really candid chunks of experience to back it up.

As for popular culture, the essayist's chronic invocation of its latest bandwagon fads, however satirically framed, comes off frequently as a pandering to the audience's short attention span—a kind of literary ambulance chasing. Take the "life-style" pages in today's periodicals, which carry commentaries that are a distant nephew of the familiar essay: there is something so depressing about this desperate mining of things in the air, such a fevered search for a generational *Zeitgeist*, such an unctuously smarmy tone of "we" which assumes that everyone shares the same consumerist-boutique sensibility, that one longs for a Hazlittean shadow of misanthropic mistrust to fall between reader and writer. One longs for any evidence of a distinct human voice—anything but this ubiquitous Everyman/woman pizzazzy drone, listing tips for how to get the most from your dry cleaner's, take care of your butcher block, or bounce back from an unhappy love affair.

The familiar essay has naturally suffered from its parasitic economic dependency on magazines and newspapers. The streamlined telegraphic syntax and homogenized-perky prose that contemporary periodicals have evolved make it all the more difficult for thoughtful, thorny voices to be tolerated within the house style. The average reader of periodicals becomes conditioned to digest pure information, up-to-date, with its ideological viewpoint disguised as objectivity, and is thus ill-equipped to follow the rambling, cat-and-mouse game of perverse contrariety played by the great essayists of the past.

In any event, very few American periodicals today support house essayists to the tune of letting them write regularly and at comfortable length on the topics of their choice. The nearest thing we have are talented columnists like Russell Baker, Ellen Goodman, Leon Hale, and Mike Royko, who are in a sense carrying on the Addison and Steele tradition; they are so good at their professional task of hit-and-run wisdom that I only wish they were sometimes given the space to try out their essayistic wings. The problem with the column format is that it becomes too tight and pat: one idea per piece. Fran Lebowitz, for instance, is a very clever writer, and not afraid of adopting a cranky persona, but her one-liners have a cumulative sameness of affect that inhibits a true essayistic movement. What most column writing does not seem to allow for is self-surprise, the sudden deepening or darkening of tone, so that the writer might say, with Lamb: "I do not know how, upon a subject which I began treating half-seriously, I should have fallen upon a recital so eminently painful. . . . "

From time to time I see hopeful panel discussions offered on "The Resurgence of the Essay." Yes, it would be very nice, and it may come about yet. The fact is, however, that very few American writers today are essayists primarily. Many of the essay collections issued each year are essentially random compilations of book reviews, speeches, journalism, and prefaces by authors who have made a name for themselves in other genres. The existence of these collections attests more to the celebrated authors' desires to see all their words between hardcovers than it does to any real devotion to the essay form. A tired air of grudgingly gracious civic duty hovers over many of these performances.

One recent American writer who did devote himself passionately to the essay was E. B. White. No one has written more consistently graceful, thoughtful essays in twentieth-century American language than White; on the other hand, I can't quite forgive his sedating influence on the form. White's Yankee gentleman-farmer persona is a complex balancing act between Whitmanian democratic and patrician values, best suited for the expression of mildness and tenderness with a resolute tug of elegiac depression underneath. Perhaps this is an unfair comparison, but there is not a single E. B. White essay that compares with the gamy, pungent, dangerous Orwell of "Such, Such Were the Joys . . . " or "Shooting an Elephant." When White does speak out on major issues of the day, his man-in-the-street, folksy humility and studiously plain-Joe air ring false, at least to me. And you would never know that the cute little wife he describes listening to baseball games on the radio was the powerful *New Yorker* editor Katharine White. The suppression or muting of ego as something ungentlemanly has left its mark on *The New Yorker* since with the result that this magazine, which rightly prides itself on its freedom to publish extended prose, has not been a particularly supportive milieu for the gravelly voice of the personal essayist. The preferred model seems to be the scrupulously fair, sporting, impersonal, fact-gathering style of a John McPhee, which reminds me of nothing so much as a colony of industrious termites capable of patiently reducing any subject matter to a sawdust of detail.

The personal, familiar essay lives on in America today in an interestingly fragmented proliferation of specialized subgenres. The form is very much with us, particularly if you count the many popular nonfiction books that are in fact nothing but groups of personal essays strung together, and whose compelling subject matter makes the reading public overlook its ordinary indifference to this type of writing. Personal essays have also appeared for years under the protective umbrella of New Journalism (Joan Didion being the most substantial and quirky practitioner to emerge from that subsidized training ground, now largely defunct); of autobiographical-political meditations (Richard Rodriguez, Adrienne Rich, Vivian Gornick, Marcelle Clements, Wilfrid Sheed, Alice Walker, Nancy Mairs, Norman Mailer); nature and ecological-regional writing (Wendell Berry, Noel Perrin, John Graves, Edward Hoagland, Gretel Ehrlich, Edward Abbey, Carol Bly, Barry Lopez, Annie Dillard); literary criticism (Susan Sontag, Elizabeth Hardwick, Seymour Krim, Cynthia Ozick, Leslie Fiedler, Joyce Carol Oates); travel writing and mores (Mary McCarthy, V. S. Naipaul, Joseph Epstein, Eleanor Clark, Paul Theroux); humorous pieces (Max Apple, Roy Blount, Jr., Calvin Trillin); food (M. F. K. Fisher). I include this random and unfairly incomplete list merely to indicate the diversity and persistence of the form in American letters today. Against all odds, it continues to attract newcomers.

In Europe, the essay stayed alive largely by taking a turn toward the speculative and philosophical, as practiced by writers like Walter Benjamin, Theodor Adorno, Simone Weil, E. M. Cioran, Albert Camus, Roland Barthes, Czeslaw Milosz, and Nicola Chiaromonte. All, in a sense, are offspring of the epigrammatic style of Nietzsche. This fragmented, aphoristic critical type of essay-writing became used as a subversive tool of skeptical probing, a critique of ideology in a time when large, synthesizing theories and systems of philosophy are no longer trusted. Adorno saw the essay, in fact, as a valuable counter-method: "The essay does not strive for closed, deductive or inductive construction. It revolts above all against the doctrine—deeply rooted since Plato—that the changing and ephemeral is unworthy of philosophy; against that ancient injustice toward the transitory, by which it is once more anathematized, conceptually. The essay shies away from the violence of dogma. . . . The essay gently defies the ideals of [Descartes'] *clara et distincta perceptio* and of absolute certainty. . . . Discontinuity is essential to the essay . . . as characteristic of the form's groping intention. . . . The slightly yielding quality of the essayist's thought forces him to greater intensity than discursive thought can offer; for the essay, unlike discursive thought, does not proceed blindly, automatically, but at every moment it must reflect on itself. . . . Therefore the law of the innermost form of the essay is heresy. By transgressing the orthodoxy of thought, something becomes visible in the object which it is orthodoxy's secret purpose to keep invisible."

This continental tradition of the self-reflexive, aphoristically subversive essay is only now beginning to have an influence on contemporary American writers. One saw it first, curiously, cropping up in ironic experimental fiction—in Renata Adler, William Gass, Donald Barthelme, John Barth. Their fictive discourse, like Kundera's, often resembles a broken essay, a personal/philosophical essay intermixed with narrative elements. The tendency of many postmodernist storytellers to parody the pedantry of the essay voice speaks both to their intellectual reliance on it and to their uneasiness about adopting the patriarchal stance of the Knower. That difficulty with assumption of authority is one reason why the essay remains "broken" for the time being.

In a penetrating discussion of the essay form, Georg Lukács put it this way, "The essay is a judgment, but the essential, the value-determining thing about it is not the verdict (as is the case with the system), but the process of judging." Uncomfortable words for an age when "judgmental" is a pejorative term. The familiar essayists of the past may have been nonspecialists—indeed this was part of their attraction—but they knew how to speak with a generalist's easy authority. That is precisely what contemporary essayists have a hard time doing, in our technical age we are too aware of the advantage specialists hold over us. (This may explain the current confidence the public has in the physician-scientist school of essayists like Lewis Thomas, Richard Selzer, Stephen Jay Gould, F. Gonzalez-Crussi, Oliver Sacks: their meditations are embedded in a body of technical information so that readers are reassured they are "learning" something, not just wasting their time on *belles lettres*.) The last of the old-fashioned generalists, men of letters who seemed able to write comfortably, knowledgeably, opinionatedly on everything under the sun, were Edmund Wilson and Paul Goodman; we may not soon see their like again.

In *The Last Intellectuals*, Russell Jacoby has pointed out the reticence of writers of the so-called generation of the sixties—my generation—to play the role of the public intellectual, as did Lionel Trilling, Harold

Rosenberg, C. Wright Mills, Irving Howe, Alfred Kazin, Daniel Bell, Dwight Macdonald, Lionel Abel, etc., who judged cultural and political matters for a large general readership, often diving into the melee with both arms swinging. While Jacoby blames academia for absorbing the energies of my contemporaries, and while others have cited the drying up of print outlets for formal polemical essays, my own feeling is that it is not such a terrible thing to want to be excused from the job of pontificating to the public. Ours was not so much a failure to become our elders as it was a conscious swerving to a different path. The Vietnam War, the central experience of my generation, had a great deal to do with that deflection. As a veteran of the sixties, fooled many times about world politics because I had no firsthand knowledge of circumstances thousands of miles away (the most shameful example that comes to mind was defending, at first, the Khmer Rouge regime in Cambodia), I have grown skeptical of taking righteous public positions based on nothing but simpatico media reports and party feeling. As for matters that I've definitely made up my mind about, it would embarrass me, frankly, to pen an opinion piece deploring the clearly deplorable, like apartheid or invading Central America, without being able to add any new insights to the discussion. One does not want to be reduced to scolding, or to abstract progressive platitudes, well founded as these may be. It isn't that my generation doesn't think politics are important, but our earlier experiences in that storm may have made us a little hesitant about mouthing off in print. We—or I should say I—have not yet been able to develop the proper voice to deal with these large social and political issues, which will at the same time remain true to personal experience and hard-earned doubt.

All this is a way of saying that the present moment offers a remarkable opportunity for emerging essayists who can somehow locate the moral authority, within or outside themselves, to speak to these issues in the grand manner. But there is also room, as ever, for the informal essayist to wrestle with intellectual confusion, to offer feelings, to set down ideas in a particularly direct and exposed format—more so than in fiction, say, where the author's opinions can always be disguised as belonging to characters. The increasing willingness of contemporary writers to try the form, if not necessarily commit themselves to it, augurs well for the survival of the personal essay. And if we do offend, we can always fall back on Papa Montaigne's "*Que sçay-je*?"; What do I know?

Against Joie de Vivre, 1989

GERALD EARLY (1952–) was born in Philadelphia but has lived for many years in St. Louis, where he is the Merle Kling Professor of Modern Letters at Washington University. A prodigiously active scholar and essayist, he has published on topics as various as sports, jazz, parenthood, boxing, beauty pageants, Shirley Temple movies, and the music of Motown. His collection of essays on prizefighting, *The Culture of Bruising*, won the 1994 National Book Critics Circle Award for criticism. He has also edited collections of essays about Muhammad Ali, Sammy Davis Jr., and Miles Davis, as well as the important two-volume anthology *Speech and Power: The African American Essay and Its Cultural Content from Polemics to Pulpit*, and has recently launched the *Best African American Essays* series. In the excerpt from his introduction to *Tuxedo Junction: Essays on American Culture* that follows, Early describes the particular situation of the African American essayist as being "anthropological" in the paradoxical sense that she or he is always both participant and observer. "The black essayist," writes Early, "is caught between acting and writing," between being "mascot and scribe."

From the Introduction to *Tuxedo Junction*

Any decent black essayist, and Douglass was often as essayistic as fictional in his autobiography (indeed, I posit that the peculiarly black literary form of the essay grew from Douglass's autobiographies and from black autobiography generally, although it is certainly related to the black sermonic tradition as Martin Luther King's "Letter from a Birmingham Jail" and Baldwin's *The Fire Next Time*, two of the famous black essays of the last thirty years, attest), is not, in effect, literary, or trying to be literary merely, but is trying quite self-consciously to be anthropological. He (or she, as the case may be) cannot help but be anthropological, as there can be no mistaking that for the African-Americans, the place where they live never ceases to be a prison-house of culture (not necessarily a bad prison as prisons go, and sometimes confinement can be strengthening), and in prison one is forced constantly to think about writing as theater. All black essayists, ultimately, with either resolution or resignation, write, as Douglass stated he did, "from sound." It is through sound, uncertain though it may be, that the anthropologist understands his work. The essays in this volume are filled with sound. They talk of little else. They try to replicate nothing so much as the sound of other things, of language bouncing off the prison-house walls. But, for the black essayist, sound must always try to be subversion, the slave's language is always undermining the master's tongue even as it imperfectly replicates it, even as it aspires to be the master's tongue. The perfect image of the black writer is Jim trapped in his prison that is not really a prison in the last chapters of Mark Twain's novel while Huck and Tom cover the walls with language and invent signs for Jim's white captors, all of which has no meaning except that the language and signs refer to novels, romances, literary conventions—that verisimilitude, in this instance and perhaps in all instances, is not a term describing how art is related to life but how life is related to books (and artistic vision), which are, in effect, more real than life. Nothing is more real than our fantasies, Twain's novel tells us. Jim, through his displays of common sense, rebels against being an instrumentality of white consciousness while succumbing to it for lack of anything better to do. I hope this singular dilemma becomes clearer as I go along. But how can one distinguish, in the case of Jim, for instance, subversion from simulation in this vastness of verisimilitude?

Consider how Douglass, in *My Bondage and My Freedom*, appropriates the terms "Nature" and "Nurture" from mid-1850s American pop-scientific, anthropological discourse and uses them to illustrate the slave's humanity, in direct opposition to their contemporary use in the hermeneutical language of the nineteenth-century white intellectual as absences of both a civilizing environment and proper genetic properties (ah, the slave, being property in a world where property was the touchstone of reality, was completely without property, and so was not only completely unreal himself but was forced to see the world as unreality). Douglass achieves this without ever using the words themselves but by appropriating the cultural symbol that compresses and decomposes both terms: mother. Douglass tells two elaborate stories of his mother, who was largely absent from his life: first, how she rescued him from a cruel black "Auntie" and gave him bread, and second, how his literary turn of mind was directly inherited from his maternal (black) side (Douglass always believed his father to be white). So, with Douglass, the absent mother (not "Mammy" or "Auntie," that lover and rearer of white sons and daughters and beloved of them) becomes the presence that repudiates the cultural absences that have been assigned the black. There is a lesson in that bit of fabrication by Douglass (literal fabrication because he could not possibly have remembered the bread incident and how does anyone know, in most instances, which source of genes produced what talents, especially in the case of someone who did not know his father as Douglass did not); a lesson that would stand any black essayist in good stead about playing with language in the prison-house of culture. For Douglass, after all, bread, the staff of life, becomes both nature and nurture and, in effect, Douglass proves the two terms are essentially interchangeable and absolutely meaningless as they both signify "mother," and everyone has one of those, as Douglass demonstrates—you can make of her whatever you wish.

But in the matters of anthropology and language on and reverberating within the prison-house walls no black writer can be more instructive than Zora Neale Hurston, a trained anthropologist/ethnographer in her own right and a novelist of some distinction. In her 1942 autobiography, *Dust Tracks on a Road*, a marvelously and shrewdly fabricated book, she tells of three successive incidents concerning language that occur when she joins a white theater company as a teenager:

> In the first place, I was a Southerner, and had the map of Dixie on my tongue. They [the theater company] were all Northerners except the orchestra leader, who came from Pensacola. It was not that my grammar was bad, it was the idioms. They did not know of the way an average Southern child, white or black, is raised on simile and invective. They know how to call names. It is an everyday affair to hear somebody called a mullet-headed, mule-eared, wall-eyed, hog-nosed, 'gator-faced, shad-mouthed, screw-necked, goat-bellied, puzzle-gutted, camel-backed, butt-sprung, battle-hammed, knocked-kneed, razor-legged, box-ankled, shovel-footed, unmated so-and-so! . . . Since that stratum of the Southern population is not given to book-reading, they take their comparisons right out of the barnyard and the woods. When they get through with you, you and your whole family look like an acre of totempoles.

As much as the white company liked young Hurston's own colorful language, they enjoyed even more having her saying things which she did not understand:

> Another sly trick they played on my ignorance was that some of the men would call me and with a very serious face send me to some of the girls to ask about the welfare and condition of cherries and spangles. They would give me a tip and tell me to hurry back with the answer. Some of the girls would send back word that the men need not worry their heads at all. They would never know the first thing about the condition of their cherries and spangles. Some of the girls sent answers full of double talk which went over my head.

Finally, this incident with written discourse:

> I got a scrapbook, and everybody gave me a picture to put in it. I pasted each one on a separate page and wrote comments under each picture. This created a great deal of interest, because some of the comments were quite pert. They egged me on to elaborate. Then I got another idea. I would comment on daily doings and post the sheets on the call-board. This took on right away. The results stayed strictly mine less than a week because members of the cast began to call aside and tell me things to put in about others. It got to be so general that everybody was writing it. It was just my handwriting, mostly. Then it got beyond that. Most of the cast ceased to wait for me. They would take a pencil to the board and set down their own item. Answers to the wisecracks would appear promptly and often cause uproarious laughter. They always started off with either "Zora says" or "The observant reporter of the Call-board asserts"—Lord, Zora said more things! I was continually astonished, but always amused.

The passages, taken together, constitute a highly complex rendering of the political realities of blacks and language in the prison-house of culture, explicating and dramatizing all the various issues that a black essayist might think about in relation to what he or she does—for here, to borrow a Roland Barthes phrase, language literally becomes theater. First, there is a political reversal occurring here as Hurston moves from being mascot to becoming something like a scribe to, in fact, something like an anthropologist; moving from being a totem of animal imagery and ritual insult language to serving as a liaison for double entendres about cherries and heads to being a headmistress of a kind of school for scandal or a gossip exchange. Literally, once she controls the call board, the actual script of the lives of the company, she becomes the one who has not only recorded the dialect but actually shaped its creation. That a black should become the central controlling figure for the discourse of whites is, ironically, both a remarkable political feat of assertion-subversion and something genuinely ignominious if we remember Jim as the central and "controlling" figure of the whites at the end of Twain's novel. The method of ritual insulting, which she describes at first as being Southern, she describes later in the book as being particularly female and Negro and refers to it as "specifying." The shift is extremely important because specifying occurs when she is in the all-black southern towns collecting data (folk stories, i.e., oral language) for her books. Among the blacks, she is purely the scientist (the objective subject), evacuating and saving a culture. Among the whites, she is purely the exhibitionist (the subjective object) signifying the tricks and trumps of language. In effect, among the whites, Hurston makes the transition from taboo to totem (which is exactly what Jim does in *Huckleberry Finn*); for Hurston, the writer is the totem who enables the language of others ("the Other") to have meaning. That Hurston should be able to write about this in such a way that she so disguises her seizing the essential instrumentality of an acting company (its language and its script), becoming not simply its conduit for discourse but its source as well while seemingly remaining an instrumentality of the whites themselves (in essence, while still remaining a creation of the white imagination: a folksy innocent) is a masterful stroke of the trickster (although it is the very strength of her trickster dissimulation that is her final undoing—because as the folksy innocent she can do nothing more than either be an exhibitionist or an observer, wavering between the anthropologist as actor to the anthropologist scribe). It is simply the problem of both being there (author) and being here (participant) that black nonfiction writers face as a kind of peculiar hazard of their game. In very stunning ways, the black nonfiction writer as anthropologist exemplifies the point of Clifford Geertz's essay "Being There: Anthropology and the Scene of Writing" better than any academic anthropologist ever could. For Hurston and Douglass—and, by extension, for most black nonfiction writers—"being there" is an ontological conundrum.

The black essayist is caught between acting and writing, between seizing the instrumentality and being trapped by the fact that he is inescapably an instrumentality; as he uses language he becomes both mascot and scribe, an odd, ambivalent coupling of the purloined and the purposeful.

Tuxedo Junction: Essays on American Culture, 1989

SUSAN SONTAG (1933–2004) was one of the most ambitious and provocative writers of her generation. A novelist and essayist, she wrote on a wide range of subjects, persistently challenging conventional forms of art and modes of understanding. She first gained widespread attention for the striking pieces in *Against Interpretation* (1966), particularly "Notes on Camp," containing fifty-eight numbered segments, tacitly critiquing high culture with a celebration of pop culture: "it's good because it's awful." On the other hand, in 1977 she produced *On Photography*, a sustained critique of the way in which "picture-taking"—a notable aspect of popular culture—had radically altered contemporary travel, family life, and conceptions of reality itself. Sontag's abiding concern with distortions of experience can also be seen in *Illness as Metaphor* (1978) and *AIDS and Its Metaphors* (1988), both of which explore the ways in which conceptions of disease and the treatment of patients have been warped by the use of metaphor. So, it is not surprising that in her Introduction to *The Best American Essays of 1992*, which follows, she defines "the influential essayist" as "someone with an acute sense of what has not been (properly) talked about, what should be talked about (but differently)."

Introduction to *The Best American Essays, 1992*

I suppose I might begin by declaring an interest.

Essays came into my life as a precocious, passionate reader as naturally as did poems and stories and novels. There was Emerson as well as Poe, Shaw's prefaces as well as Shaw's plays, and a little later Mann's *Essays of Three Decades* as well as *Stories of Three Decades,* and "Tradition and the Individual Talent" as well as "The Waste Land" and "Four Quartets," and Henry James's prefaces as well as Henry James's novels. An essay could be as much an event, a transforming event, as a novel or poem. You finished an essay by Lionel Trilling or Harold Rosenberg or Randall Jarrell or Paul Goodman, to mention only some American names, and you thought and felt forever differently.

Essays of the reach and eloquence I am describing are part of a literary culture. And a literary culture—that is, a community of readers and writers with a curious, passionate relation to the literature of the past—is just what one cannot take for granted now. The essayist is more likely a superior ironist or gadfly than a sage.

An essay is not an article, not a meditation, not a book review, not a memoir, not a disquisition, not a diatribe, not a shaggy dog story, not a monologue, not a travel narrative, not a suite of aphorisms, not an elegy, not a piece of reportage, not a—

No, an essay can be any or several of the above.

No poet has a problem saying, I am a poet. No fiction writer hesitates to say, I am writing a story. "Poem" and "story" are still relatively stable, easily identified literary forms or genres. The essay is not, in that sense, a genre. Rather, "essay" is just one name, the most sonorous name, bestowed on a wide range of writings. Writers and editors usually call them "pieces." This is not just modesty or American casualness. A certain defensiveness now surrounds the notion of the essay. And many of the best essayists today are quick to declare that their best work lies elsewhere: in writing that is more "creative" (fiction, poetry) or more exacting (scholarship, theory, philosophy).

Often conceived of as a kind of back-formation from other forms of writing, the essay is best defined by what it also is—or what it is not. The point is illustrated by the existence of this anthology, now in its seventh year. First came *The Best American Short Stories.* Then someone suggested, couldn't we also have *The Best American Short*—what?—nonfiction. The most accurate, as well as least satisfying, definition of the essay is: a short, or shorter, prose text that is *not* a story.

And yet it is a very old literary form—older than the story, arguably older than any long narrative that could be called a novel. Essay writing emerged in the high literary culture of ancient Rome, blending the energies of the oration and the formal letter. Not only did the first great essayists, Seneca and Plutarch, write what came to be known as moral essays, with titles like "On the Love of Wealth," "On Envy and Hate," "On Being a Busybody," "On the Control of Anger," "On Having Many Friends," "On Listening to Lectures," and "The Education of Children," that is, confidently prescriptive accounts of principle, attitude, and conduct —but there are also essays, such as Plutarch's account of the customs of the Spartans, that are purely descriptive. And his "On the Malice of Herodotus" is one of the earliest examples of an essay devoted to the close reading of a master text: what we call literary criticism.

The essay project exhibits an extraordinary continuity, almost to the present day. Eighteen centuries after Plutarch, Hazlitt wrote essays with titles like "On the Pleasure of Hating," "On Going a Journey," "On the Love of the Country," "On the Fear of Death," "On Depth and Superficiality," "The Prose of Poets"—the perennial topics—as well as essays on slyly trivial themes and reconsiderations of great authors and historical events. The essay project inaugurated by the Roman writers reached its climax in the course of the nineteenth century. Virtually every important nineteenth-century poet and novelist wrote essays, and several of the best writers (Hazlitt, Emerson) were principally essayists. It is also in the nineteenth century that one of the most familiar contemporary transpositions of essay writing—the essay in the guise of a book review—came to prominence. (Most of George Eliot's important essays were written as book reviews for the *Westminster Review.*) And two of the century's greatest minds, Kierkegaard and Nietzsche, could both be considered as practicing a form of the essay—made more concise and discontinuous by Nietzsche; more repetitive and verbose by Kierkegaard.

Of course, to say that a philosopher is an essayist is, from the traditional point of view of philosophy, a demotion. The culture administered by universities has always regarded the essay with suspicion, as a kind of writing that is too subjective, too accessible, merely belle-lettristic. An interloper in the solemn worlds of philosophy and polemic, the essay introduces digressiveness, exaggeration, mischief.

An essay can have any subject in the same sense that a story or a novel or a poem can have any subject. But the assertiveness of the essay-writing voice, the directness of its concern with opinion and argument, makes the essay a more perishable kind of literary enterprise. With a few glorious exceptions, the essayists from the past who were essayists only have not survived. Most essays of the past still of interest to the educated reader are by writers we already care about. One has a chance to discover that Turgenev wrote an unforgettable witness-essay against capital punishment, anticipating the famous essays on the same theme by Camus and Orwell, only because Turgenev is already present as a novelist. We relish Gertrude

Stein's "What Are Masterpieces" and her *Lectures in America* because Stein is Stein is Stein.

It is not only that the essay *could* be about anything. It usually was. The good health of essay writing depends on writers continuing to address eccentric subjects. In contrast to poetry and fiction, the nature of the essay is diversity—diversity of level, subject, tone, diction. Essays on being old and falling in love and the nature of poetry are still being written. And there are also essays on Rita Hayworth's zipper and Mickey Mouse's ears.

Sometimes the essayist is a writer, mostly otherwise occupied (with poetry or fiction), who also writes . . . polemics, accounts of travels, elegies, re-evaluations of predecessors and rivals, self-promoting manifestos. Yes. Essays.

Sometimes "essayist" seems no more or less than a sneaky euphemism for "critic." And, indeed, some of the best essayists of the twentieth century have been critics. Dance, for instance, inspired André Levinson, Edwin Denby, and Arlene Croce. Literary studies has produced a vast constellation of major essayists and still does, despite the engulfment of literary studies by academia.

Sometimes an essayist is a difficult writer who has, happily, condescended to the essay form. Would that more of the important early twentieth-century European philosophers, social thinkers, and cultural critics had done as did Simmel, Ortega y Gasset, and Adorno—who will probably continue to be read with pleasure only in their essays.

The word essay comes from the French *essai,* attempt—and many essayists, including the greatest of all, Montaigne, have insisted that the distinctive mark of the essay is its tentativeness, its disavowal of closed, systematic ways of thinking. Its most obvious trait, however, is assertiveness of one kind or another.

To read an essay properly, one must understand not only what it is arguing for but what it is arguing against. Reading the essays written by our contemporaries, we easily supply the context, the public argument, the opponent, explicit or implicit. The passage of a few decades can make this almost impossible.

Essays end up in books, but they start their lives in magazines. (It's hard to imagine a book of recent but previously unpublished essays.) The perennial comes now mainly in the guise of the topical and, in the short run, no literary form has as great and immediate an impact on contemporary readers. Many essays are discussed, debated, reacted to in a way that poets and writers of fiction can only envy.

The influential essayist is someone with an acute sense of what has not been (properly) talked about, what should be talked about (but differently). But what makes essays last is less their argument than the display of a complex mind and a distinctive prose voice.

While precision and clarity of argument and transparency of style are usually regarded as norms for essay writing, in the same way that the realistic conventions of narrative are taken as normative (and with as little justification), in fact the most durable and compelling tradition of essay writing is as a form of lyrical discourse.

All the great essays are in the first person. The writer need not say "I." A vivid, flavorful prose style with a high aphoristic content is itself a form of first-person writing: think of the essays of Emerson, Henry James, Gertrude Stein, Elizabeth Hardwick, William Gass. The writers I have mentioned are all Americans, and it would be easy to add others. Essay writing is one of the strong American literary forms. It emerges out of the sermon and its secular transposition, the public lecture. Our first great writer, Emerson, is primarily a writer of essays. And a variety of essay writing flourishes in our contemporary contentious, polyphonic culture: from essays that feature an argument to digressive meditations and evocations.

Instead of thinking of contemporary essays according to their subjects—the travel essay, literary and other kinds of criticism, the political essay, cultural criticism, etc.—one could distinguish them by their kinds of energy and rue. The essay as jeremiad. The essay as exercise in nostalgia. The essay as exhibition of a temperament. Etc.

We get out of essays everything a prancing human voice is capable of. Instruction. The bliss of eloquence deployed for its own sake. Moral correction. Entertainment. Deepening of feeling. Models of intelligence.

Intelligence is a literary virtue, not just an energy or aptitude given literary clothing.

It is hard to imagine an important essay that is not, first of all, a display of intelligence. And sheer intelligence of the highest order can in and of itself make a great essay. (Think of Jacques Rivière on the novel, the Adorno of *Prisms* and *Minima Moralia,* the major essays of Walter Benjamin and Roland Barthes.) But there are as many varieties of essay writing as there are varieties of intelligence.

Baudelaire wanted to call a collection of his essays on painters *Painters Who Think.*

This is quintessentially the essayist's point of view: to convert the world and everything in it to a species of thinking. To the reflection of an idea, an assumption—which the essayist unfolds, defends, or excoriates.

Ideas about literature—unlike ideas about, say, love—almost never arise except in response to other people's ideas. They are reactive ideas. I say *this* because it's my impression that you—or most people, or many people—are saying *that.* Ideas give permission. And I want to give permission, by what I write, to a different feeling or evaluation or practice.

This is, preeminently, the essayist's stance.

I say *this* when you are saying *that* not just because writers are professional adversaries; not just to redress the inevitable imbalance or one-sidedness of any activity that has the character of an institution (and writing is an institution); but because the practice—I also mean the nature—of literature is rooted in inherently contradictory aspirations. A truth about literature is one whose opposite is also true.

Each poem or story or essay or novel that matters, that deserves the name of literature, incarnates an idea of singularity, of the singular voice. But literature—which is an accumulation—incarnates an idea of plurality, of multiplicity, of promiscuity. Every writer knows that the practice of literature demands a talent for reclusiveness. But literature . . . literature is a party. A wake, much of the time. But a party still. Even as disseminators of indignation, writers are givers of pleasure. And one becomes a writer not so much because one has something to say as because one has experienced ecstasy as a reader.

Here are two quotations I have been gnawing on recently.

The first, by the Spanish writer Camilo José Cela: "Literature is the denunciation of the times in which one lives."

The other is by Manet, who told a visitor to his studio in 1882: "Always move in the direction of concision. And then, cultivate your memories; nature will never give you anything but hints—it's like a railing that keeps you from falling into banality. You must constantly remain the master and do as you please. No tasks! No, no tasks!"

The Best American Essays, 1992

NANCY MAIRS (1943–) is an American poet, essayist, and memoirist. Diagnosed with multiple sclerosis when she was twenty-eight, Mairs has written about her experience with MS, her chronic depression, her agoraphobia, and her marriage in the arrestingly frank and vividly detailed essays of *Plaintext* (1992) and *Carnal Acts* (1996), as well as in her memoirs *Ordinary Time* (1994), *Remembering the Bone House* (1995), and *Waist High in the World* (1997). Her irrepressible wit and self-deprecating humor are also on display in her more recent works *A Troubled Guest* (2002), *Essays Out Loud* (2004), and *A Dynamic God* (2008), which focus primarily on aspects of mortality and spirituality. In the following reflections on the essay, Mairs offers a sustained contrast of Montaigne and Bacon, exploring in particular the contemporary implications of their different essayistic modes.

From "Essaying the Feminine"

Like the French feminists, I subscribe to the premise that the world we experience is itself an immense text that in spite of its apparent complexity has been made in Western thought to rest on a too-simple structural principle opposing reason to emotion, activity to passivity, and so on, every pair reflecting the most basic dichotomy—"male" and "female." Like them, I seek to disrupt the binary structure of this text, or Logos, through *l'ecriture feminine*, which "not only combines theory with a subjectivism that confounds the protocols of scholarly discourse, it also strives to break the phallologic boundaries between critical analysis, essay, fiction, and poetry.

Hence I write essays in the Montaignesque sense of the word: not the oxymoronic "argumentative essays" beloved by teachers of composition, which formalize and ritualize intellectual combat with the objective of demolishing the opposition, but *tests*, trials, tentative rather than contentious, opposed to nothing, conciliatory, reconciliatory, seeking a mutuality with the reader which will not sway her to a point of view but will incorporate her into their process, their informing movement associative and suggestive, not analytic and declarative.

"If my mind could gain a firm footing," writes Montaigne, "I would not make essays, I would make decisions; but it is always in apprenticeship and on trial." In fact, the details of Montaigne's life demonstrate that he was fully capable of making decisions; in his essays he sets aside that capacity. "Thus his starting points are not intended to engage a war of opinions," says John O'Neill of the Montaignesque writer, "they are rather subjunctive alliances for the sake of exploring what hitherto had been shared terrain. By the same token, the conclusions reached are not meant to be absolute, but only what seems reasonable as a shared experience." And, as O'Neill points out, "Montaigne found thinking difficult because he rejected the easy assembly of philosophy and theology careless of man's embodied state," aware that the "loss in scholastic abstractions is that they can be mastered without thought and that men can then build up fantastic constructions through which they separate the mind from the body, masters from slaves, life from death, while in reality nothing matches these distinctions."

Preference for relation over opposition, plurality over dichotomy, embodiment over cerebration: Montaigne's begins to sound like a feminist project. Which is not to say that Montaigne was a feminist. ("You are too noble-spirited," he was able to write to the Comtesse de Gurson when she was expecting her first child, "to begin otherwise than with a male.") But whether intentionally or not, Montaigne invented, or perhaps renewed, a mode open and flexible enough to enable the feminine inscription of human experience as no other does. The importance of this contribution has been largely overlooked, perhaps because many of Montaigne's statements, as well as his constant reliance on prior patriarchal authority, strike one as thoroughly masculine, and also because the meaning of *essay* has traveled so far from Montaigne's that the word may be used to describe any short piece of nonfiction, no matter how rigid and combative.

"Thus, reader, I am myself the matter of my book," Montaigne writes in his preface to the essays. "You would be unreasonable to spend your leisure on so frivolous and vain a subject." In claiming this plural subjectivity, he is clearly aware that he has made writing do something new: "Authors communicate with people by some special extrinsic mark; I am the first to do so by my entire being, as Michel de Montaigne, not as a grammarian or a poet or a jurist." Not much later, Francis Bacon, the first

English writer of "essays," would shape modern scientific method thus: "Generally let every student of nature take this as a rule—that whatever his mind seizes and dwells upon is to be held in suspicion, and that so much the more care is to be taken in dealing with such questions to keep the understanding even and clear." How differently Montaigne perceives the human psyche in essays that are, as Virginia Woolf notes, "an attempt to communicate a soul . . . to go down boldly and bring to light those hidden thoughts which are the most diseased; to conceal nothing; to pretend nothing; if we are ignorant to say so; if we love our friends to let them know it."

This image of descent and retrieval echoes Woolf's description elsewhere of the experience of the woman writer as a dreaming fisherman whose imagination sweeps "unchecked round every rock and cranny of the world that lies submerged in the depths of our unconscious being," seeking "the pools, the depths, the dark places where the largest fish slumber," until it smashes against the rock of "something, something about the body, about the passions, which it was unfitting for her as a woman to know." This problem, "telling the truth about my own experiences as a body, I do not think I solved," says Woolf. In such an adventure, Montaigne has the advantage, his embodiment and his awareness of it owning at least marginal cultural acceptability. Even so, his task is hardly easy, Woolf writes, for he must be "capable of using the essayist's most proper but most dangerous and delicate tool," the self: "that self which, while it is essential to literature, is also its most dangerous antagonist."

It is this quality in Montaigne that Woolf admires, and often imitates in her own essays, despite her self-doubt: "this talking of oneself, following one's own vagaries, giving the whole map, weight, colour, and circumference of the soul in its confusion, its variety, its imperfection." Not command of the mind and the world, but communication with the mind and its world forms Montaigne's purpose. "I do not portray being: I portray passing," he states, characterizing his project as "a record of various and changeable occurrences, and of irresolute and, when it so befalls, contradictory ideas: whether I am different myself, or whether I take hold of my subjects in different circumstances and aspects." By embracing contradiction, Montaigne never permits himself a stance sturdy enough for gaining sovreignty over himself, his fellow creatures, or any of the other natural phenomena objectified by scientific discourse.

Unlike Montaigne, Bacon had no qualms about his footing. All a man need do was dislodge the idols of his mind—rooted in human nature, idiosyncracy, social intercourse, and philosophical dogma—and he would see plain the objective world, the world "out there," the world of principles uncontaminated by human flux and context. Human nature being pretty much as Bacon thought it was, "prone to suppose the existence of more order and regularity in the world than it finds," Bacon's detached view prevailed over Montaigne's messy, shifting, "domestic and private" engagement with "a life subject to all human accidents." For the past four hundred years, people may have read Montaigne for delight, even for wisdom, but most have turned to Bacon for direction to "the truth." And now, from the very products of Baconian practice, those trained in "scientific objectivity," we are learning that one cannot observe reality without changing it and that even physics, that quintessential exercise in intellectual aloofness, is not actually the impartial scrutiny of phenomena "out there" but is rather "the study of the structure of consciousness."

In rejecting the concept of himself as a self-consistent entity, purged of peculiarity, coherent through time and separate from the external processes he observes and records, Montaigne seems curiously contemporary, capable of grasping as Bacon would probably not what Michael Sprinker describes as "a pervasive and unsettling feature in modern culture, the gradual metamorphosis of an individual with a distinct, personal identity into a sign, a cipher, an image no longer clearly and positively identifiable as 'this one person.'" "We are all patchwork," Montaigne writes, "and so shapeless and diverse in composition that each bit, each moment, plays its own game. And there is as much difference between us and ourselves as between us and others." His use of the essay form reflects this sense of fragmentation.

Montaigne's essays are not strictly autobiographical if we accept the conventional definition of autobiography, the story of a person's life written by himself, wherein "story" is a narrative, that which has a beginning, middle, and (problematic) end: linear, continuous, coherent, chronological, causal. But insofar as the "life" in autobiography—selflifewriting—is a construct of the writing/written self, it has at least submerged narrative elements that may be read even when they are not explicit in the autobiographical text. With its "'stuttering,' fragmented narrative appearance," Montaigne's form helps him to avoid "the original sin of autobiography," the use of hindsight to render his narrative logically consistent, as well as to mitigate the "split intentionality" between Montaigne the man and the discursive "I." A collection of personal essays literally stutters—begins, halts, shifts, begins anew—in a partial and piecemeal literary enterprise that may go on, as Montaigne's did, for twenty years, ending or, more precisely, reaching "not their end but their suspension in full career" only with death.

Voice Lessons: On Becoming a (Woman) Writer, 1994

RACHEL BLAU DUPLESSIS (1941–) is a feminist poet, critic, scholar, and essayist who teaches at Temple University in Philadelphia. She was born in Brooklyn and grew up in New York in a nonreligious family with a strong Jewish heritage. One grandfather was a rabbi and essayist, and her father was a professor of philosophy and religion at Columbia. She earned her BA at Barnard and her PhD at Columbia, where she became involved in a feminist group that included Kate Millet. DuPlessis's main project since 1985 has been a long "life-poem" titled *Drafts*, which she has described as a kind of "essay-in-verse." She has written and edited several collections of essays, most of them focusing on modern poetry and political thought. The following excerpt from her 1996 tour de force "*f*-Words: An Essay on the Essay" focuses on the difficulties of defining the "overloaded" antigenre that is the essay and showcases DuPlessis's theoretical acumen, stunning erudition, and punning, poetical style.

From "*f*-Words: An Essay on the Essay"

Piling so many names, so many varieties of moxie, and so many directions onto one overloaded genre has a couple of effects. It tends to blur the concept, leaving the essay expiring in a hiss of other explanations, or going into overdrive. Faced with all that, one might say, "Essay? It's short but personal writing that speaks from the heart" (wherever that is). Essays tend to call the genre into question, as theory about genre also does. Yet it sometimes seems as if the essay is lots of modes, a set of intersections of intention: some essays, but not all, are "autobiographical"; some, but not all, are discursive; some, but not all, are heteroglossic; some, but not all, are theoretical—and on and on. Indeed, Réda Bensmaïa argues that the essay is not a genre, nor even several mixed genres, but "a moment of writing before the genre, before genericness—or as the matrix of generic possibilities."[1]

What an aura of specialness—the essay as the universe at the second before its dispersion, an impacted point prior to the flying off of matter into planets, fragments into texts, and over all a sense of volatile incipience. It's not that the essay is unsusceptible to genre "definition"; it's rather that the nature of the essay asks one to resist categories, starting with itself. Here the essay will be treated according to its functions (*f* is the symbol for function), presenting some activities of force, trying out some features in a trying fashion. There is some frank provocation within that function, essay being (think of Pater and Emerson and Thoreau and Du Bois, then think of Woolf and Audre Lorde) the genre of spiritual provocation, of social mourning, of political fury as a kind of melody and the sense of a new day dawning. This nexus of provocation, fury, passion, and hope, along with cunning scrutiny of social and cultural texts, a practice learned, to say it too bluntly, through the scrutiny of official lies, should tell us again why this essay function was reborn out of (loosely) the long reverberations of the sixties in U.S. thought. This generally ethical definition affronts a post- or non-humanist articulation of discursive practices and apparatuses—visual, verbal, kinetic. The contemporary essay occurs in the seam between sociality and textuality.

Is it possible to synthesize these vectors—to offer any major lines around which these writings converge—even in a fully unsystematic study?[2] Given that the array of names above—incomplete but suggestive—is strangely dazzling, one wants simply to point: Look! Look! It is also probably true that I have missed important manifestations of this form; the fault is inadvertent, but mine. I do not, for example, discuss the generic crossings between fiction and essay, a blank spot that could be filled by someone else. (Not to speak of the comic abyss that results from concentrating only on the quite contemporary or on the, mainly, United States American; one begins muttering Montaigne, Oscar Wilde, Montaigne, Christa Wolf, Montaigne, Walter Benjamin, Montaigne, Primo Levi, Montaigne. The sensation is vertiginous.) Critically, there is pleasure in variety, even when these works may be conflicting, differently motivated, and uneven in impact. (One can "like" what one does not "like.") This is exactly the kind of mindset that makes me write along facets in my own essays, getting a variety of views and claims, panning in on (for instance) Duchamp's "Etant Donnes" again and again, not settling on one way of seeing it, on one judgment of it. Speculation best be just that. Skepticism too.

But what unites essays, if it is possible to say, is probably a defining attentiveness to materiality, to the material world, including the matter of language. The essay is currently born (and borne) in some relation to a cultural moment centering on difference, on articulations of specific, local, and topographical being, on the stating of the material meanings of individual choices, practices, options, and needs, on political and social locations for identity taking shape within language as language, within form as form. While this attention to materiality can also sometimes split into two tendencies—an emphasis on either textual or biographical/historical materiality—the real interest comes when these emphases are fused: when textuality (style, rhetoric, image, resistant diction, insoucient [sic] tone, weird page space, ploys opening out the book, visual text, multiplex of genres) is presented as a social practice. So while there are probably essays in all periods (certainly journalism writes them every day, affable, kindly, vaguely analytic), it only feels like a moment for The Essay when there is some materialist adhering of meaning to mode, when critique joins with passion in language that materializes that passion as rhetoric, when interested and situated knowledge is exposed in its vibrancy, when people have undergone changes that resonate in all felt areas—ethical, intellectual, emotional, visceral—and when these areas are a nexus, mixed and unsortable. For subject position is language position. What are all the tones in which you are fluent? Add the tones in which you stutter. You're beginning to get it. The essay is elementally nontranscendent, for when it goes up, it comes back down again. The essay is both a mode of and metaphor for this nexus. The essay ruptures the conventions—especially the scientistic ethos of objectivity—of critical writing. When a situated practice of knowing made up by the untransparent situated subject explores (explodes) its material in unabashed textual untransparency, conglomerated genre, ambidextrous, switch-hitting style—as if figuring out on the ground, virtually in the time of writing—that's it: *f*-words. The essay.

1. Réda Bensmaïa, *The Barthes Effect: The Essay as Reflective Text*, trans. Pat Fedkiew (Minneapolis: U of Minnesota P, 1987): 92.

2. An alphabetical list of more systematic studies follows: Theodor W. Adorno, "The Essay as Form," trans. Bob Hullot-Kentor and Frederic Will, *New German Critique* 32 (Spring–Summer 1984): 151–71; also translated by Shierry Weber Nicholsen in Adorno, *Notes to Literature,* Vol. 1 (New York: Columbia UP, 1991), 3–23; Adorno's essay was originally written between 1954 and 1958; G. Douglas Atkins, *Estranging the Familiar: Toward a Revitalized Critical Writing* (Athens: U of Georgia P, 1992); James Bennett, "The Essay in Recent Anthologies of Literary Criti-

cism," *Sub Stance* 18, no. 3 (1989): 105–11; Réda Bensmaïa, cited above; Ruth-Ellen Boetcher Joeres and Elizabeth Mittman, *The Politics of the Essay: Feminist Perspectives* (Bloomington: Indiana UP, 1993)—a comparativist perspective with special strengths in German, French, and Hispanic materials; Alexander Butrym, ed., *Essays on the Essay: Redefining the Genre* (Athens: U of Georgia P, 1989); Robert Caserio, "The Novel As a Novel Experiment in Statement: The Anticanonical Example of H. G. Wells," in *Decolonizing Tradition: New Views of Twentieth-Century "British" Literary Canons*, ed. Karen Lawrence (Urbana: U of Illinois P, 1992), 88–109; Graham Good, *The Observing Self: Rediscovering the Essay* (London: Routledge, 1988); Anne Herrmann, "The Epistolary Essay: A Letter," in *The Dialogic and Difference: "An/Other Woman" in Virginia Woolf and Christa Wolf* (New York: Columbia UP, 1989); Georg Lukács, "On the Nature and Form of the Essay," in *Soul and Form*, trans. Anna Bostock (Cambridge: MIT P, 1971); Laurent Mailhot, "The Writing of the Essay," trans. Jay Lutz, in *The Language of Difference: Writing in Quebec(ois)*, ed. Ralph Sarkonak (New Haven: Yale UP, 1983): 74–89. [author's note]

American Literature 68.1 (March 1996)

CYNTHIA OZICK (1928–) is an American novelist, short story writer, and essayist whose immigrant Russian parents imbued her with a deep knowledge of and reverence for Jewish and Yiddish cultural traditions. Ozick in turn has written extensively about Jewish life, drawing in part on her childhood years in the Bronx, where she attended a Yiddish-Hebrew school, in part on her extensive reading of Jewish literature and history, and in part on her irrepressible concern with the Holocaust, which occurred when she was coming of age. She is known not only for the intellectually distinctive heroines she has created in such novels as *The Cannibal Galaxy* and *The Puttermesser Papers* but also for her wide-ranging collections of essays, which touch on her personal experience and engage with cultural and literary issues such as those she deals with in the following piece on the captivatingly feminine quality of the essay.

"She: Portrait of the Essay as a Warm Body"

An essay is a thing of the imagination. If there is information in an essay, it is by-the-by, and if there is an opinion in it, you need not trust it for the long run. A genuine essay has no educational, polemical, or sociopolitical use; it is the movement of a free mind at play. Though it is written in prose, it is closer in kind to poetry than to any other form. Like a poem, a genuine essay is made out of language and character and mood and temperament and pluck and chance. And if I speak of a genuine essay, it is because fakes abound. Here the old-fashioned term poetaster may apply, if only obliquely. As the poetaster is to the poet—a lesser aspirant—so the article is to the essay: a look-alike knockoff guaranteed not to wear well. An article is gossip. An essay is reflection and insight. An article has the temporary advantage of social heat—what's hot out there right now. An essay's heat is interior. An article is timely, topical, engaged in the issues and personalities of the moment; it is likely to be stale within the month. In five years it will have acquired the quaint aura of a rotary phone. An article is Siamese-twinned to its date of birth. An essay defies its date of birth, and ours too. (A necessary caveat: some genuine essays are popularly called "articles"—but this is no more than an idle, though persistent, habit of speech. What's in a name? The ephemeral is the ephemeral. The enduring is the enduring.)

A small historical experiment. Who are the classical essayists that come at once to mind? Montaigne, obviously. Among the nineteenth-century English masters, the long row of Hazlitt, Lamb, De Quincey, Stevenson, Carlyle, Ruskin, Newman, Arnold, Harriet Martineau. Of the Americans, Emerson. It may be argued that nowadays these are read only by specialists and literature majors, and by the latter only when they are compelled to. However accurate the claim, it is irrelevant to the experiment, which has to do with beginnings and their disclosures. Here, then, are some introductory passages:

> One of the pleasantest things in the world is going a journey; but I like to go by myself. I can enjoy society in a room; but out of doors, nature is company enough for me. I am then never less alone than when alone.—William Hazlitt, "On Going a Journey"
>
> To go into solitude, a man needs to retire as much from his chamber as from society. I am not solitary whilst I read and write, though nobody is with me. But if a man would be alone, let him look at the stars.—Ralph Waldo Emerson, "Nature"
>
> I have often been asked how I first came to be a regular opium eater; and have suffered, very unjustly, in the opinion of my acquaintance, from being reputed to have brought upon myself all the sufferings which I shall have to record, by a long course of indulgence in this practice purely for the sake of creating an artificial state of pleasurable excitement. This, however, is a misrepresentation of my case.—Thomas De Quincey, "Confessions of an English Opium Eater"
>
> The human species, according to the best theory I can form of it, is composed of two distinct races, the men who borrow, and the men who lend.—Charles Lamb, "The Two Races of Men"
>
> I saw two hareems in the East; and it would be wrong to pass them over in an account of my travels; though the subject is as little agreeable as any I can have to treat. I cannot now think of the two mornings thus employed without a heaviness of heart greater than I have

ever brought away from Deaf and Dumb Schools, Lunatic Asylums, or even Prisons.—Harriet Martineau, "From Eastern Life"

> The future of poetry is immense, because in poetry, where it is worthy of its high destinies, our race, as time goes on, will find an ever and surer stay. There is not a creed which is not shaken, not an accredited dogma which is not shown to be questionable, not a received tradition which does not threaten to dissolve. . . . But for poetry the idea is everything; the rest is a world of illusion, of divine illusion.—Matthew Arnold, "The Study of Poetry"

> The changes wrought by death are in themselves so sharp and final, and so terrible and melancholy in their consequences, that the thing stands alone in man's experience, and has no parallel upon earth. It outdoes all other accidents because it is the last of them. Sometimes it leaps suddenly upon its victims, like a Thug; sometimes it lays a regular siege and creeps upon their citadel during a score of years. And when the business is done, there is a sore havoc made in other people's lives, and a pin knocked out by which many subsidiary friendships hung together.—Robert Louis Stevenson, "Aes Triplex"

> It is recorded of some people, as of Alexander the Great, that their sweat, in consequence of some rare and extraordinary constitution, emitted a sweet odor, the cause of which Plutarch and others investigated. But the nature of most bodies is the opposite, and at their best they are free from smell. Even the purest breath has nothing more excellent than to be without offensive odor, like that of very healthy children.—Michel de Montaigne, "Of Smells"

What might such a little anthology of beginnings reveal? First, that language differs from one era to the next: there are touches of archaism here, if only in punctuation and cadence. Second, that splendid minds may contradict each other (outdoors, Hazlitt never feels alone; Emerson urges the opposite). Third, that the theme of an essay can be anything under the sun, however trivial (the smell of sweat) or crushing (the thought that we must die). Fourth, that the essay is a consistently recognizable and venerable—or call it ancient—form. In English: Addison and Steele in the eighteenth century, Bacon and Browne in the seventeenth, Lyly in the sixteenth, Bede in the eighth. And what of the biblical Koheleth—Ecclesiastes—who may be the oldest essayist reflecting on one of the oldest subjects: world-weariness?

So the essay is ancient and various: but this is a commonplace. There is something else, and it is more striking yet—the essay's power. By "power" I mean precisely the capacity to do what force always does: coerce assent. Never mind that the shape and inclination of any essay is against coercion or suasion, or that the essay neither proposes nor purposes to get you to think like its author—at least not overtly. If an essay has a "motive," it is linked more to happenstance and opportunity than to the driven will. A genuine essay is not a doctrinaire tract or a propaganda effort or a broadside. Thomas Paine's "Common Sense" and Emile Zola's "J'accuse" are heroic landmark writings; but to call them essays, though they may resemble the form, is to misunderstand. The essay is not meant for the barricades; it is a stroll through someone's mazy mind. Yet this is not to say that there has never been an essayist morally intent on making an argument, however obliquely—George Orwell is a case in point. At the end of the day, the essay turns out to be a force for agreement. It co-opts agreement; it courts agreement; it seduces agreement. For the brief hour we give to it, we are sure to fall into surrender and conviction. And this will occur even if we are intrinsically roused to resistance.

To illustrate: I may not be persuaded by Emersonianism as an ideology, but Emerson—his voice, his language, his music—persuades me. When we look for superlatives, not for nothing do we speak of "commanding" or "compelling" prose. If I am a skeptical rationalist or an advanced biochemist, I may regard (or discard) the idea of the soul as no better than a puff of warm vapor. But here is Emerson on the soul: "when it breathes through [man's] intellect, it is genius; when it breathes through his will, it is virtue; when it flows through his affection, it is love." And then—well, I am in thrall, I am possessed; I believe.

The novel has its own claims on surrender. It suspends our participation in the society we ordinarily live in, so that—for the time we are reading—we forget it utterly. But the essay does not allow us to forget our usual sensations and opinions; it does something even more potent: it makes us deny them. The authority of a masterly essayist—the authority of sublime language and intimate observation—is absolute. When I am with Hazlitt, I know no greater companion than nature. When I am with Emerson, I know no greater solitude than nature.

And what is most odd about the essay's power to lure us into its lair is how it goes about this work. We feel it when a political journalist comes after us with a point of view—we feel it the way the cat is wary of the dog. A polemic is a herald, complete with feathered hat and trumpet. A tract can be a trap. Certain magazine articles have the scent of so-much-per-word. What is indisputable is that all of these are more or less in the position of a lepidopterist with his net: they mean to catch and skewer. They are focused on prey—i.e., us. The genuine essay, in contrast, never thinks of us; the genuine essay may be the most self-centered (the politer word would be subjective) arena for human thought ever devised.

Or else, though still not having you and me in mind (unless as an exemplum of common folly), it is not self-centered at all. When I was a child, I discovered in the public library a book that enchanted me then, and the idea of which has enchanted me for life. I have no recollection either of the title or of the writer—and anyhow very young readers rarely take note of authors; stories are simply and magically *there*. The characters included, as I remember them, three or four children and a delightful relation who is a storyteller, and the scheme was this: each child calls out a story-element—most often an object—and the storyteller gathers up whatever is supplied (blue boots, a river, a fairy, a pencil box) and makes out of these random, unlikely, and disparate offerings a tale both logical and surprising. An essay, it seems to me, may be similarly constructed—if so deliberate a term applies. The essayist, let us say, unexpectedly stumbles over a pair of old blue boots in a corner of the garage, and this reminds her of when she last wore them—twenty years ago, on a trip to Paris, where on the banks of the Seine she stopped to watch an old fellow sketching, with a box of colored pencils at his side. The pencil wiggling over his sheet is a grayish pink, which reflects the threads of sunset pulling westward in the sky, like the reins of a fairy cart . . . and so on. The mind meanders, slipping from one impression to another, from reality to memory to dreamscape and back again.

In the same way Montaigne, in our sample, when contemplating the unpleasantness of sweat, ends with the pure breath of children. Or Stevenson, starting out with mortality, speaks first of ambush, then of war, and finally of a displaced pin. No one is freer than the essayist—free to leap out in any direction, to hop from thought to thought, to begin with the finish and finish with the middle, or to eschew beginning and end and keep only a middle. The marvel of it is that out of this apparent causelessness, out of this scattering of idiosyncratic seeing and telling, a coherent world is made. It is coherent because, after all, an essayist must be an artist, and every artist, whatever the means, arrives at a sound and singular imaginative frame—or call it, on a minor scale, a cosmogony.

And it is into this frame, this work of art, that we tumble like tar babies, and are held fast. What holds us there? The authority of a voice, yes; the pleasure—sometimes the anxiety—of a new idea, an untried angle, a snatch of reminiscence, bliss displayed or shock conveyed. An essay can be the product of intellect or memory, lightheartedness or gloom, well-being or disgruntlement. But always there is a certain quietude, on occasion a kind of detachment. Rage and revenge, I think, belong to fiction. The essay is cooler than that. Because it so often engages in acts of memory, and despite its gladder or more antic incarnations, the essay is by and large a serene or melancholic form. It mimics that low electric hum, sometimes rising to resemble actual speech, that all human beings carry inside their heads—a vibration, garrulous if somewhat indistinct, that never leaves us while we wake. It is the hum of perpetual noticing: the configuration of someone's eyelid or tooth, the veins on a hand, a wisp of string caught on a twig, some words your fourth-grade teacher said, so long ago, about the rain, the look of an awning, a sidewalk, a bit of cheese left on a plate. All day long this inescapable hum drums on, recalling one thing and another, and pointing out this and this and this. Legend has it that Titus, emperor of Rome, went mad because of the buzzing of a gnat that made her home in his ear; and presumably the gnat, flying out into the great world and then returning to her nest, whispered what she had seen and felt and learned there. But an essayist is more resourceful than an emperor, and can be relieved of this interior noise, if only for the time it takes to record its murmurings. To seize the hum and set it down for others to hear is the essayist's genius.

It is a genius bound to leisure, and even to luxury, if luxury is measured in hours. The essay's limits can be found in its own reflective nature. Poems have been wrested from the inferno of catastrophe or war, and battlefield letters too: these are the spontaneous bursts and burnings that danger excites. But the meditative temperateness of an essay requires a desk and a chair, a musing and a mooning, a connection to a civilized surround; even when the subject itself is a wilderness of lions and tigers, mulling is the way of it. An essay is a fireside thing, not a conflagration or a safari.

This may be why, when we ask who the essayists are, it turns out—though novelists may now and then write essays—that true essayists rarely write novels. Essayists are a species of metaphysician: they are inquisitive—also analytic—about the least grain of being. Novelists go about the strenuous business of marrying and burying their people, or else they send them to sea, or to Africa, or (at the least) out of town. Essayists in their stillness ponder love and death. It is probably an illusion that men are essayists more often than women (especially since women's essays have in the past frequently assumed the form of unpublished correspondence). And here I should, I suppose, add a note about maleness and femaleness as a literary issue—what is popularly termed "gender," as if men and women were French or German tables and sofas. I *should* add such a note; it is the fashion, or, rather, the current expectation or obligation—but there is nothing to say about any of it. Essays are written by men. Essays are written by women. That is the long and the short of it. John Updike, in a genially confident discourse on maleness ("The Disposable Rocket"), takes the view—though he admits to admixture—that the "male sense of space must differ from that of the female, who has such an interesting, active, and significant inner space. The space that interests men is outer." Except, let it be observed, when men write essays: since it is only inner space—interesting, active, significant—that can conceive and nourish the contemplative essay. The "ideal female body," Updike adds, "curves around the centers of repose," and no phrase could better describe the shape of the ideal essay—yet women are no fitter as essayists than men. In promoting the felt salience of sex, Updike nevertheless drives home an essayist's point. Essays, unlike novels, emerge from the sensations of the self. Fiction creeps into foreign bodies; the novelist can inhabit not only a sex not his own, but also beetles and noses and hunger artists and nomads and beasts; while the essay is, as we say, personal.

And here is an irony. Though I have been intent on distinguishing the marrow of the essay from the marrow of fiction, I confess I have been trying all along, in a subliminal way, to speak of the essay as if it—or she—were a character in a novel or a play: moody, fickle, given on a whim to changing her clothes, or the subject; sometimes obstinate, with a mind of her own; or hazy and light; never predictable. I mean for her to be dressed—and addressed—as we would Becky Sharp, or Ophelia, or Elizabeth Bennet, or Mrs. Ramsay, or Mrs. Wilcox, or even Hester Prynne. Put it that it is pointless to say (as I have done repeatedly, disliking it every moment) "the essay," "an essay." The essay—an essay—is not an abstraction; she may have recognizable contours, but she is highly colored and individuated; she is not a type. She is too fluid, too elusive, to be a category. She may be bold, she may be diffident, she may rely on beauty, or on cleverness, on eros or exotica. Whatever her story, she is the protagonist, the secret self's personification. When we knock on her door, she opens to us, she is a presence in the doorway, she leads us from room to room; then why should we not call her "she"? She may be privately indifferent to us, but she is anything but unwelcoming. Above all, she is not a hidden principle or a thesis or a construct: she is *there*, a living voice. She takes us in.

Quarrel & Quandry: Essays, 2000

VIVIAN GORNICK (1935–) was born in the Bronx, where her parents were socialist, working-class Ukrainian immigrants, and she has remained a New Yorker all her life. She attended City College and New York University, worked for years as a staff writer at the *Village Voice*, and has taught at several universities in the New York area. Gornick sees her writing as shaped by the experience of being "twice an outsider," for she is both Jewish and a woman. She has written essays, memoirs, biography, and criticism and has contributed to the *Nation*, the *New York Times*, *Tikkun*, the *Atlantic*, and several anthologies. In the following excerpt from *The Situation and the Story: The Art of Personal Narrative*, Gornick explores the problem of persona in the essay, what she calls "the twin struggle to know not only why one is speaking but *who* is speaking." The narrator of an essay is "an unsurrogated one," for the essayist must confront "those very same defenses and embarrassments that the novelist or the poet is once removed from."

From *The Situation and the Story*

The writing we call personal narrative is written by people who, in essence, are imagining only themselves: in relation to the subject at hand. The connection is an intimate one; in fact, it is crucial. Out of the raw material of a writer's own undisguised being a narrator is fashioned whose existence on the page is integral to the tale being told. This narrator becomes a persona. Its tone of voice, its angle of vision, the rhythm of its sentences, what it selects to observe and what to ignore are chosen to serve the subject; yet at the same time the way the narrator—or the persona—sees things is, to the largest degree, the thing being seen.

To fashion a persona out of one's own undisguised self is no easy thing. A novel or a poem provides invented characters or speaking voices that act as surrogates for the writer. Into those surrogates will be poured all that the writer cannot address directly—inappropriate longings, defensive embarrassments, anti-social desires—but must address to achieve felt reality. The persona in a nonfiction narrative is an unsurrogated one. Here the writer must identify openly with those very same defenses and embarrassments that the novelist or the poet is once removed from. It's like lying down on the couch in public—and while a writer may be willing to do just that, it is a strategy that often simply doesn't work. Think of how many years on the couch it takes to speak about oneself, but without all the whining and complaining, the self-hatred and the self-justification that make the analysand a bore to all the world but the analyst. The unsurrogated narrator has the monumental task of transforming low-level self-interest into the kind of detached empathy required of a piece of writing that is to be of value to the disinterested reader.

Yet the creation of such a persona is vital in an essay or a memoir. It is the instrument of illumination. Without it there is neither subject nor story. To achieve it, the writer of memoir or essays undergoes an apprenticeship as soul-searching as any undergone by novelist or poet: the twin struggle to know not only why one is speaking but *who* is speaking.

The Situation and the Story: The Art of Personal Narrative, 2001

JOHN D'AGATA (1974–), who deplores the term "creative nonfiction" and prefers to speak of himself as devoted to the essay, in particular "the lyric essay," is a professor at the University of Iowa, where he teaches courses in the art of the essay. D'Agata also serves as associate editor of the *Seneca Review*, where in collaboration with its former editor, the poet Deborah Tall, he first outlined his idea of the lyric essay in 1997. "The lyric essay partakes of the poem in its density and shapeliness, its distillation of ideas and musicality of language. It partakes of the essay in its weight, in its overt desire to engage with facts, melding its allegiance to the actual with its passion for imaginative form." Since then, he has not only exemplified those ideas in two book-length works, *Halls of Fame* and *About a Mountain*, but also developed and illustrated them at length in two striking anthologies: *The Next American Essay*, from which the following piece is excerpted, and *The Lost Origins of the Essay*.

From "2003"

The lyric essay, as some have called the form, asks what happens when an essay begins to behave less like an essay and more like a poem. What happens when an essayist starts imagining things, making things up, filling in blank spaces, or—worse yet—leaving the blanks blank? What happens when statistics, reportage, and observation in an essay are abandoned for image, emotion, expressive transformation? In this year, as we continue to wade slowly through the start of a new century, our anxiety, either real or imagined, needles us over the crest of the rest of what's left. The afterward of postmodernism waits for us there. There are now questions being asked of facts that were never questions before. What, we ask, is a fact these days? What's a lie, for that matter? What constitutes an "essay," a "story," a "poem"? What, even, is "experience"? In the words of Wallace Stevens, we have to find what will suffice. For years writers have been responding to this slippage of facts in a variety of ways—from the fragmentary forms of LANGUAGE poetry that try to mimic this loss, to the narrative-driven attempts by novelists and memorists [*sic*] to smooth over the gaps. But the lyric essay takes another approach. The lyric essay inherits from the principal strands of nonfiction the makings of its own hybrid version of the form. It takes the subjectivity of the personal essay and the objectivity of the public essay, and conflates them into a literary form that relies on both art and fact, on imagination and observation, rumination and argumentation, human faith and human perception. What the lyric essay inherits from the public essay is a fact-hungry pursuit of solutions to problems, while from the personal essay what it takes is a wide-eyed dallying in the heat of predicaments. The result of this ironic parentage is that lyric essays seek answers, yet seldom seem to find them. They may arise out of a public essay that never manages to prove its case, or may emerge from the stalk of a personal essay to sprout out and meet "the other." They may start out as travelogues that forget where they are, or begin as prose poems that refuse quick conclusions. They may originate as lines that resist being broken, or full-bodied paragraphs that start slimming down. They are unconventional essays, hybrids that perch on the fence between the willed and the felt. Facts, in these essays, are not clear-cut things. What is a lyric essay? It's an oxymoron: an essay that's also a lyric; a kind of logic that wants to sing; an argument that has no chance of proving anything.

The Next American Essay, 2003

PAUL GRAHAM (1964–) is an American computer programmer, entrepreneur, painter, venture capitalist, and essayist. After earning a PhD in computer science from Harvard, he studied painting for five years. Then, in collaboration with a Harvard friend, the notorious hacker Robert Morris, he developed an e-commerce application called Viaweb and sold it to Yahoo! in 1998 for $49 million. Since then, Graham has pioneered the field of spam filtering, developed the venture capital firm Y Combinator, and begun writing essays, which he posts on his Web site: http://www.paulgraham.com/. In the excerpt from "The Age of the Essay" that follows, Graham discusses in clear, familiar language why he writes essays. He emphasizes their origins in the skepticism and tentativeness of the scientific method. "An essay," writes Graham, "is something you write to try to figure something out." An essay prompts a conversation, meanders like a river, and, at its best, takes "off in an unexpected but interesting direction."

From "The Age of the Essay"

Trying

To understand what a real essay is, we have to reach back into history again, though this time not so far. To Michel de Montaigne, who in 1580 published a book of what he called "essais." He was doing something quite different from what lawyers do, and the difference is embodied in the name. *Essayer* is the French verb meaning "to try" and an *essai* is an attempt. An essay is something you write to try to figure something out.

Figure out what? You don't know yet. And so you can't begin with a thesis, because you don't have one, and may never have one. An essay doesn't begin with a statement, but with a question. In a real essay, you don't take a position and defend it. You notice a door that's ajar, and you open it and walk in to see what's inside.

If all you want to do is figure things out, why do you need to write anything, though? Why not just sit and think? Well, there precisely is Montaigne's great discovery. Expressing ideas helps to form them. Indeed, helps is far too weak a word. Most of what ends up in my essays I only thought of when I sat down to write them. That's why I write them.

In the things you write in school you are, in theory, merely explaining yourself to the reader. In a real essay you're writing for yourself. You're thinking out loud. But not quite. Just as inviting people over forces you to clean up your apartment, writing something that other people will read forces you to think well. So it does matter to have an audience. The things I've written just for myself are no good. They tend to peter out. When I run into difficulties, I find I conclude with a few vague questions and then drift off to get a cup of tea.

Many published essays peter out in the same way. Particularly the sort written by the staff writers of newsmagazines. Outside writers tend to supply editorials of the defend-a-position variety, which make a beeline toward a rousing (and foreordained) conclusion. But the staff writers feel obliged to write something "balanced." Since they're writing for a popular magazine, they start with the most radioactively controversial questions, from which—because they're writing for a popular magazine—they then proceed to recoil in terror. Abortion, for or against? This group says one thing. That group says another. One thing is certain: the question is a complex one. (But don't get mad at us. We didn't draw any conclusions.)

The River

Questions aren't enough. An essay has to come up with answers. They don't always, of course. Sometimes you start with a promising question and get nowhere. But those you don't publish. Those are like experiments that get inconclusive results. An essay you publish ought to tell the reader something he didn't already know.

But *what* you tell him doesn't matter, so long as it's interesting. I'm sometimes accused of meandering. In defend-a-position writing that would be a flaw. There you're not concerned with truth. You already know where you're going, and you want to go straight there, blustering through obstacles, and hand-waving your way across swampy ground. But that's not what you're trying to do in an essay. An essay is supposed to be a search for truth. It would be suspicious if it didn't meander.

The Meander (aka Menderes) is a river in Turkey. As you might expect, it winds all over the place. But it doesn't do this out of frivolity. The path it has discovered is the most economical route to the sea.[1]

The river's algorithm is simple. At each step, flow down. For the essayist this translates to: flow interesting. Of all the places to go next, choose the most interesting. One can't have quite as little foresight as a river. I always know generally what I want to write about. But not the specific conclusions I want to reach; from paragraph to paragraph I let the ideas take their course.

This doesn't always work. Sometimes, like a river, one runs up against a wall. Then I do the same thing the river does: backtrack. At one point in this essay I found that after following a certain thread I ran out of ideas. I had to go back seven paragraphs and start over in another direction.

Fundamentally an essay is a train of thought—but a cleaned-up train of thought, as dialogue is cleaned-up conversation. Real thought, like real conversation, is full of false starts. It would be exhausting to read. You need to cut and fill to emphasize the central thread, like an illustrator inking over a pencil drawing. But don't change so much that you lose the spontaneity of the original.

Err on the side of the river. An essay is not a reference work. It's not something you read looking for a specific answer, and feel cheated if you don't find it. I'd much rather read an essay that went off in an unexpected but interesting direction than one that plodded dutifully along a prescribed course.

1. Trevor Blackwell points out that this isn't strictly true, because the outside edges of curves erode faster. [Graham's note]

First published on-line, September 2004

ANDER MONSON (1975–), an experimental writer working in multiple genres and media, teaches creative writing at the University of Arizona. He is not only a fiction writer (*Other Electricities*), poet (*Vacationland* and *The Available World*), and essayist (*Neck Deep and Other Predicaments* and *Vanishing Point*), but also an editor and designer of books, journals, and Web sites, always pushing the conventional boundaries of whatever form is at hand. "Most stuff I do comes out of this basic desire to play, to hack, to open things up, whether it's language or new technologies, or the ways in which they intersect." Monson's desire to open things up is strikingly on display in the essays that compose his recent collection *Vanishing Point* (2010). These essays not only exist in the form of a printed text but also contain dagger-like symbols referring the reader to additional and expanded thoughts of Monson that can be found on his Web site: http://otherelectricities.com, which contains the following excerpt on the essay as an embodiment of mind in action.

From "The Essay as Hack"

The essay tries hard to solidify the motions of thought. It—more than most other forms of writing—is not as beholden to tradition, restriction. Sure, it's, like, old. Totally AARP. We can date it back to Montaigne, or, trying harder, Seneca. I have to admit that Montaigne bores me. Seneca, too, really, and most of what we call the moral essayists, publicly thinking about individual behavior as part of a society, offering suggestions for better living, and so on. Maybe it's my age. Maybe it's that I want to sex it up.

The essay does not rely on narrative arc (though it can). It does not rely on lyric motion (though it can). It can potentially incorporate anything, draw from anything, in search of the range of motion of human thought that it attempts to present.

It is a sticky ball. It is the video game *Katamari Damacy.* It accommodates. Like the brain.

Each essay we read is as close as we can get to another mind. It is a simulation of the mind working its way through a problem. This is not to suggest that every essay is good, revelatory, successful, fruitful, interesting. But stepping into an essay is stepping into the writer's mind. We are thrown into the labyrinth, a huge stone rolling behind us. It is a straight shot of the brain in all its immediacy, its variety, strands of half-remembered text, partly-thought-through ideas, images below the surface of memory. We are thrown into *process*: of thinking, which is like an algorithm, a machine for replicating or simulating thought:

So, a quote to add to our ball, a line to add to our algorithm, one strand of thinking: " . . . the essay is decried as a hybrid; that it is lacking a convincing tradition; that its strenuous requirements have only rarely been met: all this has been often remarked upon and censured." The quote is from Theodor Adorno's essay, "The Essay as Form."

Here we find ourselves. We find ourselves plucked out of our lives and are transplanted in the middle of a mind. A plot, really, strung together of thought. Of a linguistic situation. An argument. Given that the essay lacks tradition, what then? And later:

"Luck and play are essential to the essay. It does not begin with Adam and Eve but with what it wants to discuss; it says what is at issue and stops where it feels itself complete—not where nothing is left to say."

Adorno tries to describe what the essay does. It thinks. It plays. It discusses. It cuffs at ideas as if they were a ball. It is discursive. It cures nothing. It might occasionally curse. Naturally it is subjective, but it owns that subjectivity and strives to comprehend and transcend it. It has its stated subject (in Adorno's case, trying to work out the form of the essay in the historical situation he finds it in), but all essays' implied subjects are the essay itself, the mind of the writer, the I in the process of sifting and perceiving, even if the I is itself only implied, never apparent, hidden underneath the shroud of formal argument. *Who argues,* we ask. A pause. Silence. Awkward moment. Then: *I do,* it responds weakly.

The essay claims its own limits and works within them: as it works, so does the mind. As the argument shifts, cuts back, or redoubles, uncovering something the essay did not know it knew (for that is every essay's purpose, to wend, explore, to sidetrack as it must), so goes the processes of the mind. It freezes thought for us. Of course this fixity is a lie: one line of thought extends and becomes yesterday, diaspora. The second time through an essay in revision we are not the same combination of brain and body; the network has shifted and what we thought we thought is no longer what we think. And by thinking we erase or redouble thought, confirming or denying it. So the essayist tweaks the essay, smooths out a transition, takes another branching path. And that version of thought is fixed and left, a pathway in the brain, graphite trace on the page. And on and on until the essayist gets up and gives it up. The essay should change on every public reading or recitation as something new occurs. But it's impossible in art. Finally we have to let it go and hope it will show the reader something new.

Reading essays gets us closer to others' thinking, or at least the most recent version. Writing them gets us closer to our own. It at least allows us to interrupt the constant motion of our minds to put something down and consider it, think about it from a year removed, or from space on the shuttle, or in a different space, overlooking another view from a new hotel in a different city.

And what about the lyric essay? Have we forgotten it? It proceeds in chunks, disconnected fragments. It pauses, tacks around the subject or dead-end through white space.

In some ways the lyric essay is the most essay sort of essay.

Our lyric variety of the essay is a polyglot. It is pansexual. If the essay is a ball, the lyric essay is a super sticky power ball. But calling the essay lyric doesn't add all that much. It specifies, I guess, that this essay is a lyric one. It closes down some of the dimensions through which essay might move.

Essay itself is already polymorphic. It is oversexed in its potential union with anything: polemic, story, treatise, argument, fact, fiction, lyric.

But lyric has freshened up the essay world, it seems, so we should be grateful.

First published on-line, 2008

JOHN BRESLAND (1970–) works in radio, video, and print. His radio essays have aired on public radio, and his print essays have appeared in magazines such as the *North American Review, Hotel Amerika*, and *Minnesota Monthly*. His video pieces are available online at *Ninth Letter, Blackbird*, and *Requited*, as well as at his own Web site: http://bresland.com. A graduate of the University of Iowa's Creative Nonfiction Program, Bresland currently teaches at Northwestern University. An earlier version of Bresland's piece on the video essay serves as the introduction to an inaugural suite of video essays he edited for *Blackbird*. In it, Bresland traces the lineage of the video essay from Montaigne, author of the term *essai*, to Chris Marker, seminal filmmaker of the French New Wave, to Phillip Lopate, who heralded a "centaur," the essay-film, before the Internet made the distribution of such work viable. Bresland celebrates the new opportunities for the essay offered by the now-ubiquitous medium that is video.

"On the Origin of the Video Essay"

Beginning with this Spring 2010 edition, *Blackbird* is featuring a new form of creative nonfiction we've chosen to call the video essay. In its intent the video essay is no different from its print counterpart, which for thousands of years has been a means for writers to confront hard questions on the page. The essayist pushes toward some insight or some truth. That insight, that truth, tends to be hard won, if at all, for the essay tends to ask more than it answers. That asking—whether inscribed in ancient mud, printed on paper, or streamed thirty frames per second—is central to the essay, is the essay.

So it's been, since shortly after Christ, when a Delphic priest named Plutarch wondered which came first, the chicken or the egg. A thousand years later in Japan, Sei Shōnagon compiled a list in her *Pillow Book* of "Hateful Things" and "Things That Give a Hot Feeling." These early works of nonfiction were meditations, lists, biographies, diary entries, advice. But it took an amateur in the time of Shakespeare—a French civil servant in midlife crisis who quit his job to become a writer—to attach a name to the act of exploring the limits of what we know. He called these works *Essais*. Attempts. Trials.

Michel de Montaigne drew thematic inspiration from Plutarch, but his meditations could be associative, rambling, prickly, polyvalent. Like Shōnagon's. Which isn't to say a personal assistant to the Japanese empress during the Heian dynasty shaped the work of Montaigne. She didn't, so far as we know. But Shōnagon's essay, "Things That Quicken the Heart," is the central, soulful motif of Chris Marker's *Sans Soleil* (1982), one of the first great film essays of our time. In *Sans Soleil* Marker channels his meditation on truth and memory through Sandor Krasna, an offscreen personage whose letters (in the English-language version) are voiced by Canadian actress Alexandra Stewart. Despite the fictional scrim, *Sans Soleil* remains solidly an essay, a work of nonfiction that casts multiple lines of inquiry—among them, how images rewrite memory—and renders them as poetic evocations of lived experience. Watching *Sans Soleil*, you can almost hear Chris Marker whisper, *Here is the problem of being alive right now.*

I suspect the heart-quickening now of sound and image is what drew the otherwise reclusive Marker to film. And by reclusive I don't mean he was a poet and novelist with a promising literary career ahead of him—though he was, too, that kind of recluse, a writer, before he was anything else. Today, on the eve of his 90th birthday, Marker is still making films, yet less than a dozen photographs of the man exist. He avoids media, rarely gives interviews. When Marker appears in Agnes Varda's video essay *The Beaches of Agnes* (2008), he does so in the guise of a talking cat. Filmmakers who let their work speak for itself, who hold their audience in high esteem, do exist. But they're rare. And how like an essayist to refuse to explain his work. How like a poet to grant his audience a lasting measure of imaginative space.

Chris Marker grew up in Neuilly, on the posh rim of the Bois de Boulogne outside Paris. Probably he read Montaigne as a boy—not from any precocity we know of, but rather because French kids read their Montaigne, just as they memorize the poems of Hugo and La Fontaine. After World War II, in which he fought for the resistance, he published a collection of poetry and, in 1949, his first novel. Then, like so many other writers and critics seduced by the French New Wave—Godard, Rohmer, Truffaut—Marker turned to celluloid, and so, for that matter, did the rest of the world.

Alongside Jean Cayrol, Marker wrote uncredited for Alain Resnais's *Night and Fog* (1955), a film essay about the Holocaust, a work that welds haunting visuals (and a color scheme Spielberg later cribbed for *Schindler's List*) to a refreshingly human voiceover. In a brilliant essay he wrote for *Threepenny Review*, Phillip Lopate describes that voiceover as *worldly, tired, weighted down with the need to make fresh those horrors that had so quickly turned stale. It was a self-interrogatory voice, like a true essayist's, dubious, ironical, wheeling and searching for the heart of its subject matter.* That voice, I suspect, is Marker's. And it's the lone voice, decidedly unobjective, that resides at the heart of the visual essay. Or film essay. Or video essay.

What do we name it, anyway—this thing, this half-essay, half-film?

Lopate calls this hybrid literary form a centaur. *I have an urge to see these two interests combined,* he writes, *through the works of filmmakers who commit essays on celluloid.* The essay-film, as he terms it, barely exists as a cinematic genre. And this confounds Lopate. He puzzles over the rarity of personal films that track a person's thoughts as she works through some mental knot. Why, he asks, aren't there more of these things?

Lopate cites "promiscuity of the image" as one reason for the rarity of essay-films—the tendency of the motion picture, owing to its density of information, to defy clear expression of a filmmaker's thoughts. And he gestures toward the belief, widely held in commercial film circles, that the screen resists language in higher densities. Even if an artist were to beat the odds, the thinking goes, even if she were to combine powerful visuals with an artful text and weave it all together with economy and grace, who'd pay twelve bucks at the cinema to see an essay?

That the image resists the precision of language is indeed a complication for the essayist. Much in the way, I would argue, that pianos complicate singing. That is to say another skill is called for but the payoff can be sublime. Images and sound are visceral stimuli that even animal sensoria can tap into. When my mother's Italian Greyhound sees another dog on TV, he lunges for it, tries to maul the Samsung. And when a fish takes its last dying gasp on a sunlit pier in Ross McElwee's *Time Indefinite* (1993), I'm consumed with sadness over our capacity for cruelty. Looking that creature in the eye while a young boy stomps on it, I find myself wanting to save the fish and stomp the boy. A canny essayist, McElwee knows that a literary text—the lone voice confronting hard questions—is only the beginning. Images and sound, those engines of emotion, have their own story to tell. Promiscuity of the image isn't a weakness of the essay-film. It's a feature. A volatile one, sure. And it's changing the way we write, changing our conception of what writing means.

Film is visual; the essay is not. Film is collaborative; the essay is not. Film requires big money; the essay costs little and makes less. Essays and film, Lopate notes, are two different animals, and I agree with him on one condition: that it's 1991. That's when Lopate wrote "In Search of the Centaur" for *Threepenny*. The internet was just a baby then, nursed by dweebs. Then, financial considerations reigned. If you wanted your film made, you first needed grants, financing, distributors. Today, to make a small-scale personal film, you can shoot the thing on an inexpensive digital camera and upload it to any number of free video sharing sites. In '91 you had to hustle for eyeballs. Now, of course, the artist still hustles (post a video in the middle of a digital forest, there's no guarantee it'll make a sound) but those once formidable barriers to entry—obtaining the gear to shoot your film, and getting it in position to be seen—have been leveled by digital technology. As more literary magazines migrate online, editors are discovering that the old genre categories—fiction, nonfiction, poetry—which made perfect sense on the page, no longer do. The Internet is a conveyance for images and sound as well as text, and print media is scrambling to catch up.

Today artists have access to video editing tools that ship free on computers. A generation ago, such capability didn't exist at any price. Now all it takes for a young artist to produce a documentary is an out-of-the-box Mac, a camera, and the will to see an idea through to its resolution. The act of writing has always been a personal pursuit, a concentrated form of thought. And now filmmaking, too, shares that meditative space. The tools are handheld, affordable, no less accessible than a Smith-Corona. You can shoot and edit video, compelling video, on a cell phone.

Brave new world, right? But what do we call it?

We're calling it the video essay. Because most of us experience the motion picture as video, not film. Film is analog. Film requires a shutter to convey motion. That shutter, Chris Marker told *Libération* in 2003, is what distinguishes film from video: *Out of the two hours you spend in a movie theater, you spend one of them in the dark. It's this nocturnal portion that stays with us, that fixes our memory of a film in a different way than the same film seen on television or on a monitor.* Video, on the other hand, from the way it's acquired (on small, light digital cameras with startling image quality) to the way it's consumed (on mobile devices, on planes, as shared links crossing the ether) is now being carried everywhere, the way books and magazines once were. And there's a certain texture to video, a telltale combination of compression artifacts, blown-out whites and noisy blacks that isn't pretty. But it's not ugly, either. It's real. (It may also be, as Don DeLillo once described it, realer than real.) The video essay. *Video* in the Greek sense, from the verb *vidēre*—to see. *Essay* in the Greek sense, meaning to ask. In the Japanese sense, to quicken the heart. In the French sense, to try. I can think of no better way to take on the problems of being alive right now than to write this way, with a pen in one hand and a lens in the other.

First published in *Blackbird* 9.1 (Spring 2010); revised for this collection

JEFF PORTER (1951–) is a specialist in contemporary literature and culture, radio and film studies, and literary nonfiction. A professor at the University of Iowa, he teaches classes on radio and video essays, new media, literary journalism, history of the essay, and postmodernism. His film and radio work includes *The Men Who Dance the Giglio, Writing on Rock: N. Scott Momaday, Dublin USA, Herby Sings the Blues*, and *Mother of Invention* (an experimental sound collage). He is the author of *Oppenheimer Is Watching Me* (University of Iowa Press, 2007), a personalized cultural history of the Cold War. His essays have appeared in *Antioch Review, Isotope, Northwest Review, Shenandoah, Missouri Review, Hotel Amerika, Wilson Quarterly, Contemporary Literature, Blackbird*, and other journals. His current book project focuses on the history and practice of radiophonic literature. He is coeditor of *Understanding the Essay*, forthcoming from Broadview Press. Porter's detailed interest in the evolution of American radio art is reflected in the following piece on the radio essay.

"Essay on the Radio Essay"

A quirky voice, some music, a few sounds, a spoken text. That's the improbable formula for what's often understood as a new genre, the radio essay. Since the 1990s, the airwaves have been filled with fresh voices—cranky humorists, charming eccentrics, wry critics—that have opened up a space on radio for creative nonfiction. The radio essay got a huge boost in 1995 when, with his debut as host of *This American Life*, Ira Glass turned the genre into a national art form and created what at the time seemed to be the coolest thing ever to happen to words on the radio.

Putting one's finger on an exact point of origin for the radio essay is difficult, but it would be wrong to think that *This American Life* invented the form. Original as Glass's show may have seemed, the radio essay harks back to a much older tradition that grew out of broadcast radio's thriving partnership with literary culture from 1936 to 1950. It was a time when radio freely experimented with narrative formats, when its narrators and commentators had so much appeal that networks were encouraged to push the expressive power of the human voice in bold and imaginative ways. Far from being an innovation of the late twentieth century, the modern radio essay is in fact a survivor of an older aural culture that was significantly more daring—and literary—than most listeners of public radio might suspect.

It is impossible to grasp this culture without understanding something of radio's remarkable past. Radio came of age during the Depression and soon dominated other media, including newspapers. While it had relied on music and discussion shows early on, by the mid-1930s radio embraced short fiction and then drama, taking its lead from pulp magazines and other serial genres that drove pop culture. Before the advent of television, the evening ritual of gathering around the big wooden radio in the living room was a national custom, with families tuning into *The Jack Benny Show*, *Edgar Bergen and Charlie McCarthy*, *Burns and Allen*, *You Bet Your Life* with Groucho Marx, and *The Firestone Hour*. Radio was at the heart of popular culture and its appetite for compelling characters and diverting stories could not be satisfied.

Perhaps the most interesting development during the short span of radio's boom years was the emergence of radio drama. If much of the narrative programming serialized during radio's heyday—a wild potpourri of comedy, mystery, and melodrama—was drawn from pulp fiction, radio drama was a different life form. It flirted with greatness, with high literary art, and for a moment achieved it. In part, this was the result of bold programming at CBS with the creation of the experimental *Columbia Workshop*. But it was also an effect of World War II and the uncommon sense of common purpose the war provoked, something that proved a catalyst for serious writers such as Archibald MacLeish, Norman Corwin, and Arch Oboler.

Drama was such a dominant form during radio's peak years that even the news included theatrical reenactments of world events. Part journalism, part soap opera, the *March of Time*, for instance, featured over-the-top reenactments of historical events (such as the Spanish Civil War) that drew on professional actors, sound effects, and a full studio orchestra. There was Agnes Moorehead impersonating Eleanor Roosevelt, Art Carney playing Franklin Roosevelt, Dwight Weist imitating Adolf Hitler. Like other newsreels of the day, the show was built around a commanding announcer, often called the "voice of time," who guided listeners through a cycle of events that had already played out.

Genre-blurring, which grew out of broadcast radio's thriving partnership with literary culture, seemed to have been the rule rather than the exception. Documentary devices and essaylike tropes appeared where you least expected them. MacLeish's stylized radio plays were powered by studio announcers, on-location commentators, and reporters who evoke the presence of radio personalities such as H. V. Kaltenborn and Edward R. Murrow. Orson Welles's *The War of the Worlds* would have been a stunning flop rather than a shocking hoax without the help of radio vérité.

The radio genius who profited the most from genre-mixing was Norman Corwin. On May 8, 1945, 60 million Americans (nearly half of all the nation) tuned in to hear *On a Note of Triumph*, Norman Corwin's masterpiece marking the beginning of the end of World War II. The play opens with Bernard Hermann's brassy score and the brusque words of the narrator, played by Martin Gabel—

> So they've given up?
> They're finally done in, and the rat is dead in an alley back of the Wilhelmstrasse.
> Take a bow, GI,
> Take a bow, little guy.
> The superman of tomorrow lies at the feet of you common men of this afternoon.
> This is It, kid, this is The Day, all the way from Newburyport to Vladivostock.

A landmark in radio, the hour-long program saluted America's GIs in high colloquial style and went on to raise several questions concerning the larger meaning of victory. As expressed by the Everyman character of the GI, these questions (*who did we beat, how much did it cost, what have we learned, what do we know now, what do we do now, is it going to happen again?*) are delivered in an earnest, humble voice that contrasts markedly with the booming accents of the narrator. The play is memorable for such contrasts and mood swings. *On a Note of Triumph* progressed by sudden turns that transformed the exhilaration of victory into something more emotionally fraught and intellectually challenging. Corwin did not allow the listener the luxury of forgetting, in the joy of the moment, the human cost of war or the reluctance of Americans to get involved in the first place. In addition to the narration, other voices are introduced via remote pickup from around the nation and abroad and from miniature dramatizations, including interviews with fictional Nazis, a glimpse of the mother whose son died in the war, and an impersonation of Haile Selassie.

Corwin's play may sound like a piece of American propaganda, indulging in Nazi baiting and flag waving, but its mosaic form deepens the commemorative work it undertakes. A mix of newsreel, commentary, narration, drama, and poetry, *On a Note of Triumph* conjures up the entire history of radio in its broad effort to imagine the enormity of a war the likes of which no one had seen before. The play ends not with cheers and confetti but with a secular prayer ("Lord God of Trajectory and blast whose terrible sword has laid open the serpent so it withers in the sun for the just to see, sheathe now the swift avenging blade with the names of nations writ on it, and assist in the preparation of the ploughshare"), a burst of neobiblical prose reminiscent of the heightened writings of James Agee and Pare Lorentz.

What held all of this together was not only the vernacular lyricism of Corwin's script but also the heart-stirring zeal of Martin Gabel's remarkable narration. The voice of the narrator, rising and falling from panoramic heights to close-up intimacy, is the strong force that contains and unifies all the disparate parts of the play. It was an "unflinching voice," as Philip Roth remembers it in his novel *I Married a Communist*, the voice of "common man's collective conscience," an image of the national character inscribed in sound (40).

Where did this voice come from? Gabel's narrator wasn't created from scratch but evolved from the tradition of the radio commentator. Before the outbreak of political tension in Europe, network radio employed only a handful of commentators such as Boake Carter, but afterward hundreds of new voices were heard around the country in this role. Along with Kaltenborn came Gram Swing, Dorothy Thompson, and Lowell Thomas. And of course there were Murrow and his team. Few commentators had formal backgrounds in journalism, but many shared the same literary inclinations as essayists and columnists such as George Orwell and H. L. Mencken.

The appeal of the commentator was surely a sign of radio's rising star. By the late 1930s, radio was preferred by a wide margin to newspapers and thought to be more credible and more personal. The voice seemed to be what mattered for most listeners, as if it held the promise of authenticity.

The commentator could be trusted. His spoken words not only bore witness to history but signaled an affirmation in the face of fear and dread.

The radio commentator, as one might expect, did not survive the arrival of television or radio's own dwindling resources in the 1950s. If not for National Public Radio, the radio commentator would now be all but forgotten, an obscure footnote in the history of the wireless. NPR brought him back to life during its innovative first decade in the 1970s, though in a very different guise. Telling a good story should have little to do with varnishing your vowels or disciplining your diphthongs, NPR thought. Nobody, after all, really wants to sound like Ted Baxter, the infamously pompous newsman on *The Mary Tyler Moore Show*. An unproven entity itself, NPR had the good sense back then to develop the appeal of outliers.

It was in the spirit of outreach that NPR's *All Things Considered* went searching for voices with regional or foreign inflections, voices that, like that of Susan Stamberg (famous for her New York accent and giggle), could break through the sound barrier. There were Andrei Codrescu, who began his weekly commentaries in 1983, a foreign-born poet as renowned for his thick Romanian accent as for his ironic view of American culture; Baxter Black, the "Cowboy Poet" and humorist from Las Cruces, New Mexico, master of the southwestern drawl and homespun essays on cow bloat, barbed wire, manure, and the daily ups and downs of ordinary folks in close proximity to large, messy animals; Bailey White, from rural Georgia, who told wry tales about eccentric characters and provided vivid descriptions of small-town southern life, including her oddball mother's recipe for road kill; and Daniel Pinkwater, from Hoboken, New Jersey, a writer of children's books turned humorist, on being fat or weird. These were not detached broadcast voices, orotund and transcendent, but fully embodied voices, incarnated in a talking-self that turned its own physicality into an expressive force that was inseparable from the writing. So it is with Sarah Vowell, who sounds like a disaffected teenager scheming revenge from the basement of a library; or with David Sedaris, the man-boy whose self-ironic hilarity plumbs the joyful absurdities of his dysfunctional family; or with David Rakoff, whose sardonic, world-weary voice is as wry as the snarkiest of bloggers.

Even though the immensely popular Sedaris speaks to a younger generation than Codrescu or White (who are popular with Boomers), he is cut from the same cloth. For the most part, the success of NPR's commentators depended on the charm of their radio personae, on-air personalities that listeners grew fond of, even identified with, in the same way an earlier generation bonded with Jack Benny and H. V. Kaltenborn, not to mention the ventriloquized Charlie McCarthy. It is little wonder that Garrison Keillor's *A Prairie Home Companion* has succeeded for so long with legions of listeners (thirty-five years and running). The radiophonic personality of Keillor, America's resonant raconteur, not only sells a lot of coffee mugs but keeps alive the idea of character-based radio at a time when NPR has abandoned its interest in voice as an expressive medium.

As cultural programming lost ground to hard news coverage, NPR's short radio essays eventually began to seem irrelevant, a postscript to an aural culture that no longer existed. Throughout the 1990s, NPR moved steadily away from its commitment to sound as an evocative medium, and its dedication to hard news narrowly defined what made a good story. Often this boiled down to the sheer authority of the voice behind the news—that middle-aged, aloof, and highly educated (if somewhat self-satisfied) anchoresque sound anyone familiar with the network knows so well.

The radio essay acquired a life of its own in the mid-1990s, when Glass saw beyond the littleness of NPR's "commentaries" and gave the radio essay its own sixty-minute venue. No more three-minute stories about grandma's shoofly pie recipe salvaged from the ruination of rural farm life. With *This American Life*, Glass almost single-handedly rescued a serious kind of radiophonic literature.

Fans of *This American Life* know its format well. A fairly typical episode, "Sissies" described effeminate guys and the troubles they face—a variation on the metrosexual theme popular at the time. It consisted of five different voices, counting the hosts, and included Nancy Updike on the downfall of a family made up of sissies, John Connors on how to avoid behaving like a sissy, Dave Awl on avoiding a beating, and Dan Savage on the disdain even gay men have for sissies. Segues between the stories are helped out by music from Linda Ronstadt, Emmylou Harris, Barbra Streisand, and the Aluminum Group. The four-act format was a throwback to an older genre, the splendid tradition of drama on old-time radio (it was originally called *Your American Playhouse*), when literature, sound, voice, and music all came together in an acoustic outburst of radiophonic pop culture. Ira Glass no doubt had in mind a time when radio was more hospitable to literature and art.

Today, *This American Life* seems vulnerable to the same kind of complaints raised against NPR several years ago when critics grumbled about its lack of innovation, which is of course ironic but perhaps inevitable. Is the show, like *All Things Considered* before it, becoming monotonous, with the stories and voices all beginning to sound alike? As the *Onion* suggested in a recent send up of TAL, the show has run its course: "There is not a single existential crisis or self-congratulatory epiphany that has been or could be experienced by a left-leaning agnostic that [has not been] exhaustively documented and grouped by theme."

Where do we go from here? It is not clear that public radio, with the exception of *Radiolab* and *Studio 360*, is taking advantage of emerging technologies or listening to the mood of the times. New forms of radical editing, layering, montage, depth of field, and sound modeling could and should support an aural culture at least as interesting and demanding as that of old-time radio. Add to this recent experiments in the essay and a new generation of edgy writers, and you have to wonder how public radio could become so tone-deaf. Perhaps Boomers are content with the staid voice of NPR, but others are craving something more interesting and complicated.

When oral historian John Lomax recorded the twelve-string guitar player named Huddie Ledbetter, later known as Lead Belly, at the Louisiana State Penitentiary in 1933, he had to haul a 350-pound acetate disk recorder out of the trunk of his Ford sedan. In searing heat. Of course, things have changed radically since then. Elvis is dead, and 3M (the largest maker of analogue audio tape) shut down its facility in 1996. Everyone knows to what extent digital technology has revolutionized the making of media. Affordable, pocket-size recording gadgets have as much fidelity, if not more, than professional audio gear from the days of bulky and expensive recorders. And then there is computerized editing, which is all about cutting and pasting and laying down tracks, something anyone with a laptop probably learned how to do at the age of four. Anyone who has fiddled with GarageBand knows that making sound is significantly cheaper and easier than at any time in the past. With a small investment, there is nothing preventing you from becoming the next Antonin Artaud or at least the next Ira Glass. But writing with sound requires finesse. You will need a good ear to know when the radiophonic parts of your essay (voice, sound, music, ambience) are in tune, when its meaning is more than the sum of its tracks, and this may take greater knowledge of radio's literary and artistic past. A radio essay can be more than a mix of alternative music, a quirky story, and a deadpan voice.

The importance of the *aurality* of language should never be taken for granted. Unless on the poetry slam circuit or rehearsing Shakespearean tragedy, we do not usually think of our voices in the literal sense when writing. We have been effectively schooled in sophisticated ways to reduce the idea of voice to its message, to the elaborate process of signification through which we create form and content. The idea of voice thus gets lost in notions of textuality, and when this happens we forget that the voice is a medium in its own right.

The musicality of the vocal: words, sound, voice, aurality. These are things that reach across time, across technologies. As the poet Tristan Tzara wrote, "thought is made in the mouth." Radio essays deal with the uniqueness of sounds, and that uniqueness is grounded in the human voice. Because we fetishize the printed word in all of its glorious silence, privileging the phonic element in writing is a radical thing to do. Mixed with music and sound, the voice becomes an excess that wakens in our minds the forgotten listener in all of us, that part of aural imagination capable of finding meaning beyond the code of language—in pure sound, in music.

Written for this collection, 2011

Bibliography

COMPILED BY NED STUCKEY-FRENCH

Sixteenth and Seventeenth Centuries

Bacon, Francis. *The Advancement of Learning.* Oxford: Oxford English Texts, 1974.

———. "Dedication." *The Essays.* 1597. Ed. John Pitcher. London: Penguin, 1985. 238–39.

———. "Dedication." [Not published.] *The Essays.* 1612. Ed. John Pitcher. London: Penguin, 1985. 239.

———. "Dedication." *The Essays.* 1625. Ed. John Pitcher. London: Penguin, 1985. 57–58.

Boyle, Robert. "Proëmial Essay." *Certain Physiological Essays, written at distant times and on several occasions.* London: Henry Herringman, 1661.

Cornwallis, William. "Of Censuring," "Of Vanities," and "Of Essays and Books." *Essayes by Sir William Cornwallis, the Younger.* 1600–1601. Ed. Don Cameron Allen. Baltimore: Johns Hopkins UP, 1946.

Culpeper, Thomas, the Younger. "Of Essays." *Moral Discourses and Essays upon several subjects.* London: TC, 1655.

as [———?] "A Person of Honour." "Of Essays." *Essays or Moral Discourses on Several Subjects.* London: H. Burges for Thomas Proudlove, 1671.

as [———?] "T. C." "Prooemium." *Moral Discourses and Essayes upon Severall Select Subjects.* London: S. G. for Charles Adams, 1655.

Feltham, Owen. "To the Readers." *Resolves: A Duple Century.* 1628. London: Henry Seile, 1636.

Glanville, Joseph. "An Address to the Royal Society." *Scepsis Scientifica: or Confessed Ignorance, the way to Science; In an Essay of the Vanity of Dogmatizing, and Confident Opinion.* London: Henry Eversden, 1665.

———. "The Preface." *Essays on Several Important Subjects in Philosophy and Religion.* London: J. D. for John Baker and Henry Mortlock, 1676.

Hall, John. "To the Reverend Mr. John Arrowsmith, Master of St. John's Colledge in Cambridge" [dedication] and "Of Dissimulation." *Hora Vicavae, or, Essays. Some Occasional Considerations.* London: J. Rothwell, 1646.

Jonson, Ben. "Ingeniorum Discrimina." *Timber: or Discoveries Made Upon Men and Matters: As They have Flow'd Out of His Daily Reading; or Had Their Refluxe to His Peculiar Notion of the Times.* London: Richard Meighen, 1641.

Montaigne, Michel de. *The Complete Essays of Montaigne.* 1580. Trans. Donald M. Frame. Stanford: Stanford UP, 1958.

Scott, William. "To the Reader." *An Essay of Drapery, or The Compleate Citizen*. London: Stephen Pemell, 1635.
Temple, Sir William. "[Second Essay, Third Essay]." The Early Essays and Romances of Sir William Temple, Bt., with The Life and Character of Sir William Temple by His Sister Lady Giffard. 1652. Ed. G[eorge] C[harles] Moore Smith. Oxford: Clarendon, 1932. 149–66.
"D. T. Gent." [Daniel Tuvill]. "Dedicatory Epistle." *Essays Politic and Moral, and Essays Moral and Theological*. 1608. Ed. John Lievsay. Charlottesville: UP of Virginia, for the Folger Library, 1971. 5.
———. "Of Poverty." *Essays Politic and Moral, and Essays Moral and Theological*. 1609. Ed. John Lievsay. Charlottesville: UP of Virginia, 1971. 138–42.

Eighteenth Century

Addison, Joseph. *The Guardian*. No. 98. July 3, 1713.
———. *The Spectator*. No. 124. July 23, 1711.
———. *The Spectator*. No. 249. December 15, 1711.
———. *The Spectator*. No. 476. September 5, 1712.
———. *The Spectator*. No. 542. November 11, 1712.
———. *The Spectator*. No. 555. December 6, 1712.
———. *The Spectator*. No. 562. July 2, 1714.
———. *The Spectator*. No. 563. July 5, 1714.
Blackmore, Richard. Preface [Of Essays]. *Essays Upon Several Subjects*. London: E. Curll and J. Pemberton, 1716.
Brown, Charles Brockden. "The Rhapsodist." No. 1. *The Universal Asylum and Columbian Magazine*. [Philadelphia]. August 1789.
———. "The Man at Home." No. 1. *The Weekly Magazine*. [Philadelphia]. February 3, 1798.
"Mr. Town, Critic and Censor-General." [George Colman and Bonnell Thornton]. *The Connoisseur*. No. 27. August 1, 1754.
———. *The Connoisseur*. No. 71. June 5, 1755.
Dennie, Joseph. "The Farrago." *The Morning Ray*. No. 1. February 14, 1792.
———. "The Farrago." *The Tablet*. No. 24. June 9, 1795.
———. "The Lay Preacher." No. 1, "Design of the Preacher." *New Hampshire Journal: Or The Farmer's Weekly Museum*. 1795.
———. "The Lay Preacher." No. 2, "On the Pleasures of Study." *New Hampshire Journal: Or The Farmer's Weekly Museum*. 1795.
Goldsmith, Oliver. "New Fashions in Learning." *The Public Ledger*. August 19, 1761.
———. Preface. *Essays by Mr. Goldsmith*. London: Newberry and Griffin, 1765.
———. "A Preface to a Series of Literary Essays." *The Public Ledger*. August 22, 1761.
Hume, David. "Of Essay Writing." *Essays: Moral and Political*. Edinburgh: A. Kincaid, 1742.
Johnson, Samuel. *The Rambler*. No. 1. March 20, 1750.

———. *The Rambler.* No. 184. December 21, 1751.
"Constantina." [Murray, Judith Sargent]. *The Gleaner.* No. 1. January 1792.
———. *The Gleaner.* No. 6. August 1792.
———. *The Gleaner.* No. 12. March 1794.
———. *The Gleaner.* "Conclusion—The Gleaner Unmasked." [1794?]
———. Preface (March 16, 1797). *The Gleaner, A Miscellaneous Production in three volumes.* Boston: I. Thomas Andrews and E. T. Andrews, 1798.
Steele, Richard. *The Tatler.* No. 83. October 20, 1709.
———. *The Tatler.* No. 172. May 16, 1710.
Trumbull, John. "The Correspondent." *The Connecticut Journal.* No. 2. March 2, 1770.
———. "The Correspondent." *The Connecticut Journal.* No. 28. June 25, 1773.
———. "The Correspondent." *The Connecticut Journal.* No. 34. August 6, 1773.
———. "The Correspondent." *The Connecticut Journal.* No. 38. September 3, 1773.
———. "The Meddler." *The Boston Chronicle.* No. 1. September 4–7, 1769.
———. "The Meddler." *The Boston Chronicle.* No. 10. January 18–22, 1770.

Nineteenth Century

Bulwer-Lytton, Edward George Earle. "On Essay-writing in General, and these Essays in Particular." *Caxtonia: A Series of Essays on Life, Literature, and Manners.* New York: Harper and Brothers, 1868. Originally published in *Blackwood's Magazine* (1862).
Burton, Richard. "The Predominance of the Novel." *Dial* 16 (1894): 354–56.
Dennis, John. "The Art of Essay Writing." *National Review* 1 (1883): 744–57.
Drake, Nathan. "General Observations on Periodical Writing, Its Merit and Utility, and on the State of Literature and Manners in This Island at the Commencement of the Tatler in 1709." *Essays, Biographical, Critical and Historical, Illustrative of the Tatler, Spectator and Guardian.* 2nd ed. Vol. 1. London: Suttaby, Evance and Fox; and Sharpe and Hailles, 1814.
———. "Observations on the Effects of the Tatler, Spectator, and Guardian, on the Taste, Literature, and Morals of the Age." *Essays, Biographical, Critical and Historical, Illustrative of the Tatler, Spectator and Guardian.* 2nd ed. Vol. 3. London: Suttaby, Evance and Fox; and Sharpe and Hailles, 1814.
Emerson, Ralph Waldo. *Emerson in His Journals.* Ed. Joel Porte. Cambridge, MA: Belknap-Harvard UP, 1982.
Hazlitt, William. "A Farewell to Essay-Writing." *The London Weekly Review.* March 29, 1828. First collected in *Winterslow: Characters and Essays Written There, Collected by His Son.* London: David Bogue, 1850.
———. "On Familiar Style." *Table-Talk, or Original Essays On Men and Manners.* Vol. 2. London: Henry Colburn, 1822.
———. "On the Indian Jugglers." *Table-Talk, or Original Essays On Men and Manners.* London: John Warren, 1821.
———. "On the Periodical Essayists." *Lectures on the English Comic Writers: Delivered at the Surry Institution.* London: Taylor and Hessey, 1819.

Henley, William E. "Essays and Essayists." *Views and Reviews: Essays in Appreciation*. London: David Nutt, 1890.
Hunt, Leigh. "Difficulty of Finding a Name for a Work of This Kind." *The Indicator and the Companion: A Miscellany for the Fields and Fire-Side*. Vol. 1. London: Henry Colburn, 1834.
Jenks, Tudor. "The Essay." *Outlook* 48 (1893): 212–13.
Jones, W. Alfred. "Essay Writing—The Champion." *Essays Upon Authors and Books*. New York: Standford and Swords, 1849.
Lamb, Charles. "Imperfect Sympathies." *Elia—Essays That Have Appeared Under That Signature in the* London Magazine. London: Taylor and Hessey, 1823. Originally published in *London Magazine* (August 1821).
———. "Unpublished Review of Volume One of Hazlitt's *Table Talk* (1821)." Berg Collections, No. 220284B. New York Public Library. *Lamb as Critic*. Ed. Roy Park. London: Routledge and Kegan Paul, 1980. 299–306.
Laughlin, Clara E. "Concerning Essays." *Book Buyer* 14 (May 1897): 349–52.
Mabie, Hamilton Wright. "The Essay and Some Essayists, Part I." *Bookman* 9 (August 1899): 504–11.
———. "The Essay and Some Essayists, Part II." *Bookman* 9 (September 1899): 49–54.
Matthews, Brander. "A Note on the Essay." *Book Buyer* 16.3 (April 1898): 201–4.
Pater, Walter. "Dialectic." *Plato and Platonism: A Series of Lectures*. London: Macmillan, 1893. 156–76.
———. "Peach-Blossom and Wine" and "Suspended Judgment." *Gaston de Latour: An Unfinished Romance*. Ed. Charles L. Shadwell. London: Macmillan, 1896. 73–115. Originally published in *Macmillan's Magazine* (September–October 1889).
Repplier, Agnes. "The Passing of the Essay." *In the Dozy Hours*. Boston: Houghton Mifflin, 1894. 226–35.
Smith, Alexander. "On the Writing of Essays." *Dreamthorp: A Book of Essays Written in the Country*. 1863. Portland, ME: Thomas Bird Mosher, 1913. 22–46.
Stephen, Leslie. "The Essayists." *Men, Books, and Mountains*. Ed. S. O. A. Ullman. Minneapolis: U of Minnesota P, 1956. 45–73. Originally published in *The Cornhill Magazine* (1881).
Thackeray, William Makepeace. "A Leaf Out of a Sketch-Book." *The Victoria Regia, a Volume of Original Contributions in Poetry and Prose*. Ed. Adelaide A. Procter. London: Emily Faithfull and Co., 1861. 118–25.
———. "Ogres." *Roundabout Papers. Cornhill Magazine* 4 (August 1861): 251–56.
Thoreau, Henry David. [Journal Entries, January 27 and 28, 1852]. *The Writings of Henry David Thoreau. Vol. III. Journal: September 16, 1851–April 30, 1852*. Ed. Bradford Torrey. Boston: Riverside–Houghton Mifflin, 1906. 236–40.
Watson, E. H. Lacon. "The Essay Considered from an Artistic Point of View." *Eclectic Magazine* 123 (1894): 50–54. Originally appeared in *Westminster Review*.
Wells, H. G. "The Writing of Essays." *Certain Personal Matters: A Collection*

of Material, Mainly Autobiographical. London: Lawrence and Bullen, 1898. 180–84.
Wirt, William. "The Old Bachelor." Nos. 5, 11, 12, and 26. *The Old Bachelor.* Richmond: Thomas Ritchie and Fielding Lucas, 1814. Originally appeared in twenty-eight installments between December 22, 1810 and December 24, 1811 in the Richmond *Examiner.*
Zabriskie, Francis N. "The Essay as a Literary Form and Quality." *New Princeton Review* 4 (1888): 227–45.

Twentieth and Twenty-first Centuries

Adorno, Theodor. "The Essay as Form." Trans. Bob Hullot-Kentor. *New German Critique* (Spring–Summer 1984): 151–71. Originally published as "Der Essay als Form." *Noten zur Literatur.* Berlin: Suhrkamp, 1958. S. 9–49.
Anderson, Chris. "Essay: Hearsay Evidence and Second-Class Citizenship." *College English* 50.3 (March 1988): 300–308.
———. "Life and the Essay Compared to a Forest." *Edge Effects: Notes from an Oregon Forest.* American Land and Life Series. Iowa City: U of Iowa P, 1993. 155–85.
Anderson Imbert, Enrique. "In Defense of the Essay." *The Oxford Book of Latin American Essays.* Ed. Ilan Stavans. Oxford: Oxford UP, 1997. 221–24. Trans. Jesse H. Lytle. Originally published as "Defensa del ensayo." *Ensayos.* Tucumán: Talleres Gráficos Miguel Violetto, 1946. 119–24.
Arciniegas, Germán. "El ensayo en nuestra América." *Cuadernos* 19 (1956): 125–30.
———. "Nuestra América es un ensayo." *Cuadernos* 73 (1963): 9–16.
Arthur, Chris. "An Essay on the Esse." *Irish Elegies.* New York: Palgrave MacMillan, 2009. 155–68.
Atkins, G. Douglas. *Estranging the Familiar: Toward a Revitalized Critical Writing.* Athens: U of Georgia P, 1992.
———. *On the Familiar Essay: Challenging Academic Orthodoxies.* New York: Palgrave MacMillan, 2009.
———. *Reading Essays: An Invitation.* Athens: U of Georgia P, 2008.
———. *Tracing the Essay: Through Experience To Truth.* Athens: U of Georgia P, 2005.
Atwan, Robert. "The Essay—Is it Literature?" *What Do I Know? Reading, Writing, and Teaching the Essay.* Ed. Janis Forman. Portsmouth, NH: Heinemann-Boynton/Cook, 1996. 21–37.
———. "Essayism." *Iowa Review* 25 (1995): 6–14.
———. Foreword. *The Best American Essays of the Century.* Ed. Robert Atwan and Joyce Carol Oates. Boston: Houghton Mifflin, 2000. x–xvi.
———. Forewords. *The Best American Essays.* 1987–present. Series ed. Robert Atwan. New York: Ticknor and Fields, 1987–93. Boston: Houghton Mifflin, 1994–present.

Belleau, André. "Petite Essayistique." *Surprendre les voix: Essais*. Montreal: Boréal, 1986. 85–89. Originally published in *Liberté* 150 (December 1983).
Belloc, Hilaire. "By Way of Preface: An Essay upon Essays upon Essays (1929)." *One Thing and Another. A Miscellany from his Uncollected Essays selected by* Patrick Cahill. London: Hollis and Carter, 1955. 11–14.
Bense, Max. "Über den Essay und seine Prosa." *Plakatwelt: Vier Essays*. Stuttgart: Deutsche Verlags-Anstalt, 1952. 23–37. Originally published in *Merkur* 1 (1947): 414–24.
Benson, Arthur C. "The Art of the Essayist." *Modern English Essays*. Vol. 5. Ed. Ernest Rhys. London: J. M. Dent, 1922. 50–63.
———. "On Essays at Large." *Living Age* 46.3423 (February 12, 1910): 408–15. Originally published in *Cornhill Magazine*.
Berry, Wendell. Preface. *Home Economics: 14 Essays*. San Francisco: North Point P, 1987. ix–x.
Bloom, Lynn Z. "The Essay Canon." *College English* 61.4 (March 1999): 401–30.
Bourne, Randolph. "The Light Essay." *Dial* 65 (November 16, 1918): 419–20.
Braley, Berton. "On Being an Essayist." *Bookman: A Review of Books and Life* 51 (August 1920): 646–48.
Bresland, John. "On the Origins of the Video Essay" and "Video Suite." *Blackbird* 9.1 (Spring 2010). http://www.blackbird.vcu.edu/v9n1/gallery/ve-bresland_j/index.shtml.
Brooks, Charles S. "Lazy Ink-Pots." *Like A Summer's Cloud*. New York: Harcourt, 1925.
———. "The Writing of Essays." *Hints to Pilgrims*. New Haven: Yale UP, 1921. 59–76.
Burton, Richard. "The Essay: A Famous Literary Form and Its Conquests." *New York Times* (April 5, 1914): BR166.
———. "The Essay as Mood and Form." *Forces in Fiction*. Indianapolis: Bowen-Merrill, 1902. 85–99.
Canby, Henry Seidel. "The Essay as Barometer." *Saturday Review of Literature* (February 16, 1935): 488.
———. "Out with the Dilettante." *Definitions: Essays in Contemporary Criticism*. New York: Harcourt, 1922. 246–48.
Chesterton, G. K. "The Essay." *Essays of the Year, 1931–32*. London: Argonaut, 1932. xi–xviii.
———. "On Essays." *Come to Think of It*. London: Methuen, 1930. 1–5. Originally published in the *Illustrated London News* (February 16, 1929).
Crothers, Samuel McChord. "Making Friends with the Essay." *World Review* 4 (1927): 190.
D'Agata, John. Introduction and Headnotes. *The Lost Origins of the Essay*. Ed. John D'Agata. St. Paul: Graywolf Press, 2009.
———. Introduction and Headnotes. *The Next American Essay*. Ed. John D'Agata. St. Paul: Graywolf Press, 2003.
Daiches, David. "Reflections on the Essay." *A Century of the Essay: British and American*. New York: Harcourt, 1951. 1–8.

Depp, Michael. "On Essays: Literature's Most Misunderstood Form." *Poets & Writers* (July–August 2002): 14–17.
Díaz-Plaja, Guillermo. "Los límites del ensayo." *La Estafeta Literaria* 582 (February 15, 1976): 236–39.
Dickson, Edith. "Women and the Essay." *Dial* 369 (November 1901): 309–10.
Dillard, Annie. Introduction. *The Best American Essays 1988.* Ed. Annie Dillard. Series ed. Robert Atwan. New York: Ticknor and Fields, 1988. xiii–xxii.
DuPlessis, Rachel Blau. "*f*-Words: An Essay on the Essay." *American Literature* 68.1 (March 1996): 15–45.
Early, Gerald. "Dispersion, Dilation, Delation." *Speech and Power: The African American Essay and Its Cultural Content from Polemics to Pulpit.* Vol. 2. New York: Ecco, 1993. ix–xi.
———. "Gnostic or Gnomic?" *Speech and Power: The African American Essay and Its Cultural Content from Polemics to Pulpit.* Vol. 1. New York: Ecco, 1992. vii–xv.
———. Introduction. *Tuxedo Junction: Essays on American Culture.* New York: Ecco, 1989. vii–xvii.
Eaton, Walter Prichard. "On Burying the Essay." *Virginia Quarterly Review* 24 (1948): 574–83.
Eiseley, Loren. "The Ghost World." *All the Strange Hours.* 1975. Lincoln: Bison-U of Nebraska P, 2000. 172–79.
Epstein, Joseph. Introduction. *The Best American Essays, 1993.* Ed. Joseph Epstein. Series ed. Robert Atwan. New York: Ticknor and Fields, 1993. xiii–xviii.
———. "Introduction: The Personal Essay as a Form of Discovery." *The Norton Book of Personal Essays.* Ed. Joseph Epstein. New York: Norton, 1997. 11–24.
———. "Piece Work: Writing the Essay." *Plausible Prejudices: Essays on American Writing.* New York: Norton, 1985. 397–411. Originally published in *New Criterion* (1984).
Erdman, Irwin. "The Art of the Unhurried Essay in a Hurry-Up World." *New York Times Book Review* (January 18, 1953): BR3.
Fadiman, Anne. Introduction. *The Best American Essays, 2003.* Ed. Anne Fadiman. Series ed. Robert Atwan. Boston: Houghton Mifflin, 2003. xiv–xxiv.
Fadiman, Clifton. "A Gentle Dirge for the Familiar Essay." *Party of One: The Selected Writing of Clifton Fadiman.* Cleveland: World, 1955. 349–53. Originally appeared as "Party of One" *Holiday* (January 1955).
Faery, Rebecca Blevins. "On the Possibilities of the Essay: A Meditation." *Iowa Review* 20.2 (Spring–Summer 1990): 19–27.
Foster, Patricia. "The Intelligent Heart." *Fourth Genre: Explorations in Nonfiction* 3.2 (Fall 2001): 175–77.
Frazier, Ian. Introduction. *The Best American Essays, 1997.* Ed. Ian Frazier. Series ed. Robert Atwan. Boston: Houghton Mifflin, 1997. xv–xxi.
Freeman, John. "The English Essayist." *English Portraits and Essays.* Edinburgh: Morrison and Gibb, 1924. 223–44.
Gass, William. "Emerson and the Essay." *Habitations of the Word.* New York: Simon and Schuster, 1985. 9–49.

Gerould, Katharine Fullerton. "An Essay on Essays." *North American Review* 240.3 (December 1935): 409–18.
———. "Information, Please! A Call for a Plebiscite of Magazine Readers." *Saturday Review of Literature* (December 29, 1934): 393, 395.
Gillett, Eric. "A Word for the Essay." *Fortnightly* 156 (July 1941): 82–90.
Gold, Herbert. "Introduction: How Else Can the Novelist Say It?" *First Person Singular: Essays for the Sixties*. New York: Dial, 1963. 9–14.
Gopnik, Adam. Introduction. *The Best American Essays, 2008*. Ed. Adam Gopnik. Series ed. Robert Atwan. Boston: Houghton Mifflin, 2008. xiv–xxiii.
Gornick, Vivian. *The Situation and the Story: The Art of Personal Narrative*. New York: Farrar, Straus and Giroux, 2001. 3–85.
Gould, Gerald. "The Happy Essayist." *Saturday Review* 139 (1925): 549.
Gould, Stephen Jay. "Introduction: To Open a Millennium." *The Best American Essays, 2002*. Ed. Stephen Jay Gould. Series ed. Robert Atwan. Boston: Houghton Mifflin, 2002. xiii–xvii.
Graham, Paul. "The Age of the Essay (Sept. 2004)." http://www.paulgraham.com/essay.html.
Hall, James Norman. "A Word for the Essayist." *Yale Review* 32 (September 1942): 50–58.
Hamburger, Michael. "An Essay on the Essay." *Art as Second Nature: Occasional Pieces, 1950–74*. Manchester: Carcanet, 1975. 3–5. Originally appeared as "Essay über den Essay" in *Akzente* 12 (1965): 290–93.
Hardison, O. B. "Binding Proteus: An Essay on the Essay." *Essays on the Essay: Redefining the Genre*. Ed. Alexander J. Butrym. Athens: U of Georgia P, 1989. 11–30.
Hardwick, Elizabeth. Introduction. *The Best American Essays, 1986*. Ed. Elizabeth Hardwick. Series ed. Robert Atwan. New York: Ticknor and Fields, 1986. xiii–xxi.
Hewett, Heather. "In Search of an 'I': Embodied Voice and the Personal Essay." *Women's Studies* 33.6 (2004): 719–41.
Hewlett, Maurice. "The Maypole and the Column." [Preface.] *Extemporary Essays*. London: Oxford UP, 1922. 7–12.
Hilsbecher, Walter. "Essay über den Essay." *Wie modern ist eine Literatur: Aufsätze*. Munich: Nympenburger Verlaghandlung, 1965. 139–50.
Hoagland, Edward. Foreword. *Balancing Acts*. New York: Simon and Schuster, 1992. 9–10.
———. "Introduction: Writers Afoot." *The Best American Essays, 1999*. Ed. Edward Hoagland. Series ed. Robert Atwan. Boston: Houghton Mifflin, 1999. xiii–xix.
———. "To the Point: Truths Only Essays Can Tell." *Harper's* (March 1993): 31–40.
———. "What I Think, What I Am." *The Tugman's Passage*. New York: Random House, 1982. 24–27. Originally appeared in *New York Times Book Review* (June 27, 1976).

Holliday, Robert Cortes. "An Article Without an Idea." *Broome Street Straws.* New York: George H. Doran, 1919. 80–87.

Howard, Maureen. Introduction. *The Penguin Book of Contemporary American Essays.* New York: Penguin, 1985. xi–xix.

Howarth, William. "Itinerant Passages: Recent American Essays." *Essays on the Essay: Redefining the Genre.* Ed. Alexander J. Butrym. Athens: U of Georgia P, 1989. 241–49.

Howells, William Dean. "The Old-Fashioned Essay." *Harper's Magazine* (October 1902): 802–3.

Huxley, Aldous. Preface. *Collected Essays.* New York: Harper and Row, 1960.

Kazin, Alfred. "Introduction: The Essay as a Modern Form." *The Open Form: Essays for Our Time.* New York: Harcourt, 1961. vii–xi.

Kirkland, Winifred M. "Foreword: The Ego in the Essay." *Joys of Being a Woman, and Other Papers.* Boston: Houghton Mifflin, 1918. v–ix.

Klaus, Carl. "The Chameleon 'I': On Voice and Personality in the Personal Essay." *Voices on Voice: Definitions, Perspectives, Inquiry.* Ed. Kathleen Blake Yancey. Urbana: National Council of Teachers of English, 1994. 111–29.

———. "Embodying the Self: Malady and the Personal Essay." *Iowa Review* 25.2 (Spring–Summer 1995): 177–92.

———. "Essayists on the Essay." *Literary Nonfiction: Theory, Practice, Pedagogy.* Ed. Chris Anderson. Carbondale: Southern Illinois UP, 1989. 155–75.

———. "Excursions of the Mind: Toward a Poetics of Uncertainty in the Disjunctive Essay." *What Do I Know? Reading, Writing, and Teaching the Essay.* Ed. Janis Forman. Portsmouth, NH: Heinemann-Boynton/Cook, 1996. 39–53.

———. *The Made-up Self: Impersonation in the Personal Essay.* Iowa City: U of Iowa P, 2010.

———. "Montaigne on His Essays: Toward a Poetics of Self." *Iowa Review* 21 (1991): 1–23.

———. "On Virginia Woolf on the Essay." *Iowa Review* 20 (Fall 1990): 28–34.

———. "The Put-Ons of Personal Essayists." *Chronicle Review* (November 19, 2010): B14–B15.

Kostelanetz, Richard. "Essaying the Essay." *Book Forum* 1.3 (May 1975): 417–23.

Kott, Jan. Introduction. Trans. Jadwiga Kosicka. *Four Decades of Polish Essays.* Ed. Jan Kott. Evanston: Northwestern UP, 1990. 1–6.

Kriegel, Leonard. "The Observer Observing: Some Notes on the Personal Essay." *Truth in Nonfiction: Essays.* Ed. David Lazar. Iowa City: U of Iowa P, 2008. 93–99.

Krutch, Joseph Wood. "No Essays, Please!" *Saturday Review of Literature* (March 10, 1951): 18–19, 35.

Lapham, Lewis. "Notebook: Figures of Speech." *Harper's* 321.1926 (November 2010): 7–9.

Lazar, David. "Occasional Desire: On the Essay and the Memoir." *Truth in Nonfiction: Essays.* Ed. David Lazar. Iowa City: U of Iowa P, 2008. 100–113.

Le Gallienne, Richard. "Sad Demise of Pleasurable Reading." *New York Times Book Review* (July 1, 1923): BR2.
Levine, Sara. "What in the Wide Wide World is the Essay For?" *River Teeth: A Journal of Nonfiction Narrative* 1.2 (2000): 106–22.
Lopate, Phillip. "The Essay Lives—in Disguise." *New York Times Book Review* (November 18, 1984): 1+.
———. "In Search of the Centaur: The Essay-Film." *Beyond Document: Essays on Nonfiction Film*. Ed. Charles Warren. Middletown: Wesleyan University Press, 1998. 243–70. Originally appeared in the *Threepenny Review* 48 (Winter 1992): 19–22.
———. Introduction. *The Art of the Personal Essay*. New York: Anchor Doubleday, 1994. xxiii–liv.
———. "Notes Toward an Introduction." *Selected Writings*. New York: Basic Books, 2003. ix–xii.
———. "What Happened to the Personal Essay?" *Against Joie De Vivre*. New York: Poseidon Press, 1989. 75–86.
Loveman, Amy. "Arm Chair Philosophy." *Saturday Review of Literature* 5 (August 23, 1930): 65.
———. "A Disappearing Art." *Saturday Review of Literature* 9 (July 23, 1932): 1.
Lukács, Georg. "The Nature and Form of the Essay: Letter to Leo Popper [written in Florence, October 1910]." *Soul and Form*. Trans. Anna Bostock. Cambridge, MA: MIT P, 1974. 1–18.
Mabie, Hamilton Wright. "Why the Essay is Valuable as Reading." *Ladies' Home Journal* (April 1908): 36.
Macy, John Albert. "The Reading of Essays." *A Guide to Reading for Young and Old*. Garden City: Doubleday, Page and Company, 1913. 179–92.
Madden, Patrick. "The Infinitive Suggestiveness of Common Things." *Quotidiana: Essays*. Lincoln: U of Nebraska P, 2010. 1–10.
Mairs, Nancy. "But First . . . " *Carnal Acts: Essays*. New York: Harper, 1990. 1–18.
———. "Carnal Acts." Mairs, *Carnal Acts*. 81–96.
———. "Essaying the Feminine: From Montaigne to Kristeva." Mairs, *Voice Lessons: On Becoming a (Woman) Writer*. Boston: Beacon, 1994. 71–87.
———. "On Uttering the Unspeakable." Mairs, *Carnal Acts*. 53–64.
———. "Prelude." Mairs, *Voice Lessons*. 1–14.
———. "Trying Truth." *Truth in Nonfiction: Essays*. Ed. David Lazar. Iowa City: U of Iowa P, 2008. 89–92.
Malinowitz, Harriet. "Business, Pleasure, and the Personal Essay." *College English*, Special Issue: Creative Nonfiction 65.3 (January 2003): 305–22.
Matthews, Brander. Introduction. *The Oxford Book of American Essays*. New York: Oxford, 1914. v–xi.
———. "Modern Essays." *Munsey's Magazine* 49 (1913): 268–72.
McCord, David. "Once and for All." *Saturday Review of Literature* (October 5, 1929): 208.
Mehta, Ved. "Introduction: Lightning and the Lightning Bug." *A Ved Mehta Reader: The Craft of the Essay*. New Haven: Yale UP, 1998. xi–xxi.

Menand, Louis. "Introduction: Voices." *The Best American Essays, 2004*. Ed. Louis Menand. Series ed. Robert Atwan. Boston: Houghton Mifflin, 2004. xiv–xviii.

Miller, Brenda. "A Braided Heart: Shaping the Lyric Essay." *Writing Creative Nonfiction: Instruction and Insights from the Teachers of the Associated Writing Programs*. Ed. Carolyn Forché and Philip Gerard. Cincinnati: Story Press, 2001. 14–24.

———. "'Brenda Miller Has a Cold,' or, How the Lyric Essay Happens." *The Fourth Genre: Contemporary Writers of/on Creative Nonfiction*. Ed. Robert L. Root and Michael Steinberg. 5th ed. New York: Longman, 2009. 378–84.

Monson, Ander. "The Designed Essay (Essay as Design)." http://otherelectricities.com/swarm/spatiality1d.pdf [2008?].

———. "Essay as Hack." http://otherelectricities.com/swarm/essayashack.html [2008].

Morley, Christopher. Preface. *Modern Essays*. New York: Harcourt, Brace, 1921. iii–x.

Murdoch, Walter. "The Essay." *Collected Essays*. 1938. Sydney: Angus and Robertson, 1945. 284–87.

———. Preface. *Collected Essays*. 3–5.

Musil, Robert. [Essayism]. *The Man Without Qualities*. Trans. Sophie Wilkins and Burton Pike. New York: Knopf, 1995. 273–74. Originally appeared as *Der Mann ohne Eigenschaften* in 1930, 1942.

———. [On the Essay] [1914?]. *Precision and Soul*. Trans. Burton Pike and David S. Luft. Chicago: U of Chicago P, 1990. 48–51.

Nicolson, Harold. "On Writing an Essay." *Of Men and Manners: The Englishman and His World*. Ed. Katherine Feldberg. Coral Gables: U of Miami Press, 1970. xiii–xv. Originally appeared in the *Observer* (October 18, 1952).

Norris, Kathleen. "Introduction: Stories Around a Fire." *The Best American Essays, 2001*. Ed. Kathleen Norris. Series ed. Robert Atwan. Boston: Houghton Mifflin, 2001. xiv–xvi.

Oates, Joyce Carol. Introduction. *The Best American Essays, 1991*. Ed. Joyce Carol Oates. Series ed. Robert Atwan. New York: Ticknor and Fields, 1991. xiii–xxiii.

———. "Introduction: The Art of the (American) Essay." *The Best American Essays of the Century*. Ed. Robert Atwan and Joyce Carol Oates. Boston: Houghton Mifflin, 2000. xvii–xxviii.

Ortega y Gasset, José. "To the Reader." *Meditations on Quixote*. Trans. Evelyn Rugg and Diego Marín. New York: Norton, 1961. 31–53 (especially 40–41).

Ouellette, Fernand. "Divagations sur l'essai." *Etudes Littéraires* 5 (1972): 9–13. Collected in *Écrire en notre temps: Essais*. Vol. 39, Collection Constantes (Cité de LaSalle: Éditions Hurtubise HMH, 1979).

Ozick, Cynthia. "Forewarning." *Metaphor and Memory*. New York: Knopf, 1989. ix–xii.

———. Foreword. *Art and Ardor*. New York: Knopf, 1983.

———. "It Takes a Great Deal of History to Produce a Little Literature." *Partisan Review* 60 (Spring 1993): 195–200.

———. "She: Portrait of the Essay as a Warm Body." *Quarrel & Quandary: Essays.* New York: Knopf, 2000. 178–87. Originally published as "Introduction: Portrait of the Essay as a Warm Body." *The Best American Essays, 1998.* Ed. Cynthia Ozick. Series ed. Robert Atwan. Boston: Houghton Mifflin, 1998. xv–xxi.
Percy, H. R. "The Essay: An Art in Eclipse." *Queen's Quarterly* (Winter 1959): 642–49.
Perry, Jennette Barbour. "The Romantic Essay." *Critic* 40 (April 1902): 358–60.
Pickering, Samuel. "Being Familiar." *Texas Review* (1986): 74–81.
Picón-Salas, Mariano. "En torno al ensayo." *Cuadernos* 8 (1954): 31–33. Reprinted as "Y va de ensayo" in *Crisis, cambio, tradición: Ensayos sobre la forma de nuestra cultura*. Madrid: Ediciones Edime, 1955. 140–45; as "Formula del ensayo" in *La Nueva Democracia* 42 (January 1962): 18–20.
Podhoretz, Norman. "The Article as Art." *Harper's* (July 1958): 74–81.
Porter, Jeff, and Patricia Foster, eds. *Understanding the Essay*. Calgary: Broadview Press, 2012.
Priestley, J. B. "In Defence." *Saturday Review* 148 (1929): 235–37.
———. "On Beginning." *I for One*. London: John Lane, The Bodley Head, 1923. 3–12.
Rascoe, Burton. "What of Our Essayists?" *Bookman* 55 (1922): 74–75.
Repplier, Agnes. "The American Essay in Wartime." *Yale Review* 7.2 (January 1918): 249–59.
Reyes, Alfonso. "Las nuevas artes." *Obras Completas*. Vol. 9. Mexico: Fondo de Cultura Económica, 1959. 400–403. Originally appeared in *Tricolor* 16 (September 1944).
Root, Robert L., Jr. *E. B. White: The Emergence of an Essayist.* Iowa City: U of Iowa P, 1999.
———. *The Nonfictionist's Guide: On Reading and Writing Creative Nonfiction.* Lanham: Rowman and Littlefield, 2008.
Sampson, George. Introduction. *Nineteenth Century Essays.* Cambridge: Cambridge UP, 1917. vii–xi.
Sanders, Scott Russell. Introduction. *The Paradise of Bombs*. New York: Simon and Schuster, 1987. xi–xiv.
———. Preface. *Staying Put: Making a Home in a Restless World*. Boston: Beacon, 1993.
———. "The Singular First Person." *Essays on the Essay: Redefining the Genre*. Ed. Alexander J. Butrym. Athens: U of Georgia P, 1989. 31–42. Reprinted in Scott Russell Sanders, *Secrets of the Universe*: *Scenes from the Journey Home*. Boston: Beacon, 1991. 187–204.
Scholes, Robert, and Carl H. Klaus. *Elements of the Essay*. New York: Oxford UP, 1969.
Scott, Gail. Preface. *Spaces Like Stairs: Essays*. Toronto: Women's P, 1989. 9–12.
Sheed, Wilfred. "Program Notes." *Essays in Disguise*. New York: Knopf, 1990. vii–xvii.
Sherman, Stuart. "An Apology for Essayists of the Press." *Points of View*. New York: Scribner's, 1924. 173–85.

Shields, David. "Reality, Persona." *Truth in Nonfiction: Essays*. Ed. David Lazar. Iowa City: U of Iowa P, 2008. 77–88.

Sontag, Susan. Introduction. *The Best American Essays, 1992*. Ed. Susan Sontag. Series ed. Robert Atwan. New York: Ticknor and Fields, 1992. xiii–xix.

Squire, J. C. "The Essay." *Flowers of Speech*. 2nd ed. New York: Books for Libraries Press, Inc., 1967. 108–15.

———. "An Essay on Essays." *Essays of the Year, 1929–1930*. London: Argonaut, 1930. ix–xviii.

Starobinski, Jean. "Peut-on definer l'essai?" *Cahiers pour un temps*. Paris: Centre Georges Pompidou, 1985. 185–96. Originally published as "Les enjeux de l'essai." *La Revue de Belles-Lettres* 106.2–3 (1983): 93–105. Trans. and reprinted as "¿Es posible definir el ensayo?" *Cuadernos Hispanoamericanos* 575 (1998): 31–32.

Strunsky, Simeon. "The Essay of Today." *English Journal* 17.1 (January 1928): 8–16.

Stuckey-French, Ned. *The American Essay in the American Century*. Columbia: U of Missouri P, 2011.

———. "'An Essay on Virginia': William Carlos Williams and the Modern(ist) Essay." *American Literature* 70.1 (March 1998): 97–130.

———. "Why Does the Essay Keep Dying, and What Do Little Lord Fauntleroy and the Lavender-Scented Little Old Lady Have to Do with It?" *CEA Critic* (Winter and Spring–Summer 1999): 30–36.

Talese, Gay. Introduction. *The Best American Essays, 1987*. Ed. Gay Talese. Series ed. Robert Atwan. New York: Ticknor and Fields, 1987. xiii–xxii.

Thomas, Lewis. "Essays and Gaia." *The Youngest Science*. New York: Viking Penguin, 1983. 239–48.

Van Doren, Carl. "Day In and Day Out: Manhattan Wits." *Many Minds*. New York: Knopf, 1924. 181–99.

———. "A Note on the Essay." *Essays of Our Times*. Ed. Sharon Brown. Chicago: Scott, Foresman, 1928. 396–98.

Wallace, David Foster. "Introduction: Deciderization 2007—A Special Report." *The Best American Essays, 2007*. Ed. David Foster Wallace. Series ed. Robert Atwan. Boston: Houghton Mifflin, 2007. xii–xiv.

Waters, John P. "A Little Old Lady Passes Away." *Forum and Century* 90.1 (July 1933): 27–29.

Weeks, Edward. "The Peripatetic Reviewer." *Atlantic Monthly* (August 1954): 81–82.

White, E. B. Foreword. *Essays of E. B. White*. New York: Harper Colophon, 1977. vii–ix.

Williams, William Carlos. "An Essay on Virginia." *Imaginations*. Ed. Webster Scott. New York: New Directions, 1970. 321–24. Originally published in *This Quarter* 1.1 (Spring 1925): 173–75. First collected in *A Novelette and Other Prose (1921–1931)*. Toulon: To Publishers, 1932.

Williams, William Emrys. "The Essay." *The Craft of Literature*. 1925. London: Methuen, 2nd ed., 1930.

Wolfe, Tom. "The New Journalism." *The New Journalism*. Ed. Tom Wolfe and E. W. Johnson. New York: Harper and Row, 1973. 3–52.

Wolff, Geoffrey. "Introduction: An Apprentice." *The Best American Essays, 1989.* Ed. Geoffrey Wolff. Series ed. Robert Atwan. New York: Ticknor and Fields, 1989. xiii–xxxv.

Woolf, Virginia. "A Book of Essays." *The Collected Essays. Vol. II: 1912–1918.* Ed. Andrew McNeillie. New York: Harcourt Brace Jovanovich, 1988. 212–13.

———. "The Decay of Essay-writing." *The Collected Essays. Vol. I: 1904–1912.* Ed. Andrew McNeillie. London: Hogarth, 1986. 24–27. Originally appeared in a slightly different form in *TLS* (November 22, 1922).

———. "The Modern Essay." *The Common Reader: First Series.* 1925. Ed. Andrew McNeillie. New York: Harcourt Brace Jovanovich, 1953. 216–27.

Zaid, Gabriel. "La carretilla alfonsina." *Ensayo literario mexicano.* Ed. John Brushwood et al. Mexico: UNAM-Universidad Veracruzana-Aldus, 2001. 331–33. Originally appeared in *Proceso* 583 (January 4, 1988): 50–51.

Thematic Guide to Entries in the Bibliography

COMPILED BY NED STUCKEY-FRENCH

The Essay

The essay as an embodiment of consciousness or of mind in the process of thought: Sixteenth and seventeenth centuries: Montaigne, 2, 108–9, 278–79, 504, 595–96, 610–12, 667, 720–21; Temple; Eighteenth and nineteenth centuries: Stephen; Zabriskie; Twentieth and twenty-first centuries: Atwan, Foreword (2003); Canby, "The Essay as Barometer"; Gass; Gold; Kazin; Klaus, "Essayists on the Essay," *Literary Nonfiction*, "Montaigne on His Essays: Toward a Poetics of Self," "Embodying the Self: Malady and the Personal Essay," "Excursions of the Mind: Toward a Poetics of Uncertainty in the Disjunctive Essay," *The Made-up Self*; Lopate, Introduction; Mairs, "Essaying the Feminine: From Montaigne to Kristeva"; Monson, "Essay as Hack"; Musil, [On the Essay]; Ozick, "Introduction: Portrait of the Essay as a Warm Body"; Repplier, "The American Essay in Wartime"; Strunsky; Woolf, "The Modern Essay."

The essay as an embodiment of personality or projection of self: Eighteenth and nineteenth centuries: Bulwer-Lytton; Goldsmith, "A Preface to a Series of Literary Essays"; Hazlitt, "On the Indian Jugglers"; Henley; Jenks; Jones; Mabie, "The Essay and Some Essayists" (Parts I and II); Matthews; Smith; Stephen; Thackeray, "Ogres"; Wells; Twentieth and twenty-first centuries: Atwan, Foreword (1995), Foreword (2001); Benson, "The Art of the Essayist"; Burton, "The Essay as Mood and Form," "The Essay: A Famous Literary Form and Its Conquests"; Daiches; Early, "Dispersion, Dilation, Delation"; Eaton; Epstein, "Piece Work: Writing the Essay," Introduction to *The Best American Essays, 1993*, "Introduction: The Personal Essay as a Form of Discovery"; Fadiman, Clifton; Foster; Freeman; Gass; Gillett; Hamburger; Hewett; Hoagland, "Introduction: Writers Afoot"; Howells; Huxley; Kirkland; Klaus, "On Virginia Woolf on the Essay," *The Made-Up Self*; Kriegel; Krutch; Le Gallienne; Lopate, "The Essay Lives—in Disguise," "What Happened to the Personal Essay?" Introduction to *The Art of the Personal Essay*, "In Search of the Centaur: The Essay-Film"; Loveman, "Arm Chair Philosophy," "A Disappearing Art"; Mabie; Mehta; Murdoch, "The Essay"; Nicolson; Perry; Priestley, "On Beginning"; Sanders, Introduction to *The Paradise of Bombs*, "The Singular First Person"; Starobinski, "Les enjeux de l'essai"; Van Doren, "Day In and Day Out: Manhattan Wits," "A Note on the Essay"; Weeks; White; Wolff; Woolf, "The Decay of Essay-writing," "A Book of Essays," "The Modern Essay."

The essay as mode of discovery: Sixteenth and seventeenth centuries: Montaigne, 100, 242, 272–74, 425–26, 721; Eighteenth and nineteenth centuries: Steele, *The Tatler*, No. 172; Brown, "The Man at Home"; Bulwer-Lytton; Pater, "Dialectic"; Twentieth and twenty-first centuries: Early, Introduction (1989); Eiseley; Epstein, Introduction (1993), "Introduction: The Personal Essay as a Form of Discovery"; Graham, Paul, "The Age of the Essay (Sept. 2004)"; Hoagland, "To the Point: Truths Only Essays Can Tell"; Howarth; Klaus, "Montaigne on His Essays: Toward a Poetics of Self"; Kriegel; Lopate, "Notes Toward an Introduction"; Mairs, "Essaying the Feminine: From Montaigne to Kristeva"; Oates, "Introduction: The Art of the (American) Essay"; Ouellette; Ozick, Foreword (1983); Scott.

Essay as personal or intimate expression: Sixteenth and seventeenth centuries: Montaigne, 503, 595–96, 750–51; "D. T. Gent" [Daniel Tuvill], "Dedicatory Epistle"; Eighteenth and nineteenth centuries: "Constantina" [Murray, Judith Sargent], Preface; Dennie, "The Farrago," No. 1; Henley; Jenks; Stephen; Twentieth and twenty-first centuries: Crothers; Gillett; Klaus, "On Virginia Woolf on the Essay"; Macy; Woolf, "The Decay of Essay-writing," "A Book of Essays," "The Modern Essay."

Essay as an open, unmethodical genre: Sixteenth and seventeenth centuries: Hall, "To the Reverend Mr. John Arrowsmith, Master of St. John's Colledge in Cambridge" [Dedication], "Of Dissimulation"; Jonson; Montaigne, 26–27, 107, 135, 219, 229, 482–84, 494–96, 734–37, 761; Eighteenth and nineteenth centuries: Addison, *The Spectator*, Nos. 124, 249, 476; Bulwer-Lytton; Dennie, "The Farrago" No. 24, "The Lay Preacher" No. 1; Hazlitt, "On the Indian Jugglers"; Johnson, *The Rambler*, No. 184; Lamb, "Imperfect Sympathies"; Matthews; "Mr. Town, Critic and Censor-General" [George Colman and Bonnell Thornton], *The Connoisseur*, No. 71; Pater, "Dialectic"; Thoreau; Watson; Zabriskie; Twentieth and twenty-first centuries: Adorno; Anderson, "Life and the Essay Compared to a Forest"; Arthur; Atwan, Foreword (1990), "The Essay—Is it Literature?"; Benson, "On Essays at Large"; Chesterton, "On Essays," "The Essay"; Depp; Dillard; DuPlessis; Fadiman, Anne; Faery; Frazier; Gopnik; Graham; Hamburger; Hardison; Holliday; Howells; Huxley; Kazin; Klaus, "Essayists on the Essay," "The Chameleon 'I': On Voice and Personality in the Personal Essay," "Excursions of the Mind: Toward a Poetics of Uncertainty in the Disjunctive Essay"; Lopate, "The Essay Lives—in Disguise," "In Search of the Centaur: The Essay-Film"; Lukács; Mairs, "Essaying the Feminine: From Montaigne to Kristeva"; Matthews, Introduction to *The Oxford Book of American Essays*; Musil, [On the Essay], [Essayism]; Nicolson; Oates, Introduction (1991); Sanders, "The Singular First Person"; Sontag; Squire, "An Essay on Essays"; Strunsky; Van Doren, "A Note on the Essay"; Wallace; Weeks; White; Williams, "An Essay on Virginia."

Essay as pointed and purposeful genre: Sixteenth and seventeenth centuries: Montaigne, 21; Eighteenth and nineteenth centuries: Zabriskie; Twentieth and twenty-first centuries: Atwan, Foreword (1992); Erdman; Gass; Gerould, "An Essay on Essays"; Hoagland, "To the Point: Truths Only Essays Can Tell," "What I Think,

What I Am"; Huxley; Klaus, "Essayists on the Essay," "On Virginia Woolf on the Essay"; Kostelanetz; Lukács; Oates, "Introduction: The Art of the (American) Essay"; Sontag; Van Doren, "A Note on the Essay"; Woolf, "The Modern Essay."

Essay as pleasurable rather than polemical genre: Eighteenth and nineteenth centuries: Wirt, *The Old Bachelor*, No. 5; Twentieth and twenty-first centuries: Benson; Bourne; Brooks, "Lazy Ink-Pots"; Daiches; Gerould, "Information, Please!"; Hall; Holliday; Klaus, "On Virginia Woolf on the Essay," "Embodying the Self: Malady and the Personal Essay"; Loveman, "Arm Chair Philosophy"; Malinowitz; McCord; Monson, "Essay as Hack"; Murdoch, Preface to *Collected Essays*, "The Essay"; Ozick, "Introduction: Portrait of the Essay as a Warm Body."

Essay as skeptical, antidogmatic genre: Sixteenth and seventeenth centuries: Montaigne, 234, 251, 253; Eighteenth and nineteenth centuries: Hazlitt, "On the Periodical Essayists"; "Mr. Town, Critic and Censor-General" [George Colman and Bonnell Thornton], *The Connoisseur*, No. 71; Pater, "Dialectic"; Stephen; Twentieth century: Adorno; Atwan, Foreword (2003); DuPlessis; Gass; Hardison; Klaus, "Essayists on the Essay"; Ortega y Gasset; Sherman, "An Apology for Essayists of the Press."

Essay as an attempt, trial, or experiment: Sixteenth and seventeenth centuries: Bacon, "Dedication" (1612), Boyle; Cornwallis, "Of Essays and Books"; Culpeper; Glanville, "An Address to the Royal Society"; Mabie, "The Essay and Some Essayists" (Parts I and II); Scott; Thackeray, "A Leaf Out of a Sketch-Book"; "D. T. Gent." [Daniel Tuvill], "Dedicatory Epistle"; Eighteenth and nineteenth centuries: Lamb, "Imperfect Sympathies"; Zabriskie; Twentieth and twenty-first centuries: Anderson Imbert; Berry; Bloom; DuPlessis; Epstein, "Piece Work: Writing the Essay"; Mabie; Ozick, Foreword to *Art and Ardor*, "Forewarning"; Sanders, Introduction to *The Paradise of Bombs*; Starobinski, "Les enjeux de l'essai."

Essay as conversational and familiar in style: Sixteenth and seventeenth centuries: Boyle; Montaigne, 127, 184–85, 482–84, 503, 666; Scott; Eighteenth and nineteenth centuries: Dennie, "The Farrago," No. 1; Goldsmith; Hazlitt, "On the Periodical Essayists"; Hume; Lamb, "Unpublished Review of Volume One of Hazlitt's *Table Talk* (1821)"; Pater, "Peach-Blossom and Wine," "Dialectic"; Twentieth and twenty-first centuries: Arthur; Belloc; Benson, "On Essays at Large"; Berry; Burton, "The Essay as Mood and Form," "The Essay: A Famous Literary Form and Its Conquests"; Epstein, "Piece Work: Writing the Essay"; Gass; Kirkland; Kostelanetz; Klaus, "On Virginia Woolf on the Essay," "The Chameleon 'I': On Voice and Personality in the Personal Essay"; Le Gallienne; Lopate, "The Essay Lives—in Disguise," "What Happened to the Personal Essay?" Introduction to *The Art of the Personal Essay*; Matthews, "Modern Essays," Introduction to *The Oxford Book of American Essays*; Menand; Murdoch, "The Essay"; Nicolson; Percy; Priestley, "In Defence"; Woolf, "The Decay of Essay-writing," "The Modern Essay."

Essay as allusive, intertextual genre: Sixteenth and seventeenth centuries: Feltham; Jonson; Montaigne, 818, 824; Eighteenth and nineteenth centuries: Smith;

Zabriskie; Twentieth century: Brooks, "The Writing of Essays"; DuPlessis; Gass; Hardison; Kott; Lopate, "The Essay Lives—in Disguise," Introduction to *The Art of the Personal Essay*; Oates, Introduction (1991).

The Essayist

The essayist as candid, genuine, and truthful: Sixteenth and seventeenth centuries: Montaigne, 32, 108–9, 610–12, 642, 644, 677–78, 720–21, 749, 824–25; Eighteenth and nineteenth centuries: Addison, *The Spectator*, No. 562; Johnson, *The Rambler*, No. 1; Twentieth century: Atwan, Foreword (1987, 1993); Eiseley; Epstein, "Introduction: The Personal Essay as a Form of Discovery"; Hoagland, "What I Think, What I Am"; Klaus, *The Made-up Self*; Lopate, Introduction to *The Art of the Personal Essay*; Ozick, "Forewarning"; Priestley, "In Defence"; Sanders, "The Singular First Person"; Shields, "Reality, Persona"; White; Wolff; Woolf, "The Modern Essay."

The essayist's self as made-up, as impersonation: Sixteenth and seventeenth centuries: Montaigne; Eighteenth and nineteenth centuries: Lamb; Twentieth and twenty-first centuries: Gornick; Hoagland; Klaus, *The Made-up Self*; Lopate, Introduction to *The Art of the Personal Essay*; Mairs; Sanders; Shields, "Reality, Persona"; White; Wolff; Woolf, "The Modern Essay."

The essayist as possessing a distinctive voice or style: Eighteenth and nineteenth centuries: Smith; Wells; Zabriskie; Twentieth century: Atwan, Foreword (1994, 1999); Burton, "The Essay: A Famous Literary Form and Its Conquests"; Daiches; Gass; Hamburger; Hoagland, "What I Think, What I Am," "Introduction: Writers Afoot"; Klaus, *The Made-Up Self*; Lopate, "Notes Toward an Introduction"; Lukács; Mabie; Malinowitz; Menand; Oates, "Introduction: The Art of the (American) Essay"; Van Doren, "A Note on the Essay"; Weeks; Woolf, "The Modern Essay."

The essayist as distinctly male or female, the essay as a gendered form: Eighteenth and nineteenth centuries: Matthews; Twentieth century: Atwan, Foreword (2004); Braley; Dickson; DuPlessis; Faery; Hewett; Howarth; Kirkland; Mairs, "Prelude," "Essaying the Feminine: From Montaigne to Kristeva"; Malinowitz; Ozick, "Introduction: Portrait of the Essay as a Warm Body"; Scott; Waters.

The Essay in Context

The essay versus methodical discourse, academic theme, and the article: Sixteenth and seventeenth centuries: Boyle; Cornwallis; Glanville; Montaigne; Eighteenth and nineteenth centuries: Addison; Johnson; Twentieth and twenty-first centuries: Anderson, "Life and the Essay Compared to a Forest"; Atwan, Foreword (1987, 1990, 1998); Bloom; Canby, "Out with the Dilettante," "The Essay as Barometer"; DuPlessis; Eiseley; Erdman; Foster; Frazier; Gass; Gerould, "Information, Please!"; Gold; Graham; Hall; Hoagland, "What I Think, What I Am"; Howard; Howells; Kazin; Klaus, "Essayists on the Essay"; Krutch; Lopate, "What

Happened to the Personal Essay?"; Loveman, "A Disappearing Art"; Macy; Mairs, "Prelude"; Malinowitz; Mehta; Oates, Introduction (1991); Percy; Podhoretz; Priestley, "On Beginning"; Waters; Weeks.

The "death" (or revival) of the essay: Eighteenth and nineteenth centuries: Jenks; Jones; Laughlin; Repplier; Twentieth century: Atwan, Foreword (1988); Braley; Canby, "The Essay as Barometer"; Eaton; Erdman; Fadiman, Clifton; Foster; Hamburger; Hardison; Krutch; Lopate, "The Essay Lives—in Disguise," "What Happened to the Personal Essay?"; Loveman, "A Disappearing Art"; Percy; Repplier; Woolf, "The Modern Essay."

Essay as modern: Eighteenth and nineteenth centuries: Emerson; Pater, "Dialectic," "Peach-Blossom and Wine"; Twentieth century: Atwan, Foreword (2000); Chesterton, "On Essays," "The Essay"; Epstein, Introduction to *The Best American Essays, 1993*; Hardison; Kazin; Lopate, "In Search of the Centaur: The Essay-Film"; Williams, William Carlos; Woolf, "The Decay of Essay-writing," "The Modern Essay."

Essay as middle-class or intended for a middle-class audience: Sixteenth and seventeenth centuries: Montaigne, 826; Eighteenth and nineteenth centuries: Dennie, "The Farrago," No. 1; Drake, "Observations on the Effects of the Tatler, Spectator, and Guardian"; Twentieth century: Hoagland, "What I Think, What I Am"; Murdoch, Preface to *Collected Essays*; Sherman, "An Apology for Essayists of the Press."

Essay as genteel, old-fashioned, organic, and quaint, outpaced by the speed of the modern, mechanistic era: Eighteenth and nineteenth centuries: Dennis; Laughlin; Repplier; Stephen; Twentieth century: Atwan, Foreword (1988, 1997, 2000, 2002, 2004; *Century*, 2000); Belloc; Braley; Erdman; Gould, Stephen Jay; Hall; Lopate, "What Happened to the Personal Essay?"; Matthews; Percy; Priestley, "In Defence"; Sanders, "The Singular First Person"; Woolf, "The Modern Essay."

Essay vis-à-vis magazines, journalism, mass culture, and new media: Eighteenth and nineteenth centuries: Drake, "General Observations on Periodical Writing"; Goldsmith, "New Fashions in Learning"; Jones; Trumbull, "The Meddler," No. 1; Twentieth century: Atwan, Foreword (1996, 2000, 2008); Belloc; Bourne; Braley; Canby, "Out with the Dilettante," "The Essay as Barometer"; Crothers; Depp; Early, Introduction to *Tuxedo Junction*; Epstein, "Piece Work: Writing the Essay," Introduction to *The Best American Essays, 1993*, "Introduction: The Personal Essay as a Form of Discovery"; Frazier; Gerould, "Information, Please!"; Gould, Gerald; Graham; Hewlett; Hoagland, "Introduction: Writers Afoot"; Holliday; Howard; Howarth; Kostelanetz; Le Gallienne; Lopate, "The Essay Lives—in Disguise," "What Happened to the Personal Essay?"; Monson; Norris; Podhoretz; Priestley, "In Defence"; Sherman; Talese; Van Doren, "Day In and Day Out: Manhattan Wits"; Waters; Williams, William Emrys; Wolff; Woolf, "The Modern Essay."

Essay as having a lesser status, as the fourth genre, as ephemeral: Sixteenth and seventeenth centuries: Montaigne, 227; Eighteenth and nineteenth centuries: Goldsmith, Preface to *Essays by Mr. Goldsmith*; Trumbull, "The Meddler," No. 1; Twentieth century: Anderson, "Essay: Hearsay Evidence and Second-Class Citizenship"; Anderson Imbert; Atwan, "The Essay—Is it Literature?" Foreword (2005, 2009); Bloom; Depp; Dillard; Epstein, "Piece Work: Writing the Essay," Introduction to *The Best American Essays, 1993*; Gopnik; Hoagland, "To the Point: Truths Only Essays Can Tell"; Klaus, "On Virginia Woolf on the Essay"; Lukács; Monson, "Essay as Hack"; Podhoretz; White.

Permissions

It is our pleasure to acknowledge a number of authors, publishers and estates for their permission to reprint the following.

Excerpt from "The Essay as Form" by T. W. Adorno, translated by Bob Hullot-Kentor and Frederic Will, in *New German Critique* 32 (Spring/Summer), pp. 151–71. Copyright © 1984, New German Critique, Inc. All rights reserved. Reprinted by permission of the publisher, Duke University Press.

Excerpt from "In Defense of the Essay" by Enrique Anderson Imbert, from *The Oxford Book of Latin American Essays,* edited by Ilan Stavans and translated by Jesse H. Lytle. Copyright © 1997 by Oxford University Press. Reprinted by permission of Oxford University Press, Ilan Stavans, and Jesse H. Lytle.

"Petite Essayistique" in *Surprendre les voix* by André Belleau. Copyright © 1986 by Les Éditions du Boréal. Translated as "Little Essayistic" by Lindsey Scott. Reprinted by permission of Les Éditions du Boréal.

"On the Origins of the Video Essay" by John Bresland is a revised version of an essay that first appeared in *Blackbird* 9.1 (Spring 2010). Copyright © 2010 by John Bresland. Used by permission of John Bresland.

"The Essay" by G. K. Chesterton, from *Come to Think of It.* Copyright © 1930 by Metheun. Reprinted by permission of A. P. Watt Ltd., London.

Excerpt from "2003" from *The Next American Essay* by John D'Agata. Copyright © 2002 by John D'Agata. Reprinted with the permission of the Permissions Company, Inc. on behalf of Graywolf Press, Minneapolis, Minnesota, www.graywolfpress.org.

"Los límites del ensayo" by Guillermo Díaz-Plaja. Copyright © 1976. Translated as "The Limits of the Essay" by David Hamilton. Copyright © 2012, David Hamilton. Reprinted here by permission of Ana Díaz-Plaja and the Estate of Guillermo Díaz-Plaja.

Excerpt from the introduction to *Tuxedo Junction: Essays on American Culture* by Gerald Early. Copyright © 1989 by Gerald Early. Reprinted by permission of Gerald Early.

Excerpt from "The Age of the Essay" by Paul Graham. Copyright © 2004 by Paul Graham. Reprinted by permission of Paul Graham.

"An Essay on the Essay" by Michael Hamburger, from *Art as Second Nature: Occasional Pieces, 1950–74*. Copyright © 1975 by the author. Reprinted by permission of the Michael Hamburger Trust.

"What I Think, What I Am," from *The Tugman's Passage* by Edward Hoagland. Published by the Lyons Press. Copyright © 1979, 1982, 1995 by Edward Hoagland. Reprinted by permission of Lescher & Lescher, Ltd. All rights reserved.

Excerpt from author's preface from *Collected Essays* by Aldous Huxley. Copyright © 1923, 1925, 1926, 1928, 1929, 1930, 1931, 1934, 1937, 1941, 1946, 1949, 1950, 1951, 1952, 1953, 1954, 1955, 1956, 1957, 1958, 1959 by Aldous Huxley. Reprinted by permission of HarperCollins Publishers.

"What Happened to the Personal Essay?" from *Against Joie de Vivre: Personal Essays*, first published by Poseidon Press, reprinted by University of Nebraska Press. Copyright © 1989, 2008 by Phillip Lopate. Reprinted by permission of the Wendy Weil Agency, Inc.

"Essaying the Feminine: From Montaigne to Kristeva" from *Voice Lessons* by Nancy Mairs. Copyright © 1994 by Nancy Mairs. Reprinted by permission of Beacon Press, Boston.

Excerpt from "The Essay as Hack" by Ander Monson. Copyright © 2008 by Ander Monson. Reprinted by permission of Ander Monson.

Excerpt from "The Essay" by Walter Murdoch, from *Collected Essays*. Copyright © 1945 by Angus and Robertson. Reprinted by permission of HarperCollins.

From *The Man without Qualities, Vol. I* by Robert Musil, translated by Sophie Wilkins and Burton Pie, translation copyright © 1995 by Alfred A. Knopf Inc. Used by permission of Alfred A. Knopf, a division of Random House, Inc.

From *Meditations on Quixote* by José Ortega y Gassett, translated by Evelyn Rug and Kiego Marin. Copyright © 1961 and renewed 1989 by W. W. Norton & Company, Inc. Reprinted by permission of W. W. Norton & Company, Inc.

"Divagations sur l'essai" by Fernand Ouellette, from *Écrire en notre temps: essais*, Montreal, Éditions Hurtubise, HMH, "Constantes" pp. 9–13. Copyright © 1979 by Éditions Hurtubise NMH (Constantes). Translated as "Ramblings on the Essay" by Carl Klaus, Ned Stuckey-French, and Lindsey Scott. Reprinted by permission of Éditions Hurtubise NMH (Constantes).

"She: Portrait of the Essay as a Warm Body" from *Quarrel & Quandary* by Cynthia Ozick. Copyright © 2000 by Cynthia Ozick. Used by permission of Alfred A. Knopf, a division of Random House, Inc.

Excerpt from "On the Essay" by Mariano Picón-Salas, translated by David Hamilton. Copyright © 2012. Reprinted by permission of Universidad Católica Andrés Bello, Caracas, Venezuela.

"Essay on the Radio Essay" by Jeff Porter. Copyright © 2011 by Jeff Porter. Used by permission of Jeff Porter.

Excerpt from "The Singular First Person," from *Secrets of the Universe* by Scott Russell Sanders. Copyright © 1991 by Scott Russell Sanders. Reprinted by permission of Beacon Press, Boston.

Excerpt from "Peut-on definer l'essai?" in *Cahiers pour un temps* by Jean Starobinski, composed originally as a public address delivered in Lausanne in 1983 on the occasion of receiving the Le Prix européen de l'essai Charles Veillon. Copyright © 1983 by Jean Starobinski. Translated here as "Can One Define the Essay?" by Lindsey Scott. Reprinted by permission of Jean Starobinski.

Excerpt from E. B. White's foreword from *Essays of E. B. White* by E. B. White. Copyright © 1977 by E. B. White. Reprinted by permission of HarperCollins Publishers.

"An Essay on Virginia," by William Carlos Williams, from *Imaginations.* Copyright ©1932 by William Carlos Williams. Reprinted by permission of New Directions Publishing Corp.

Excerpt from "The Modern Essay," from *The Common Reader: First Series* by Virginia Woolf, edited by Andrew McNeillie. Copyright © Houghton Mifflin Harcourt Publishing Company 1984. Reprinted by permission of Houghton Mifflin Harcourt Company.

Excerpt from "La carretilla alfonsina" by Gabriel Zaid. Copyright © 1988 by Gabriel Zaid. Translated as "Alfonso Reyes' Wheelbarrow" by Maria Willstedt and Gabriel Zaid. Reprinted by permission of Gabriel Zaid.

Index